The Pursuit
of a Just
Social Order

J. BRIAN BENESTAD is assistant professor of political theory and social ethics in the Department of Theology and Religious Studies at the University of Scranton, Scranton, Pennsylvania. He has a Ph.D. in political science from Boston College and an S.T.L. (licentiate in theology) from the Gregorian University in Rome. He is the co-editor of *Quest for Justice*, a compendium of statements on the political and social order by the American Catholic bishops.

The Pursuit of a Just Social Order

Policy Statements of the U.S. Catholic Bishops, 1966–80

J. Brian Benestad

Foreword by Avery Dulles, S.J.

Ethics and Public Policy Center
Washington, D.C.

Library of Congress Cataloging in Publication Data
Benestad, J. Brian.
   The pursuit of a just social order.
   Includes index.
   1. Sociology, Christian (Catholic)—History of
doctrines—20th century. 2. Church and social problems
—United States—History—20th century. 3. Church
and social problems—Catholic Church—History—20th
century. 4. Catholic Church—United States—Pastoral
letters and charges—History—20th century. 5. United
States Catholic Conference—History—20th century.
6. Catholic Church. National Conference of Catholic
Bishops—History—20th century. I. Ethics and Public
Policy Center (Washington, D.C.) II. Title.
BX1753.B44   1982   261.8'08822   82-18326
ISBN 0-89633-060-5
ISBN 0-89633-061-3 (pbk.)

$12 cloth, $7 paper

To my wife

Contents

Appendixes

Notes   *183*

Index of Names and Documents   *201*

Foreword

By Avery Dulles, S.J.

IN CATHOLIC THEOLOGY, especially since Vatican Council II, it is universally agreed that the Church has a responsibility to exert a Christian influence on the political and social order. The American bishops, particularly through the United States Catholic Conference, have been commendably striving to set forth Catholic positions on national and international issues, but their policy statements are relatively unknown, even to clergy and persons professionally engaged in social service. To illustrate this, I might mention a recent incident. In conversation with a professor of social studies at a major Catholic university, I found that my friend, although teaching courses concerned with housing, health care, and other welfare issues, was totally unaware that the American Catholic bishops had ever spoken on such issues. He asked me where such statements might be found, but when I referred him to the periodical *Origins* he confessed that he had never heard of it.

J. Brian Benestad, a young and promising professor of political theory and social ethics, is helping to remedy this situation. In collaboration with Francis J. Butler he edited *Quest for Justice,* an excellent compendium of statements by the United States hierarchy on social and political issues.* The present book, especially in chapters three and four, may be viewed as a companion piece to this compendium. It provides a concise and informative survey of what the bishops have been saying about many crucial public issues of our day, such as world hunger, nuclear armament, military conscription, conscientious objection, multinational corporations,

---

Quest for Justice: A Compendium of Statements by the American Catholic Bishops on the Political and Social Order, 1966–1980 (Washington: United States Catholic Conference, 1981).

national health insurance, capital punishment, abortion legislation, and public aid to non-public education. Benestad both presents the positions of the bishops and analyzes the reasoning behind these positions. In so doing he indicates, to some extent, the views of certain individuals who have contributed to the bishops' statements—for example, Bishop James S. Rausch, Monsignor George Higgins, and Father Bryan Hehir. Because the bishops are addressing issues not simply of Catholic but of general concern, this account should be of interest to every American seriously interested in the religious and ethical dimensions of public policy.

Benestad, however, is not content to be informative. He seeks also to give an evaluation and to propose constructive measures. In many cases, he has words of praise for particular statements of the hierarchy, especially those that are more educational in character. But in what will probably prove to be the most controversial portion of this book, he raises a number of difficulties. Among the criticisms he and others have made, the following may be especially noted:

- The bishops and clergy who write and issue the statements lack sufficient expertise to speak with authority about many of the questions addressed. While sometimes disclaiming special competence they nevertheless advocate positions that presuppose such competence—for example, in promoting the so-called New International Economic Order, the ratification of SALT II, and the adoption of universal national health insurance.

- By issuing policy statements on matters that lie beyond their specific competence, and that pertain rather to experts in secular disciplines, the bishops diminish their own credibility in speaking about matters with which they are specially charged as spiritual leaders of the Church.

- The bishops, or those who compose policy statements on their behalf, can hardly avoid introducing their own political and economic biases, which should on no account be confused with the teaching of the Church.

- By opting for certain positions on matters legitimately debated among committed Catholics, the bishops tend to marginalize church members who have different social or political orientations.

• By framing official church positions on social and political policy matters, the bishops and clergy arrogate to themselves functions that more properly belong to the laity, as persons regularly and continuously involved in secular affairs.

• By seeking relevance for the Church on terms set by secular trends, the bishops unwittingly give support to the opinion that evangelization, prayer, worship, and religious doctrine are of secondary importance.

Notwithstanding these and other difficulties, Dr. Benestad does not on principle oppose the issuance of policy statements on secular matters in the name of the Church. He holds, however, that the issues should be more carefully selected, that the statements should be drawn up by a politically balanced staff consisting of truly competent persons, that the laity should normally participate in the process, and that the positions advocated should be clearly presented as applications of Catholic social principles.

These suggestions, which seem eminently reasonable from the author's own perspective, will have to be appraised by many minds and from many points of view. Benestad's recommendations with regard to restructuring the relationships between the National Conference of Catholic Bishops and the United States Catholic Conference, very succinctly set forth, will no doubt have to be worked out in greater detail by himself or by others.

From the criticisms listed above one might get the impression that Dr. Benestad is in favor of a partial withdrawal of the Church from public issues and greater concentration on private piety and worship. More correctly, his position could be characterized, I think, as calling for an increase of the Church's influence on the social and political order without any reduction of the importance of personal religious practice. He has specific recommendations as to how this might be achieved.

Following the teaching of the twentieth-century popes, especially John Paul II, Benestad forcefully argues that the primary responsibility of bishops and clergy in the social sphere is to evangelize and to teach Catholic social doctrine. No transformation of social structures, he believes, will be of lasting value unless it is accompanied by the personal conversion of individuals to the way of the Gospel. Contrary to Kant, Benestad is convinced that good laws will be of little use if the people are corrupt and self-seeking. In continuity with the classical tradition of political philosophy and theology, he contends that the primary goal of secular government is to promote the personal and civic virtue of the citizens.

Catholic social doctrine, Benestad reminds his readers, is not the same thing as the formulation of social policy. Church doctrine, consciously based on revelation and on the Christian understanding of the divine order, is primarily addressed to believers, and is free from the kinds of compromise that are frequently necessary in addressing transitory issues. The social implications of the Gospel have been spelled out in the great tradition of Christian political philosophy stretching back to Augustine and Aquinas—a tradition carried forward in our own century by the recent popes and by Christian philosophers such as Jacques Maritain.

Unconsciously infected by contemporary trends, the American bishops, according to Benestad, have tended to underemphasize the importance of personal faith, character formation, and discipleship. Insufficiently familiar with the great tradition of Catholic political thought, they have failed to pass on the patrimony of social and political wisdom to which they are the rightful heirs. For this reason they have in many cases used policy statements as a substitute for social teaching, and neglected to give a coherent rationale for the policies they have advocated. Too often the cardinals and bishops have descended to the level of lobbyists rather than presenting themselves as authentic spiritual leaders.

Benestad's study, however, does not end on this negative note. He points to the social teaching of recent popes as exemplifying what spiritual leaders in the Church can and should do. A close student of the thought of John Paul II, he devotes a major section of his final chapter to examining how this pope understands the relation of the Church to the sociopolitical order. While warning the clergy against engaging in "partisan politics," the present pope advocates principles that, if implemented, cannot fail to exert a transforming influence on secular society.

Dr. Benestad strongly emphasizes the importance of presenting traditional and papal social teaching. This task can be an important one, but if the discipline of theological social ethics is seriously cultivated in this country, the American bishops and theologians might be able to do more than to transmit a heritage gratefully received. Thanks to men such as Monsignor John A. Ryan and John Courtney Murray, S.J., American Catholic thinkers have already made a distinctive contribution to official church doctrine in the social sphere. By deeper reflection on the American experience, others may make comparable contributions in the years to come.

In the current climate of opinion, readers will inevitably ask whether the author of this study is liberal or conservative. The issues he raises, I submit, transcend the debate between these opposing factions. Avoiding both the liberalism of the new left and the conservatism of the new right, Benestad does not settle for a weak compromise between the two. Instead, he offers a sustained critique of all the prevailing tendencies. He is conservative in the sense that he stands firmly within the great tradition of Catholic political philosophy, and offers no apologies for so doing. He is liberal in the sense of being devoted to the dignity and authentic freedom of every human person as created by God and redeemed by the blood of Jesus Christ.

This book might even be called radical in the original meaning of that term. It goes to the roots. Instead of uncritically adopting the agenda and *modus operandi* dictated by current fashions, Benestad is convinced that the Church, in loyalty to Christ, can draw up a better agenda of its own. His critique of recent episcopal policy statements is not that they are too radical but that they are not radical enough; they fail to expose the roots of the present disorders.

As an ecclesiologist I should like to express my gratitude to the author for introducing some distinctions that greatly help to clarify the current controversies about the mission of the Church. If Benestad is correct, evangelization and social doctrine pertain to the essential nature of the Church in a way in which policy statements on transitory secular issues do not. In his inevitably brief exposition he perhaps gives the impression that social theory can be constructed without any dependence on practical experience, but I do not think that his position necessarily implies this. Even if the theory-praxis relationship is seen as a dialectical one of mutual priority and interdependence, Benestad's distinctions are still valuable, even essential. In any future discussions of the Church's involvement in social reconstruction, account should be taken of the three phases that are so lucidly distinguished in the present work.

I enthusiastically welcome *The Pursuit of a Just Social Order* as a positive contribution to the study of the questions it raises. If this book has the kind of influence I should wish for it, the clergy and spiritual leaders of the coming generation may be able to retrieve, and develop further, the forgotten riches of the classical and Christian tradition of political wisdom. Such wisdom is sorely needed in our day.

Acknowledgments

I AM VERY GRATEFUL to all those who assisted me in various ways to prepare the initial and subsequent drafts of this manuscript: Professors Ernest Fortin and Robert Scigliano from Boston College; Professor Wilson Carey McWilliams, Rutgers University; Dean William Parente and Professors Thomas Garrett and John McGinley from the University of Scranton; the Reverend George Aschenbrenner, St. Joseph's University; the Reverend William J. Byron, S.J., Catholic University of America; and the Most Reverend John J. O'Connor, Military Ordinariate, New York City. I am also indebted to the three people who were kind enough to write formal evaluations of the first draft: Monsignor George Higgins, the Reverend James Schall, S.J., and Mr. Patrick Riley. I owe a special debt of gratitude to the Reverend Avery Dulles, S.J., of Catholic University, who read two drafts of my manuscript and who wrote the foreword; to the Reverend Ernest Fortin, A.A., who has enlightened and encouraged me from my first years in college; and to my wife, Janet, who read each version of the manuscript and patiently gave me wise counsel at every stage along the way.

I wish to thank my editor, Carol Friedley Griffith, who made helpful suggestions and conscientiously prepared the manuscript for publication, and my typist, Mrs. Cynthia Knott, who did an outstanding job in a very short time.

Finally, I would like to pay tribute to the memory of my college French teacher, the Reverend Denys Gonthier, A.A., who attained a rare level of excellence in teaching languages and literature, who motivated many students to take learning and the spiritual life seriously, and whose friendship was cherished by those who were close to him.

It goes without saying that none of the above is responsible for any deficiencies in my book.

PART ONE

Religion and Politics
in the Catholic Tradition

CHAPTER ONE

Addressing the Political Order

FOR OVER SIXTY YEARS the Catholic bishops of the
United States have collectively sought to promote justice by addressing public issues. They make statements primarily through
the United States Catholic Conference (USCC) and also through
the National Conference of Catholic Bishops (NCCB), both of
which are in Washington, D.C. These two parallel organizations,
established in 1966, replaced the National Catholic Welfare Conference (NCWC), through which the bishops as a body spoke
between 1919 and 1966.[1] This study focuses on the political and
social statements issued by the USCC and the NCCB between
1966 and 1980.[2] The structure of these two bodies and their
statement-making procedures are described in appendix A.

The bishops have stressed the development of specific policy
statements for the guidance of individual citizens and policymakers. While not usually endorsing specific legislation by name, the
bishops do endorse specific legislative proposals. Through these
statements the bishops have made a commendable effort to promote human rights, justice, and peace. In the realm of foreign
policy, they have opposed the violation of human rights abroad,
defended both conscientious and selective conscientious objection, advocated arms control, urged the alleviation of hunger in the
world, opposed the reinstitution of the draft, and condemned the
use of nuclear weapons. In domestic policy, they have condemned

3

abortion and racism, sought federal aid for parochial schools, defended the rights of farm workers, urged the government to fight inflation without causing greater unemployment, endorsed national health insurance, and offered proposals for prison and welfare reform, the preservation of the family farm, and a more humane immigration policy. In brief, the bishops have energetically sought economic and social justice for all.[3]

Interest groups like the USCC in the American political process usually issue policy statements that propose specific legislation. These statements may also be used to state principles that can serve as the basis for solutions to particular problems. While the American bishops have focused on supporting or opposing specific legislation, they also, to a limited extent, have attempted to evangelize and educate through their policy statements.

Unlike most interest groups, the bishops do not present their own policy positions as the only possible solutions to particular problems.

> The principles of revelation do not provide specific solutions to many social problems, nor do they constitute a blueprint for organizing society. In proposing concrete policies in the social order, the Church is aware that often the more specific a proposal or program, the more room there may be for persons of sincere faith to disagree.[4]

The bishops realize that the Gospel and Catholic social thought—a teaching that is shaped mainly by papal writings from 1891 to the present and by the documents of the Second Vatican Council[5]—do not provide specific recipes for resolving public policy dilemmas.[6] The Gospel and Catholic social thought do provide guiding principles, but the formulation of a policy position requires precise knowledge of many particulars. For example, the answers to inflation and unemployment require expertise in American politics and economics.

As there is widespread agreement that contemporary problems require a good deal of specific government action on a national level, the policy statement seems the most logical vehicle by which to work for justice. Let us assume that all the bishops' policy proposals do indeed offer the best solutions to the nation's problems. Let us further assume that the future will reveal that the bishops' stands on abortion and nuclear weapons are much wiser than many currently realize. What more could one ask of the Catholic bishops?

To state the answer simply, the legislation and structural changes suggested by policy statements, however wise, are the necessary but not the sufficient condition of moral order in political and social life. Catholic social thought teaches that formation of character, a certain kind of education, strong religious beliefs, and the preservation of worthy traditions and mores are indispensable to the well-being of society. Good laws and structures will not benefit a people ill prepared to receive them. Jean-Jacques Rousseau makes this point in his *Social Contract:*

> As an architect, before erecting a large edifice, examines and tests the soil in order to see whether it can support the weight, so a wise lawgiver does not begin by drawing up laws that are good in themselves, but considers first whether the people for whom he designs them are fit to endure them ... and it is on this account that good laws and worthless men were to be found in Crete, for Minos had only disciplined a people steeped in vice.[7]

Citizens need character formation, and there is a steep price to pay for neglecting to foster and maintain appropriate qualities of soul in the body politic. Pope John Paul II said in Brazil:

> A transformation of political, social, or economic structures would never be consolidated if it were not accompanied by a sincere "conversion" of the mind, the will, and the heart of man in all his truth.[8]

The Latin American bishops took considerable pains to stress this point in the final document of their Third General Conference (Puebla, Mexico; 1979):

> The Church realizes that even the best structures and the most idealized systems quickly become inhuman if human inclinations are not improved, if there is no conversion of heart and mind on the part of those who are living in those structures or controlling them.[9]

The close relation between the quality of the political order and the personal virtue of citizens has been a principal theme of Augustine,

Thomas Aquinas, and others, and also of modern Catholic social thought beginning with Pope Leo XIII.[10]

The Church in fact has consistently taught that it makes a significant contribution to the political and social order by fulfilling its fundamental mission, evangelization. The Second Vatican Council cited the words of Pope Pius XI to Father M. D. Roland Gosselin: "It is necessary never to lose sight of the fact that the objective of the Church is to evangelize, not to civilize. If it civilizes, it is by evangelization."[11] The Council Fathers asserted that "by the very fulfillment of her own mission the Church stimulates and advances human and civic culture."[12] Elsewhere in that document (*Gaudium et Spes*) they said, " . . . the force which the Church can inject into the modern society of man consists of that faith and charity put into vital practice, not in any external dominion exercised by merely human means."[13] By teaching the whole Christian message, the Church sheds light on all areas of human activity; it thereby promotes the transcendence of the human person and fosters political freedom and the responsibility of citizens.

Pope Paul VI reaffirmed this teaching of the Second Vatican Council. Pope John Paul II has done so also, using almost the same words as the Council to describe the relation of evangelization to civilization:

> Nor let it be said that evangelization should necessarily follow the process of humanization. The true apostle of the Gospel is he who humanizes and evangelizes at the same time, in the certainty that he who evangelizes also civilizes. It is necessary to proceed in this way.[14]

John Paul II teaches that the Church always and everywhere strives to make people better, more conscious of their dignity, and more devoted family members, workers, professionals, and citizens. By teaching virtue and a sense of obligation to family, friends, neighbors, country, and the international community, the Church shapes the customs of nations. John Paul II has stated this thought forcefully:

> We cry out once more: Respect man! He is the image of God! Evangelize so that this may become a reality; so that the Lord

may transform hearts and humanize the political and economic systems, with man's responsible commitment as a starting point.[15]

Certainly, Catholic Action loves the world, but with a love that draws inspiration from the example of Christ. His way of serving the world and promoting the values of man is *primarily* that of evangelizing, in logical consistency with the conviction that in the Gospel is contained the most overwhelming power, capable of really making all things new [emphasis added].[16]

The Catholic Church is anxious to put the solicitude of Christ into practice and therefore, while working for man's eternal salvation as her first duty, she cannot fail to take an active interest also in the welfare and progress of peoples in this world. The Church's *principal* contribution in this field is through the *formation of consciences,* by making people more spiritually mature, more open to others and ready to assist them in need [emphasis added].[17]

The Church forms the consciences of human beings; it especially seeks changes in the political order through evangelization.

In the final document from their conference at Puebla, the bishops of Latin America also stressed the close relation between evangelization and just political structures:

Evangelization seeks to get to the very core of a culture, the realm of its basic values, and to bring about a conversion that will serve as the basis and guarantee of a transformation in structures and the social milieu.[18]

Evangelization, properly understood, does not legitimize an unjust status quo, as some argue, but is really a critique of culture. Evangelization seeks to address both the personal and the social evils present in a culture. The Gospel, properly preached, has economic, social, cultural, and political implications. John Paul II said in Brazil:

Evangelization, the *raison d'être* of any ecclesial community, would not be complete if it did not keep in mind the relations existing between the message of the Gospel and man's personal and social life, between the commandment of love for one's suffering neighbor and the concrete situations of injustice to be combatted and of justice and peace to be established.[19]

French philosopher Jacques Maritain, who had a significant influence on both Paul VI and John Paul II, argued that "a vitally Christian social renewal will be a work of sanctity or it will be nothing: a sanctity, that is, turned toward the temporal, the secular, the profane."[20]

> You can only transform the social regime of the world by effecting at the same time, and first of all within yourselves, a renewal of spiritual life and of moral life, by digging down to the spiritual and moral foundations of human life, by renewing the moral ideas which govern the life of the social group as such, and by awakening in the depths of the latter a new *élan*.[21]

For the sake of clarity, it is helpful to distinguish evangelization, Catholic social teaching, and policy statements.

Evangelization is the proclamation of the life and teaching of Jesus Christ. Pope Paul VI described it in this way:

> To evangelize is first of all to bear witness, in a simple and direct way, to God revealed by Jesus Christ, in the Holy Spirit; to bear witness that in his Son God loved the world—that in his Incarnate Word he has given being to all things and has called men to eternal life. . . .
>
> Evangelization will also contain . . . a clear proclamation that, in Jesus Christ, the Son of God made man, who died and rose from the dead, salvation is offered to all men, as a gift of God's grace and mercy.[22]

Catholic *social teaching,* found primarily in papal social encyclicals and in several documents issued by the Second Vatican Council, is based on Scripture, tradition, and reason. In that body of teaching, the popes and the Council Fathers carefully explain a number of basic concepts as guides for understanding the relation between Christianity and the political order, and for rightly judging social, political, and economic phenomena. Examples of these concepts are: the dignity of the human person, the social nature of man, the purpose of politics, war and peace, the common good, the value of work, the duties of individuals toward one another and toward society, the right to a living wage, the right to private property, the right to development, the relation of rights to duties, and the role of the family. Pope John Paul II carefully distinguishes specific policy proposals or partisan politics from Catholic social teaching and relates the latter to evangelization:

> In her social doctrine, the Church does not propose a concrete political or economic model, but indicates the way, presents principles. And she does so in accordance with her evangelizing mission, in accordance with her evangelical message which has as its aim man in his eschatological dimension, but also in the concrete context of his historical contemporary situation. She does so because she believes in the dignity of man, created in the image of God: a dignity which is intrinsic in every man, every woman, every child, whatever may be his place in society.[23]

Catholic social teaching is really a subdivision of evangelization broadly understood.

Specific *policy statements* are an application of Catholic social teaching to particular issues. Reliance on Catholic social teaching does not insure that a policy statement will be wise or effective. Drawing guidance from Catholic social principles in order to propose specific solutions to public problems requires keen perception of many particulars and the virtue of political prudence. Policy statements, whether issued by bishops, clergy, or laypersons, must be submitted to careful scrutiny. Bishops *qua* bishops have no greater insight into policy matters than anyone else. Besides, there is room for legitimate disagreement among reasonable Christians. As Paul VI pointed out, "In concrete situations, and taking account of solidarity in each person's life, one must recognize a legitimate variety of possible options. The same Christian faith can lead to different commitments."[24]

Jacques Maritain, in his influential book *Integral Humanism,* also made a distinction between Catholic social teaching and policy positions based on Christian principles. He said that Christian wisdom on political, economic, and social matters, as elaborated by the encyclicals of Leo XIII and Pius XI, "does not descend to the particular determinations of the concrete."

> Let us denounce therefore the equivocation contained in a formula like the following, which is not uncommon to meet: "We wish to judge from the Catholic point of view all temporal, political or economic, national or international, artistic or scien-

tific questions." Such a formula, in order not to be illusory, must necessarily be taken in two different ways: for there is a judgment of Catholicism on these questions, but this judgment bears only on certain lofty principles on which they depend, or on certain spiritual values implied in them, and cannot tell me whether it is fitting to support or to oppose the wheat policy of M. Flandin or the foreign policy of M. Laval.[25]

Karl Rahner, a well-known Jesuit theologian, says that the "task of criticizing society which belongs to the official church has still not achieved any theological definition, and so too any recognized position in society."[26] Rahner has no doubt that the official Church should be a critic of society, but he insists that this function has not been well thought out on the theological level. It cannot, he says, be subsumed under the teaching office or pastoral office, because "the task of the teaching office strictly as such is to preach the Gospel in its abiding and permanent validity" and "the role of the pastoral office is to instruct the faithful in the specifically religious sphere."

Rahner suggests calling the function of social criticism "prophetic instruction," a function performed not as a matter of faith and morals but as a recommendation. These instructions "of their very nature [would be] (whether explicitly or implicitly) subject to criticism on the part of the faithful of the world." Rahner adds that those primarily responsible for social criticism should be "Christians in general" and their formal and informal groupings within the Church—in other words, the laity.

In brief, *evangelization* is the proclamation of the life and teaching of Jesus Christ, Catholic *social teaching* offers an education in political and social principles, and *policy statements* are an application of Catholic social teaching to particular issues. There are therefore three ways by which the Church addresses the public order.

It has been the constant teaching of the popes from Leo XIII to John Paul II and the teaching of the Second Vatican Council that the hierarchical Church makes its best contribution to the political order through the first two of these ways, evangelization and education in Catholic social teaching.[27] These two activities enable the Church to work for a slow, deep transformation of society. John Paul II has said:

> The Church indicates how to build society in accordance with man, in respect for man. Her task is to put the leaven of the Gospel in all fields of human activity. It is in Christ that the Church is an "expert in humanity. . . ." She does not claim to interfere in politics, she does not aspire to take part in the management of temporal problems. Her specific contribution will be *to strengthen the spiritual and moral bases of society,* doing her utmost so that all and any activity in the field of the common good will develop in harmony and consistency with the guidelines and requirements of human and Christian ethics. . . . This service is *first and foremost a service of formation of con- sciences:* to proclaim the moral law and its requirements, to denounce errors and attacks on the moral law and on the dignity of man on which it is based, to clarify and convince [emphasis added].[28]

This book is an exposition and critique of the bishops' mode of addressing political issues. Chapter two explains the theological foundation of the bishops' concern for politics, the role of the Church in the political and social orders, and the general moral perspective behind the bishops' political statements. Chapter three presents the bishops' positions on foreign policy issues under the rubrics of military and strategic policy, human rights, and de- velopment. Chapter four explains the bishops' positions on domes- tic social justice issues such as the economy and examines their views on abortion, aid for parochial schools, and the family. The concluding sections of the third and fourth chapters comment briefly on the educational value of the bishops' policy state- ments—more precisely, to what extent these statements provide guidance in looking at politics from the point of view of Catholic social teaching.

Chapter five briefly discusses the general characteristics of the bishops' political statements; evaluates the bishops' policy state- ments according to the criteria of logical development, consis- tency, completeness of argument, and fidelity to Catholic social teaching; suggests ways of making future policy statements more effective instruments for promoting justice; and discusses the role the laity should play in the political and social order. Chapter six makes a case for drawing political and social benefits from evangelization and education, briefly and therefore inadequately explains why the study of political philosophy is indispensable, and concludes with some observations on teaching Catholic social thought.

Given the charged atmosphere that envelops discussions of religion and politics, it is important to make two additional comments. First, according to the Second Vatican Council, bishops and laypersons have different roles to play in the political and social order. Their activities sometimes overlap, but each group has certain specific duties that ought to predominate. The Council's *Dogmatic Constitution on the Church* (*Lumen Gentium*) states the distinction this way:

> Among the principal duties of bishops, the preaching of the Gospel occupies an eminent place. . . . What specifically characterizes the laity is their secular nature. It is true that those in holy orders can at times be engaged in secular activities, even have a secular profession. But they are by reason of their particular vocation especially and professedly ordained to the sacred ministry. . . . But the laity, by their very vocation, seek the kingdom of God by engaging in temporal affairs and by ordering them according to the plan of God.[29]

Let this brief description suffice for now. I wish to make this distinction very clear so as to avoid possible misunderstanding. In arguing that the task of bishops is to pursue justice primarily through evangelization and education, I am not saying that these activities exhaust the political and social responsibilities of the Catholic Church. Catholic laypersons should be involved in the political and social life of the nation to the measure of their capacity. They should perform their familial and professional duties well and exercise their responsibilities as citizens. In the latter role, the laity may contribute in various ways to the formulation of public policy; they may push for preserving, changing, adding to, or removing structures and laws. The bishops themselves may address particular issues in general educational statements that do not require specific legislative proposals. They may also make conventional policy statements, but not at the expense of seeking justice through evangelization and education. There are times when the bishops' mission to promote justice will require a denunciation of clear evils. This kind of policy statement will be, in a sense, easier to formulate than those statements that propose specific solutions to complicated problems.

The second point I want to add here is that there is a widespread tendency to devalue the importance of pursuing justice through evangelization and education. The idea of seeking justice in these ways is dismissed as ineffective or conservative, or as a sanctification of the status quo. This is really an old argument, the full dimensions of which cannot be understood without a knowledge of political philosophy. It is unlikely that an informed discussion of the relation among evangelization, education, and justice will take place unless we all become more familiar with the quarrel between the ancient and the modern philosophers about the nature of politics.[30] In this very difficult task we are aided by the work of Leo Strauss, about whom Ernest Fortin has said:

> By resurrecting classical political theory, Strauss has paved the way for a genuine recovery of the Christian classics as well. One regrets that with few exceptions, Christian scholars have yet to avail themselves of his pioneering work in order to gain fresh insight into their own heritage.[31]

Most Christian theologians have neglected not only Strauss but political philosophy as well, and especially the views of ancient, medieval, and early modern political philosophers.

CHAPTER TWO

Political Principles

THIS CHAPTER WILL FIRST deal with one principle not thematically discussed but rightly named as the root concept underlying every political statement by the bishops: human dignity.[1] It will then present the bishops' reflections on the relation of the Catholic Church to the political order and, lastly, expound the bishops' political principles, insofar as they have explained them.

The bishops have not systematically explained in detail all the principles of Catholic social teaching upon which their social ministry is based, principles found, for the most part, in papal writings beginning with Pope Leo XIII and in several documents of the Second Vatican Council. However, the bishops have presented some significant aspects of that teaching in statements on political responsibility and in two pastoral letters, "Human Life in Our Day" (NCCB, November 1968)[2] and "To Live in Christ Jesus: A Pastoral Reflection on the Moral Life" (NCCB, November 1976).[3] In these documents we find general reflections on the political order, both domestic and international, as well as a discussion of the way in which the Church understands its specific contributions to the political order.

These episcopal documents are not confined, however, to explaining Catholic social teaching. The bishops also apply that teaching to the United States. Hence I will speak of the American bishops' moral perspective on the international and domestic political order. Furthermore, I will distinguish the bishops' exposition

14

of Catholic social teaching from their own pronouncements, because the latter are not the only possible applications of the former.

THE DIGNITY OF THE HUMAN PERSON

The theological foundation of the Catholic Church's interest in the political order is the dignity of the human person. The Catholic Church believes that man was created in the image and likeness of God and was so loved by God that God gave his Son Jesus Christ to redeem man from sin. In his book on the Second Vatican Council, Pope John Paul II says it is apparent that man was made in God's image "not only because of the spiritual nature of his immortal soul but also by reason of his *social* nature if by this we understand the fact that he 'cannot fully realize himself except in an act of pure self-giving.' "[4] In other words, man is a social being who needs to live in association with other human beings if he is to live a fully human life. Without community, a person cannot fulfill his obligation to grow in faith, charity, and knowledge

The human person, created in God's image with both a spiritual and a social nature, has both rights and duties. The chief duty of public authorities is, in the words of Pope Pius XII, "to safeguard the inviolable rights of the human person in order to facilitate the fulfillment of his duties."[5] Pope John Paul II argues that the Church functions as a sign and safeguard of the transcendent dimension of the human person, not only by defending human rights but also by encouraging fulfillment of the corresponding duties and the right use of the freedom afforded by the protection of rights.

Rights, however, must be conceived in their correct meaning. The right to freedom, for example, does not of course include the right to moral evil, as if it were possible to claim, among other things, the right to suppress human life, as in abortion, or the freedom to use things harmful to oneself or others. Likewise one should not deal with the rights of man without envisaging also his corresponding duties, which express his own responsibility and his respect for the rights of others and of the community.[6]

The political significance of the Church's theological affirmations about the nature of the human person is evident in comments on modern civilization made by Pope John Paul II. In Mexico, the Pope said:

> Perhaps one of the most obvious weaknesses of present day civilization lies in an inadequate view of man. Without doubt, our age is the one in which man has been most written and spoken of, the age of the forms of humanism and anthropocentrism. Nevertheless it is paradoxically also the age of man's abasement to previously unsuspected levels, the age of human values trampled on as never before.[7]

John Paul II attributes misperceptions about human nature to certain forms of humanism that deny man's longing for the infinite. In the West, the absence of a genuine belief that human beings are created in God's image manifests itself in materialism and moral permissiveness. In the Soviet Union, the doctrine of atheistic humanism denies that man is made in God's image and therefore has a spiritual nature and infinite longings. This sort of humanism claims that man acquires dignity by working for the state, and that he does indeed live by bread alone.[8]

Speaking at the United Nations, John Paul II argued that modern civilization, while successfully promoting material development over the last hundred years, has failed to foster respect for the spiritual dimension of the human person. The resulting materialism has not only personal but also political consequences. When people are insensitive to the spiritual dimension of life, their struggle to obtain material goods gives "rise to tension, dissension, and division that will often turn into open conflict."[9] The values of the spirit give "the proper sense of earthly material goods" and enable people to make the sacrifices required for the common good.[10]

Since it is insensitive to the spiritual dimension of life, modern civilization is unlikely to overcome its inadequate view of the human person, and societies are unlikely to attain peace and unity. The neglect of the spiritual feeds on itself and thus constitutes a very deep temptation:

> It goes further than anything constituting man's temptation in past history, and it shows at the same time, we might say, the deepest reality of all temptation. Man today is submitted to the temptation of refusing God.[11]

Political systems based upon an inadequate view of man lead inevitably to injustice. John Paul II discerns two threats to human rights from these deficient political systems. The first is the unjust distribution of material goods within nations and among nations. The dignity of the human person requires that a political system be judged by its capability to restrain exploitation and to insure, through work, a just distribution of material goods as well as participation in the process of production. That same criterion requires that all nations cooperate to overcome the disparity between rich and poor nations, including efforts to eliminate belts of hunger, malnutrition, underdevelopment, disease, and illiteracy.[12]

The second systematic threat to man from deficient political systems is the abridgment or denial of such civil and political liberties as the right to participate in political life, freedom of thought and expression, religious freedom of conscience, and freedom from discrimination on the grounds of origin, race, sex, nationality, religion, political convictions, and the like.

Further insight into the political implications of the Church's vision of the human person may be gleaned from Pope Paul VI's reflections on Marxism, socialism, and liberalism in *Octogesima Adveniens* (May 1971). Concrete historical movements such as Marxism and various kinds of socialism, though originating in ideologies, are in part distinct from them, said Paul VI. He quoted from John XXIII's *Pacem in Terris:*

> Who can deny that those movements, insofar as they conform to the dictates of right reason and are interpreters of the lawful aspirations of the human person, contain elements that are positive and deserving of approval.[13]

This passage implies that Christians may cooperate, to some degree, with parts of Marxist and socialist movements. However, in succeeding paragraphs Pope Paul became more specific. He did not rule out cooperation with Marxists, especially insofar as they employ Marxist teachings as a rigorous method of examining social and political conditions and as the rational link tested by history between theoretical knowledge and the practice of revolutionary transformation. But he stressed the intimate link between Marxist movements and ideology. He condemned the kind of violent,

totalitarian society that results from the practice of class struggle
and its Marxist interpretation.

Pope Paul was more sanguine about cooperation with socialists,
though he similarly warned of the link between these movements
and ideology. Christians must understand, he continued, the precise nature of the link so that their cooperation will not jeopardize
certain values, "especially those of liberty, responsibility, and
openness to the spiritual which guarantee the integral development of man." [14]

Paul VI was also critical of liberal ideology, for this reason:

> Liberal ideology . . . believes it exalts individual freedom by
> withdrawing it from every limitation, by stimulating it through
> exclusive seeking of interest and power, and by considering
> social solidarities as more or less automatic consequences of
> individual initiatives, not as an aim and a major criterion of the
> value of social organization.[15]

Pope Paul did not entirely rule out cooperation with proponents of
liberal ideology: in fact, he believed that "personal initiative must
be maintained and developed" in economic and political affairs.
However, he did not give details as to the nature of this personal
initiative. He did point out that Christians easily forget that the
"very root of philosophical liberalism is an erroneous affirmation
of the autonomy of the individual in his activity, his motivation,
and the exercise of his liberty." [16] The error of liberalism has two
harmful consequences: it encourages the individual to seek power
and his own self-interest, and it leads him to think that social
solidarity follows more or less automatically from the private pur-
suits of individuals. In other words, Pope Paul denied the liberal
axiom that an invisible hand invariably extracts public benefits
from private vice.

Because of its view of the human person, the Catholic Church is
opposed to total state control, unlimited individualism, and the
reduction of man to a consumer of economic goods. Catholic
principles lead people to choose the form of government that most
effectively allows, and even encourages, the human person to
develop his spiritual and social nature.

Many American liberals and conservatives subscribe to the

philosophical liberalism criticized by Pope Paul VI. Segments of both groups erroneously affirm the autonomy of the individual. Liberals tend to stress the freedom from any interference with personal morals, while conservatives argue that the public interest will emerge from the untrammeled pursuit by individuals of their private economic interests.

THE CATHOLIC CHURCH AND THE POLITICAL ORDER

Clergy, religious congregations, and orders have become increasingly involved in politics during the past decade and a half. Perhaps the best known of the new Catholic activists were the priests Daniel Berrigan, a Jesuit, and his brother Philip. When the American hierarchy (a term that generally refers to the bishops, though technically it includes priests and deacons also) organized as the United States Catholic Conference and the National Conference of Catholic Bishops in 1966, it began to increase its political activity. Since then, the hierarchy has taken positions on numerous domestic and international issues. The bishops have testified on Capitol Hill, met with presidents, and communicated with the secretary of state and other officials.

The bishops' understanding of the Church's relation to the political order was briefly presented in two statements issued by the USCC's Administrative Board: in February 1976, "Political Responsibility: Reflections on an Election Year," and in October 1979, "Political Responsibility: Choices for the 1980s." The two statements made the same points (almost word for word) on the relation of the Church to the political order. The Church's role includes: educating the faithful in the social teachings of the Church; calling upon citizens to revitalize public life and to approach public affairs from positions grounded in moral convictions and religious belief; promoting human rights and social justice; denouncing violations of human rights; calling attention to the moral and religious dimension of political issues; showing what changes are required by the Christian faith to bring about a just society; and analyzing public policy in the light of gospel values. This last task entails offering specific solutions to political problems. Principles to be observed include these: statements on human rights and social justice should be comprehensive and consistent; they should be competent, showing awareness that issues are complex; and they should be developed in dialogue with concerned parties.

The USCC board said in the 1979 statement that the Church's participation in political affairs may appear to some as a threat to pluralism and to the political process. But "advocating the critical values of human rights and social justice" does not interfere with the legitimate autonomy of government. In support of this position, the board quoted a passage from Vatican II's *Gaudium et Spes:*

> By preaching the truth of the Gospel and shedding light on all areas of human activity through her teaching and the example of the faithful, [the Church] shows respect for the political freedom and responsibility of citizens and fosters these values. She also has the right to pass moral judgments, even on matters touching the political order, whenever basic personal rights or the salvation of souls make such judgments necessary.[17]

The USCC board also quoted from *Justice in the World,* a statement by the 1971 worldwide Synod of Bishops: "insofar as the Church is a religious and hierarchical community," it is not her role "to offer concrete solutions in the social, economic, and political spheres for justice in the world."[18] Nevertheless, the Church still has the right to apply religious and moral principles to individual cases and thus to make concrete proposals. In support of this position, the board quoted a passage from Pope John's *Pacem in Terris:*

> It must not be forgotten that the Church has the right and duty not only to safeguard the principles of ethics and religion, but also to intervene authoritatively with her children in the temporal sphere when there is a question of judging the application of principles to concrete cases.[19]

The USCC board expressed the belief that the Constitution of the United States gives religious bodies the right not only to state principles but also to take specific positions on matters of public policy. The board went on to say that, when taking concrete positions on matters about which reasonable Christians may disagree, the bishops do not impose their views by dint of authority. Hence they are not planning to form a religious voting bloc, do not endorse candidates, and are not telling people how to vote. They hope to move all citizens to take politics more seriously and to look at political issues from a moral and religious viewpoint.

> We seek to promote a greater understanding of the important link between faith and politics and to express our belief that our nation is enriched when its citizens and social groups approach public affairs from positions grounded in moral conviction and religious belief.[20]

The USCC board stated that "the laity has major responsibility for the renewal of the temporal order"[21] but did not indicate how the layman's role in the political order differs from the clergy's.

What is the relation of the Church's social ministry to the rest of its mission? The NCCB's *National Catechetical Directory* (1977) shows the importance of the social ministry by citing excerpts from three sources. From the Second Vatican Council statement *Gaudium et Spes:*

> The expectation of a new earth must not weaken but rather stimulate our concern for cultivating this one.[22]

From an address of Pope Paul VI:

> Yes, the cause of human dignity and of human rights is the cause of Christ and his Gospel.[23]

From the 1971 Synod of Bishops statement *Justice in the World:*

> Action on behalf of justice and participation in the transformation of the world fully appear to us as a constitutive dimension of the preaching of the Gospel, or, in other words, of the Church's mission for the redemption of the human race, and its liberation from every oppressive situation.[24]

Without comment, the *Catechetical Directory* also adds the following very important qualification by quoting from Pope Paul VI's 1975 statement *On Evangelization in the Modern World:* "The Church links human liberation and salvation in Jesus Christ, but she never identifies them."

In November 1974, the entire body of bishops reminded Catho-

lics that hunger in the world presented the Church with an opportunity "to experience an essential dimension of its mission: acting
on behalf of justice and participating in the transformation of the
world" ("Statement on the World Food Crisis: A Pastoral Plan of
Action," NCCB).[25] The bishops were citing and interpreting the
key passage from the 1971 Synod of Bishops statement quoted
above. This passage was cited again by Bishop James Rausch,
general secretary of the USCC, in *Homily: The Red Mass* (1975)[26]
and in the 1976 statement on political responsibility by the USCC
Administrative Board.[27] But the board's 1979 statement on political responsibility did not mention this passage, probably because of
the debate that had arisen over its exact theological significance.[28]

In a short article entitled "The Ministry for Justice," the Reverend J. Bryan Hehir, director of the USCC's Office of International
Justice and Peace and the bishops' principal advisor on political
matters, interpreted the remarks of the 1971 Synod to mean that
action on behalf of justice "should be regarded as a constitutive
dimension" of the Church's ministry. This means that "work for
justice is essential to the whole Church [not just specialists], pertaining to its innermost nature and mission":

> The constitutive tasks of the Church traditionally have been
> understood as the celebration of the sacraments and the preach-
> ing of the Gospel. In our day the teaching authority through the
> Synod has expanded this vital category of constitutive tasks to
> include the ministry for justice.[29]

Hehir's interpretation of the Synod document has very significant
theological implications. He is really saying that the Church has a
new understanding of itself, a new ecclesiology or doctrine of the
Church. Working for justice is of the same importance as preaching
the Gospel and administering the sacraments. The bishops have
never formally accepted Hehir's interpretation. Nor have they
formally addressed the theological questions that the ministry for
justice has provoked.

In 1977 the International Theological Commission, an advisory
body serving the Pope, issued a statement entitled "Declaration on
Human Development and Christian Salvation," in which the following reflection on Christianity and politics is offered:

It must remain beyond doubt that for the Christian politics is not the final ground that gives ultimate meaning to all of life; it is not an absolute in the Christian eon; and so its nature is to be an instrument, a servant.[30]

The theological commission admitted that the interpretation of the key passage from *Justice in the World,* that working for justice is a "constitutive dimension of the preaching of the Gospel," was still being debated. Commission members suggested that a more accurate interpretation of "constitutive dimension" *(ratio constitutiva)* would be "an integral, not an essential, part of proclaiming the faith." The commission said it did not intend to discourage Christians from infusing a Christian spirit into political, economic, and social structures; on the contrary, it urged them to take politics seriously. But it also said that political action for justice must be seen in a different theological perspective from that suggested by Hehir.

The understanding of justice in the 1971 Synod of Bishops document *Justice in the World,* which may be the prevailing view today, is mainly limited to economic and social development and the protection of human rights. These are worthy goals, but their attainment by the people of a nation does not directly lead to conversion of citizens. Persons who have sufficient material goods and socio-economic, political, and civil rights may be atheists, or may simply be dedicated to their own self-interest. In other words, justice as it is popularly understood today does not imply transformation in the individual soul, conversion or *metanoia.* To create a just man in the biblical sense of the word, one who exhibits in his life "faith working through love," a much more comprehensive understanding of justice is needed. Augustine described justice as primarily order in the soul:

And it is when the soul serves God that it exercises a right control over the body; and in the soul itself the reason must be subject to God if it is to govern as it ought the passions and other vices. Hence, when a man does not serve God, what justice can we ascribe to him, since in this case his soul cannot exercise a just control over the body, nor his reason over his vices; and if there is no justice in such an individual, certainly, there can be none in a community of such persons.[31]

Given the limited content of the present understanding of justice, the International Theological Commission was right in saying
that working for justice cannot give ultimate meaning to life.
Certainly it cannot take precedence over working for Christian
salvation. The commission argued rightly that the relation between
human development and Christian salvation is distorted

> . . . if the practice of social and political liberation has such
> priority that divine worship, prayer, the Eucharist, and other
> sacraments, individual ethics and all questions about the final
> destiny of man and woman (death and eternal life), and the
> exhausting struggle within history against the powers of dark-
> ness take second place.[32]

While the American bishops do not subordinate sacred things to
political and social liberation, they do not adequately relate
evangelization and education (to which they are fully committed)
to the quest for justice.

Pope Paul VI showed by word and deed that he was not satisfied
with the 1971 Synod's reflections on the Church and justice. He
never signed the document *Justice in the World,* and his closing
address to the 1974 Synod of Bishops revealed his belief that
thinking on human liberation needed further refinement:

> Human liberation . . . has been rightly emphasized. It forms part
> of that love which Christians owe to their brethren. But the
> totality of salvation is not to be confused with one or other aspect
> of liberation, and the Good News must preserve all of its own
> originality: that of a God who saves us from sin and death and
> brings us to divine life. Hence, *human advancement, social prog-
> ress, etc., is not to be excessively emphasized on a temporal level* to
> the detriment of the essential meaning which evangelization has
> for the Church of Christ: the announcement of the Good News
> [emphasis added].[33]

In his opening statement to that synod, Pope Paul asked that the
bishops define more accurately the relation between "evangelization properly so called and the whole human effort towards development for which the Church's help is rightly expected, even
though this is not her specific task." He warned against the tendency to reduce the message of the Church to political and social
action. Finally he said:

There is no opposition or separation, therefore, but a com-
plementary relationship between evangelization and human
progress. While distinct and subordinate, one to the other, each
calls for the other by reason of their convergence toward the
same end: the salvation of man.[34]

Pope Paul considered the question so important that he published
another major statement on the issue in December 1975 entitled
On Evangelization in the Modern World. It warned of the growing
tendency among sincere Christians to identify Christianity with
political liberation:

[Generous Christians] in their wish to commit the Church to the
liberation effort are frequently tempted to reduce her mission to
the dimensions of a simply temporal project. They would reduce
her aims to a man-centered goal; the salvation of which she is the
messenger would be reduced to material well-being. Her activity, forgetful of all spiritual and religious preoccupation, would
become initiatives of the political or social order.[35]

The pontiff insisted very strongly on the primacy of the Church's
spiritual vocation:

There is no true evangelization if the name, the teaching, the life,
the promises, the Kingdom, and the mystery of Jesus of
Nazareth, the Son of God, are not proclaimed.[36]

Despite these remarks, Pope Paul VI was careful not to underesti-
mate the close link between evangelization and human advancement. It is the Church's right and duty to promote human progress.
Pope Paul wanted it to be crystal clear that he was not trying to
keep the Church out of the temporal arena and that he recognized
the Church's obligation to promote human rights and progress—
but not at the expense of the Church's unique mission.

The reflections of Pope Paul VI and the International Theological Commission make clear not only why the NCCB's *Catechetical
Directory* says that "the Church links human liberation and salvation in Jesus Christ but she never identifies them," [37] but also why
the USCC Administrative Board chose not to quote the key passage from *Justice in the World* in the 1979 statement on political
responsibility. The American bishops probably did not want to
quote a statement that demanded so much nuanced explanation in
the light of recent debates.

This whole debate may seem to be theological nitpicking, but it has to do with the very nature of Christianity and the Church. Pope John Paul II shares the reservations expressed by Pope Paul VI, but he has chosen to address the issues raised in the debate without explicitly referring to it. In his trip to Mexico, John Paul made a special point of citing Paul VI's *On Evangelization in the Modern World,* referring to those passages where the late pontiff discussed the nature of Christianity and the Church's mission to promote justice. In short, John Paul II encourages the Church to promote justice but not to identify Christianity with political action, nor to reduce the work of justice merely to the promotion of human rights and social justice. He also stresses that bishops and clergy pursue justice most effectively through evangelization and education.[38]

It is noteworthy that the bishops never developed any statements to explain the theological debates over the Church's ministry for justice. They never clearly indicated that they were even aware of Pope Paul VI's thinking on the relation between evangelization and justice.

THE BISHOPS' PERSPECTIVE ON FOREIGN POLICY

The second part of the NCCB's November 1968 pastoral letter, "Human Life in Our Day," represented the bishops' view of the international order and American foreign policy.[39] Much of it simply repeated the teaching on war and peace of the Second Vatican Council's *Gaudium et Spes.* However, the bishops also made specific recommendations on their own authority.

The American hierarchy echoed *Gaudium et Spes* in condemning wars of aggression, genocide, wars fought without limitation, and the use of weapons of mass destruction, i.e., nuclear weapons and probably some conventional weapons.

> Every act of war directed to the indiscriminate destruction of whole cities or vast areas with their inhabitants is a crime against God and man which merits firm and unequivocal condemnation.[40]

The Vatican II document did not condemn the possession of nuclear weapons as a means of deterring "possible enemy attack."[41]

The bishops also reiterated the Council's teaching on arms control and arms reduction. The Council Fathers warned that the arms race was not a safe way to preserve the peace. They called not for unilateral disarmament but for reciprocal disarmament "proceeding at an equal pace according to agreement and backed up by authentic and workable safeguards." [42] While stressing the importance of arms control, the bishops pointed out that *Gaudium et Spes* explicitly recognized the right of legitimate self-defense and that it even praised members of the armed forces as agents of security and freedom. "As long as they fulfill this role properly, they are making a genuine contribution to the establishment of peace." [43] The bishops also joined the Council Fathers in praising "those who renounce the use of violence in the vindication of their rights and who resort to methods of defense which are otherwise available to weaker parties, provided that this can be done without injury to the rights and duties of others or of the community itself." [44]

The bishops reaffirmed the Council's call for a change in the behavior of sovereign nation-states. *Gaudium et Spes* urged political leaders to be concerned about the whole of humanity, the international common good. In particular, the Council Fathers argued that the best chance for achieving peace among nations was to establish a universal public authority "acknowledged as such by all, and endowed with effective power to safeguard, on the behalf of all, security, regard for justice, and respect for rights." [45]

On their own authority in the pastoral letter, the bishops called all Americans to support efforts to make the United Nations a more effective instrument of justice and peace. They urged ratification of the United Nations convention on genocide, pressed for acceptance of policies that would help implement the U.N. Declaration of Human Rights, and urged support of all international programs that promote the sanctity of human life and the dignity of the human person. Furthermore, they expressed, also in their own name, a strong desire to hear the leaders of all nations endorse the idea of a worldwide public authority.

The bishops commended the efforts of all statesmen, especially those in the United States, who promote cooperation in international agencies and regional associations, and who work not only to build a body of international law but also to remove the causes of war. Referring specifically to public policy in the United States, the bishops deplored "the lack of a stable, persevering concern for the promotion of the international common good." [46] They found evidence of this lack in the American people's reluctance to support foreign-aid programs and in their apparent insensitivity to the importance of granting favorable trade agreements to developing nations. The bishops expressed the belief that aid programs should become increasingly multilateral. They also deplored the policy of making foreign aid contingent upon acceptance of contraceptive programs.

The bishops questioned the value of seeking military superiority. In their eyes, the struggle for nuclear superiority was nothing but an irrational resolve "to keep ahead in 'assured destruction' capability." [47] They saw no advantage to such a policy and were sure it would lead to a quickening of the arms race. They also criticized an anti-ballistic-missile system for the United States because it was likely to cause other nations to develop additional offensive nuclear weapons.

The bishops suggested aids to the prevention of war. One was to eliminate peacetime conscription in the United States, which they believed tended to breed wars, and to have instead an all-volunteer army. They also called for modification of the U.S. Selective Service Act: selective conscientious objectors, provided they perform some other service for the human community, should be able to refuse to participate in wars that they consider unjust or in branches of service (e.g., the strategic nuclear forces) that would obligate them to perform actions contrary to deeply held moral convictions about indiscriminate killing. The bishops suggested also that Catholic intellectuals undertake systematic studies of new theories and practices in warfare, including guerrilla warfare, revolution, and wars of liberation.

Finally, the bishops argued that the military power of the United States brought a special responsibility to the local Catholic churches to exercise moral leadership by evaluating war with an entirely new attitude. This statement was meant to be an example of that moral leadership. It should also be noted that the bishops emphasized the importance of prayer in bringing about peace. They quoted from Psalm 27: "If the Lord does not build the house, in vain the masons toil; if the Lord does not guard the city, in vain the sentries watch."

In 1973, Bishop James S. Rausch, then general secretary of the NCCB/USCC, gave a speech entitled "Human Rights: Reflections on a Twin Anniversary" to commemorate the twenty-fifth anniversary of the U.N. Universal Declaration of Human Rights and the tenth anniversary of *Pacem in Terris*.[48] In it he explained the principles beneath the bishops' statements on foreign policy issues.

Bishop Rausch's specific purpose was to show "how the Church's teaching on human rights, as found in *Pacem in Terris,* can contribute to the theoretical basis for promoting human rights." The Church's teaching on human rights is based upon its understanding of international affairs, he said. According to the modern theory of international relations, the sovereign nation-state is the basic unit of international politics. Each state is generally regarded as sovereign in its own jurisdiction. It is wrong for one state to interfere in the affairs of another.

However, the present church teaching on international relations, put forth by Pope John XXIII in *Pacem in Terris,* is not the concept of the sovereign state, said Rausch, but "the ideal of the human community bound together by reciprocal rights and duties which are articulated on the level of individuals and states." According to Pope John XXIII, nations in their relations with one another must observe the same moral law that governs relations among human beings. This moral law, which limits national sovereignty, is universally applicable and can be invoked by anyone in the international community. Hence, violations of human rights in any nation are and must be the concern of all other nations. Individuals and governments should be concerned about human rights violations wherever they might occur in the world. Furthermore, special responsibility falls upon not only nations and their citizens who are involved in the violations but also those who are in a position to affect the course of events. The United States, then, has a special role to play in promoting human rights.

Thanks to Pope John XXIII, Rausch continued, the Church has a further contribution to make to the theory and practice of human rights, namely the concept of the universal common good, elaborated by the Holy Father for the guidance of nations. This is helpful because, while "the objective needs of the common good exist on a worldwide basis, . . . there exists no public authority suitably constituted to meet these needs."

Bishop Rausch mentioned three problems as examples of those whose solutions surpass the capacities of any single state. First, at least two of the superpowers possess a second-strike nuclear capability; consequently, neither nation can assure the protection of its population; each can only deter the other through the balance of terror. Second, the international economic order is so structured that justice is impossible as long as the affluent make policy without regard to the needs of poorer nations. Third, the problems of environmental pollution cannot be solved without international cooperation.

Pope John XXIII, according to Rausch, hoped the concept of the universal common good would replace the idea of national interest as the guiding principle of foreign policymaking. Using the concept of the universal common good is "not simply an ethical necessity" but "also an empirical requirement for successful policy," said Rausch. In other words, it is not only right but useful for nations to replace national self-interest with concern for the common good. For example, the bishop suggested that the United States would benefit from formulating its economic policies in such a way as not to place a burden on the poor nations of the world.

Bishop Rausch insisted that the nation-state, though still the main actor in the international system, was slowly becoming obsolete because of the international situation and would soon be, if it was not already, incapable of dealing with international problems. For an explanation of this position, we can examine a 1975 paper entitled "A Challenge to Theology: American Wealth and Power in the Global Community" by the Reverend J. Bryan Hehir, director of the USCC's Office of International Justice and Peace and the principal author of Bishop Rausch's speech. "Little if any evidence points toward a qualitative leap toward transnational institutions

of action which could supplant the state," said Father Hehir.[49]
However, he insisted that under current conditions of international
interdependence the state could not do an adequate job politically,
strategically, or economically.

> [This] is the fundamental problem of foreign policy today. . . .
> Finding ways to live with this structural gap in the international
> system [i.e., how to act with inadequate means of action] may be
> the crucial problem of international relations in the last quarter
> of this century.[50]

Catholic social thought, continued Hehir, adapted easily to this
problem. It was easy for the Catholic Church to recognize the
emerging limits of the nation-state because Catholic thought has
never accorded the state an absolute value. As early as 1963, Pope
John XXIII had pointed out the limited value of the state and had
sought "to link its responsibilities and policies to the larger human
community." Hence, said Hehir, a decade before political analysts
began highlighting the enormous gap between transnational problems and the nation-state's ability to cope with them, Pope John
had declared that the international situation forced new ethical
obligations upon the state. The first of these obligations was that
the nation-state could no longer simply pursue its own interest
without taking into account the needs of other nations. To do so
was, according to the Pope, immoral.

Because Pope John's statement on the role of the nation-state in
the international situation is skeletal, Hehir concluded that what
needs to be done is to clarify the "conceptual model we use to
define the globe and our place in it." Since our conception or model
of the state and its responsibilities toward the rest of the world
determines our moral response to international crises, this clarifi-
cation is very important.

The food crisis, for example, calls forth varying ethical responses
depending upon the respondent's conception of the nation-state.
Hehir said there were two alternatives:

> One approach is to cast the food crisis in terms of a relief effort,
> thereby confining the moral problem to the realm of charity and
> limiting the scope of inquiry to how generous we choose to be.
> Another approach casts the same question in terms of social

justice, thereby opening up a range of structural questions for analysis, and describing the moral choice in terms of basic obligations to be fulfilled, not superogatory works to be chosen.[51]

The first approach views the individual state as separate from the larger community. The second, advocated by Hehir, views the nation-state as part of the world community, which can make claims upon it. This view is also accepted by the developing nations. These nations try to avoid appeals based on humanitarian charity and concessional aid. They try instead to "recast the issues in structural terms, using social and distributive justice as the categories of analysis," said Hehir.

> In a sense what is being sought is a redefinition of the rules of discourse and standards of evaluation before specific issues of trade, monetary relations, commodity prices, and practices of the multinationals are considered.[52]

Hehir's model of the nation-state and his approach to development received the bishops' imprimatur in "To Live in Christ Jesus: A Pastoral Reflection on the Moral Life" (NCCB, November 1976).[53] The bishops wrote:

> The discussion of international justice and of institutions for its realization has become more specific as a result of the call at the United Nations for a New International Economic Order. Its significance lies in its effort to change the language of the debate from that of aid and charity to that of obligation and justice. The traditional question about foreign aid has been how much we of the industrial nations would choose to give others within the framework of the existing international order. By contrast, a discussion cast in terms of justice would examine the rules by which the system works—such things as trade treaties, commodity prices, corporate practices, and monetary arrangements—with a view to making them more just. New rules would clarify obligations among the parties. Politically, they would be designed to improve the bargaining position of the developing nations in relation to the industrialized countries.[54]

This statement is an application of Pope John XXIII's principles by the American bishops. There are, of course, other legitimate ways for Catholics to seek the international common good. Acceptance of the policy proposals implied in the call for a New International

Economic Order must not be considered the *only* way of being faithful to Pope John's thought.

In the same 1976 pastoral letter, the bishops spoke briefly of human rights and stated their view of U.S. responsibilities:

> This nation's traditional commitment to human rights may be its most significant contribution to world politics. Today, when rights are violated on the left and the right of the international political spectrum, the pervasive presence of our nation's political power and influence in the world provides a further opportunity and obligation to promote human rights. How this should be done will vary from case to case; at the very least, however, national policy and our personal consciences are challenged when not only enemies but close allies use torture, imprisonment, and systematic repression as measures of governance.[55]

This statement indicates an abhorrence of human rights violations in both leftist and rightist regimes. The bishops' policy statements, however, mainly address human rights violations on the right.

On the subject of war and peace, this 1976 pastoral letter reiterated things the bishops had said in their 1968 pastoral letter. The tone, however, was even more insistent on the dangers of both conventional and nuclear war. The bishops added one new facet to their teaching on nuclear weapons by stating that "not only is it wrong to attack civilian populations, but it is also wrong to threaten to attack them as part of a strategy of deterrence."[56]

THE BISHOPS' PERSPECTIVE ON DOMESTIC POLICY

The bishops do not have a formally stated moral perspective on domestic politics. The beginnings of one, however, may be found in the November 1973 "Resolution of the United States Catholic Conference on the Twenty-Fifth Anniversary of the Universal Declaration of Human Rights." "Catholics should be in the forefront speaking in defense of and acting for the fulfillment of the rights of men and women at the local, national, and international level," said the bishops.[57] The rights they referred to include the entire spectrum—political, cultural, and economic rights—as enumerated by John XXIII in *Pacem in Terris:* "that catalogue stands before us today as an unfinished agenda."

What rights are included in this catalogue of rights that the bishops said must be implemented throughout the globe? According to Pope John, man has a natural right to life and to those means suitable for its proper development, especially food, clothing, shelter, rest, medical care, and the necessary services dispensed by the state.

> From this it follows that man also enjoys the right to look after himself if he is seized by ill health, disabled by work and labor, left in widowhood, worn out by old age, is forced into unemployment, or lastly, if in any way he is deprived of the means to subsistence through no fault of his own.[58]

Pope John implied that the state must intervene if private efforts do not adequately protect the enumerated rights.

Furthermore, said Pope John, man has the natural right to due honor and a good reputation, as well as the right to seek the truth; within the limits set by the moral order and the common advantage of all, he has the right to declare his opinions publicly and to pursue any kind of art; and he has the right to be informed truthfully about public events.

Man also has the right to education, including both technical and professional training "in keeping with the stage of educational development in his own country." Other natural rights, according to Pope John XXIII, are: the right to practice one's religion in private or in public, to have private property, to marry or to remain single, to enter the religious life, to have the opportunity to work, and "to demand working conditions in which strength is not disabled, nor the integrity of morals ruined, nor the normal development of the young harmed." Furthermore, the worker has a right to a wage that enables him and his family to have a standard of living that accords with human dignity.

Moreover, since man is by nature social, said Pope John, he has a natural right to assemble, to form private associations, to live where he chooses in his own country, and, unless there are countervailing just reasons, to emigrate to other countries. He also has the right to participate in public affairs. And finally, he has the right to have all his rights legally protected.[59]

The 1976 pastoral letter ("To Live in Christ Jesus") offered only a few glimpses of the bishops' moral vision of domestic politics. They asserted that there is a relation between personal morality and good public policy:

> Law and public policy do not substitute for the personal acts by which we express love of neighbor; but love of neighbor impels us to work for laws, policies, and social structures which foster human goods in the lives of all persons.[60]

The bishops added that even good policies are insufficient to bring about a just political order:

> Just laws and policies, taxes and programs are necessary, but they will not by themselves secure justice and peace. Such values must be built upon the foundations of good and dedicated individual human lives.[61]

These points do not receive much attention in the USCC's policy statements.

The bishops addressed a number of domestic issues in this letter, for the most part stating general principles. They affirmed the right to life of the unborn, condemned abortion as an unspeakable crime, and argued that the right to life must be protected by law. They asserted that women have the same dignity and fundamental rights as men but rejected those views "which would ignore or deny significant differences between the sexes, undermine marriage and motherhood, and erode family life and the bases of society itself."[62]

The bishops condemned discrimination against black Americans, Hispanic Americans, and American Indians, and called for programs to undo the consequences of past injustices. Self-help is not sufficient, said the bishops; they explicitly recognized the role of law in fighting racial discrimination, and even in educating citizens to distinguish right from wrong in other matters as well. They also mentioned the problem of unemployment and the exploitation of agricultural workers and implied that the nation should do its best to solve these problems.

On the subjects of housing and crime, the bishops became more specific. They argued that "all Americans should be able to live where they wish and their means allow." An obstacle to this goal is action by government, banks, and the real estate industry "to deprive some racial groups of financing for housing and to manipulate real estate values for the profit of insiders with the result that our cities remain divided and hostile." Society should make decent housing available to the poor and not isolate public housing from the rest of the community.

As for crime, the bishops mentioned both the dangers of violent urban crime and the increasing frequency of white-collar fraud. They directed attention to four causes of crime: poverty, injustice, society's spirit of acquisitiveness, and the present penal system with its long delays, unequal application of the law, and prisons that confirm inmates "in criminal attitudes and practices."

Lastly, the bishops suggested that government should take "responsible, constitutional steps to stem the flood of pornography, violence, and immorality in the media."[63]

In the same pastoral letter, in a section entitled "The Family," the American hierarchy reaffirmed certain aspects of Catholic teaching that, in the words of Pope John Paul II, "had been challenged, denied, or in practice violated" in the United States.[64] These are the immorality of contraception, sexual intercourse outside marriage, homosexual activity as distinguished from homosexual orientation, and euthanasia. (They condemned abortion and called for laws to prohibit it in another section of the letter, "The Nation.") The bishops also upheld the indissolubility of marriage and taught that marriage should be open to the bearing of children. They did not, however, explain why adherence to Catholic teaching on the above matters would be beneficial for society, nor did they attempt to draw out any possible public policy implications of the Catholic principles they affirmed. It is informative to note that the bishops treated euthanasia and homosexuality in a non-political, non-social context.

PART TWO

Policy Statements

CHAPTER THREE

Foreign Policy

THE AMERICAN CATHOLIC BISHOPS spoke out on numerous matters of foreign policy between 1966 and 1980. After presenting an overview of their positions, this chapter will look more closely at several topics they addressed.

Vietnam War. In 1971 the bishops called upon the United States to withdraw from Vietnam. A little later they condemned U.S. bombing operations in Cambodia. They urged the government to grant amnesty to those imprisoned as conscientious objectors to the war and to give those who left the country to avoid military service a chance to return, with the understanding that they should remain open to some form of service to the community.

The draft. The bishops acknowledged the government's right to require young men to register. They opposed the registration of women. And they opposed the reinstitution of compulsory military service except for a national defense emergency.

Nuclear weapons. The bishops have consistently condemned any *use* of nuclear arms against cities and other populated areas but have varied in their approach to the *deployment* of such arms for deterrence, moving from acceptance of nuclear deterrence to apparent condemnation and back to limited acceptance. They opposed a deterrent strategy that targets enemy forces (counterforce), and they opposed deployment of the MX missile, the cruise missile, and the so-called neutron bomb (high radiation warhead).

Other military matters. The bishops accepted in principle the use of conventional military forces for self-defense. They favored limiting as much as possible the export of U.S. arms. They supported the ratification of SALT II (the Strategic Arms Limitation Treaty).

Human rights. The USCC urged the U.S. Senate to consent to the following conventions: the Genocide Convention, the International Covenant on the Elimination of All Forms of Racial Discrimination, the International Covenants on Human Rights, and the Inter-American Convention on Human Rights. In 1974, the USCC's Administrative Board denounced human rights violations in Chile and Brazil and urged the U.S. government to bring pressure on both countries to restore human rights. The board encouraged policymakers in multinational corporations and institutions "to assess the social consequences of their present or contemplated investments in Brazil" and urged stockholders to exert moral influence on corporation policies.

In congressional testimony the USCC drew attention to human rights violations in Bolivia, Nicaragua, Paraguay, South Korea, and the Philippines. The bishops urged that military aid to the three Latin American nations be ended and that such aid to the two Asian nations be reduced; they also recommended that no economic assistance be given to any of these countries unless it was directed to the neediest citizens. More recently the bishops criticized the violation of human rights in El Salvador and urged the U.S. government to cut off military aid.

The bishops spoke out in favor of religious liberty in a 1977 statement. They accused all Eastern European countries of using the state to support atheism and mentioned oppressive conditions in the Ukraine, Albania, Poland, and Czechoslovakia.

The Panama Canal. The bishops argued that "it is a moral imperative—a matter of elemental social justice—that a new and more just treaty be negotiated," because every nation has a right to be the primary agent of its own development.

Southern Africa. In a 1976 letter from then USCC General Secretary James Rausch to Secretary of State Henry Kissinger, the bishops urged the following measures: repeal of the 1971 Byrd Amendment to the Military Procurement Act (the amendment required that the government could not ban imports of a strategic material from a non-Communist country—e.g., for political purposes such as protest against the country's human rights record—if the importing of the material from a Communist country were permitted); restrictions on U.S. business and investment in Rhodesia, Namibia, and South Africa; the extension of economic aid to Mozambique and Angola because of the hardship they suffered for refusing to do business with Rhodesia; and an announcement to Rhodesia and South Africa that they would receive no aid or moral support from the United States until black majorities fully participated in both governments. On another occasion the bishops suggested that the United States tell the U.N. Security Council of the threat to world peace posed by South Africa's apartheid policy.

The Middle East. The bishops called for a comprehensive political solution, involving the following policies: recognition of Israel's right to exist as a sovereign state with secure boundaries; acceptance of the right of the Palestinians to have a state, to participate in any negotiations, and to be compensated for their losses by Israel and other members of the international community; and, finally, acceptance by all parties of U.N. Resolution 242 (Security Council, 1967) as a basis for negotiations.

Developing nations. The bishops criticized U.S. policy toward less developed nations for not being sufficiently compassionate. In 1973 the USCC asserted that the wealthy nations "because of their cupidity and waste are in large measure responsible for the poverty in Third World Nations." This statement described in detail policies that Congress should adopt in order to end exploitation of the developing nations by American business and the U.S. government. The bishops later argued that multinational corporations and U.S. foreign policy serve jointly to keep Third World countries underdeveloped and dependent.

Hunger. Between November 1974 and February 1976 the USCC issued five statements on the world food crisis. The bishops recommended: greater agricultural and technical assistance for the less industrialized nations; increased funding of Food for Peace (PL 480); the separation of food aid from political and strategic considerations; and a guaranteed annual minimum of food aid, with priority given to nations that the U.N. designates "most severely affected." The bishops also promised to work against hunger through their educational system, the liturgy, and church relief agencies. They encouraged people to adopt a more frugal life-style and to avoid wasting food and energy. They reminded American Catholics that the problems of world hunger and malnutrition presented the whole Church with the opportunity "to experience an essential dimension of its mission, acting on behalf of justice and participating in the transformation of the world."

This brief survey gives a general idea of the foreign policy matters on which the bishops have spoken and the types of positions they have taken. We will now look more closely at a few of these topics in the three categories of military and strategic policy, human rights, and the problems of developing nations.

MILITARY AND STRATEGIC POLICY

Three foreign policy topics that have been of particular concern to the bishops are conscientious objection, nuclear strategy, and SALT II.

Conscientious Objection

The bishops' support for *selective* conscientious objection (i.e., conscientious objection to a particular war but not to all wars) met with some favorable response when it was first expressed formally in a November 1968 pastoral letter called "Human Life in Our Day."[1] James Finn commented that in the past the Church had given more weight to the civic obligations of citizens in time of war than to the rights of the individual conscience. As an example, Finn quoted a statement by Pius XII:

If, therefore, a body representative of the people and a government—both having been chosen by free election—in a moment of extreme danger decide, by legitimate instruments of internal and external policy, on defensive precautions, and carry out the plans which they consider necessary, they do not act immorally; *so that a Catholic citizen cannot invoke his own conscience in order to refuse to serve and fulfill those duties the law imposes* [emphasis added].[2]

Now, said Finn, the bishops supported "the role of conscience and individual responsibility in judging the morality of modern war";[3]

the stress was now on the rights of the human person rather than the duties of the good citizen.

Gordon Zahn, a professor of sociology and a long-time pacifist, said the bishops' position put them far ahead of the great majority of American Catholics.[4] Most Catholics, Zahn wrote, still thought individual citizens were not competent to decide whether a particular war was just, but the bishops clearly supported the individual's right to make up his own mind.

This support for selective conscientious objection was reiterated in 1969 by the International Justice and Peace division of the USCC and in 1971 by the USCC as a whole. The latter statement ("Declaration on Conscientious Objection and Selective Conscientious Objection," USCC, October 1971) proclaimed the moral right of Catholics to be conscientious objectors to all wars or to certain wars:

> In the light of the Gospel and from an analysis of the Church's teaching on conscience, it is clear that a Catholic can be a conscientious objector to war in general or to a particular war "because of religious training and belief."[5]

American Catholics were acting in accord with Catholic teaching if they took advantage of the law granting exemption from military service because of conscientious opposition to all war, argued the bishops. They suggested that the law should require selective objectors to perform some other service to the community.

As support for its position, the USCC quoted from two documents issued by the Second Vatican Council, the *Declaration on Religious Freedom (Dignitatis Humanae)* and the *Pastoral Constitution on the Church in the Modern World (Gaudium et Spes)*. The quotation from the former had to do with man's duties to seek knowledge of the divine law so that he may form a right and true judgment of conscience. From the latter, the USCC quoted a passage declaring the duty of conscience to seek knowledge of God's law and holding that a correct conscience is guided by objective norms of morality. The bishops cited these passages because "individual conscience is crucial in this issue of [general] conscientious objection and selective conscientious objection."[6]

The bishops quoted these key passages from *Gaudium et Spes*:

We cannot fail to praise those who renounce the use of violence in the vindication of their rights and who resort to methods of defense which are otherwise available to weaker parties too, provided this can be done without injury to the rights and duties of others or of the community itself.[7]

It seems right that laws make humane provisions for those who for reasons of conscience refuse to bear arms, provided however that they accept some other form of service to the human community.[8]

The first passage qualifies the defense of individual rights by requiring that the prior rights of the political community be upheld. The second passage clearly indicates a preference for laws allowing general and selective conscientious objection but does not assert that morality *requires* such laws.[9]

Commenting on the section of *Gaudium et Spes* from which the second quotation was taken, French theologian René Coste pointed out that Catholic doctrine recognizes conscientious objection—providing it is not inspired by egoism, comfort, or anarchy—as "an exceptional vocation of a prophetic kind." As for selective conscientious objection, Coste wrote: "Catholic tradition not only regards it as permissible, but expressly forbids participation in an unjust war."[10]

In response to the bishops' statements on general and selective conscientious objection, Major General Thomas Lane suggested that the Church was "departing from its historic teaching on war to indulge sentiments of pacifism. . . ."[11] I disagree. In their 1971 "Declaration on Conscientious Objection" the bishops explicitly gave moral approval to "the participation of Christians in the legitimate defense of their nation."[12] They even quoted the Second Vatical Council's reference to the possibility of a just war: ". . . governments cannot be denied the right to legitimate defense once every means of peaceful settlement has been exhausted."[13]

From Lane's criticism emerged a dialogue between a committee of five USCC representatives, called the Dougherty Committee after its chairman, Bishop John J. Dougherty, and a committee of four representing no particular organization, with General Lane as chairman. The Dougherty Committee held that various kinds of pacifism had been and still were consonant with Catholic teaching. It pointed out that neither the just war theory nor pacifism had been declared by the Church "to be *the* Catholic position" and that it was up to each person to decide which position he would adopt.[14] The individual should no longer presume the state correct when it judged that a particular war was necessary and just. In this respect, the Dougherty Committee echoed the bishops' 1971 rejection of the position that a Catholic citizen could not invoke his own conscience to refuse military service.

The Dougherty Committee said the individual was free to choose any one of three forms of pacifism: general conscientious objection (opposition to all war), selective conscientious objection (opposition to a particular war on the grounds that it is unjust), and nuclear pacifism (opposition to the use of nuclear weapons on the grounds that they are inherently immoral). The last may also be considered a form of selective conscientious objection. The American hierarchy, the Dougherty Committee stressed, believes that these forms of pacifism "deserve to be recognized and respected under the teachings of the Church—and under the constitutional guarantees of religious freedom."[15]

In arguing for pacifism, the Dougherty Committee recognized the predominance of the just war doctrine in the Church's tradition. However, it insisted that the early Christians were pacifist and that "a strain of pacifist theory and action" had always been alive in the Catholic Church. A minority of contemporary theologians, it continued, believed that the early churches had attained a "peak of moral purity" from which the Church has since declined by its acceptance of the just war doctrine. According to the committee, the bishops thought pacifism deserved to be included in the teachings of the Church.

In examining this issue we need to distinguish between two kinds of pacifism. Catholic doctrine has always recognized that an individual may feel called by the Gospel to renounce the use of force for any reason. For example, Catholic clergy throughout history have abstained from participating in wars, even so-called just wars. This kind of pacifism, always acknowledged in the Christian tradition, does not hold that the Gospel requires all men or all states to be pacifist. In other words, it says nothing at all about whether a state should refuse to defend itself against an unjust aggressor. A second and *rare* kind of pacifism holds that all individuals and states *ought* to be pacifist if they want to be faithful to the Gospel.

Do the American bishops think that Catholics may, without violating Catholic doctrine, hold this second kind of pacifism? The Dougherty Committee's answer is that, according to the American hierarchy, the following kinds of pacifism deserve recognition in the teachings of the Church:

> (1) A pacifism based on the teachings of scripture and the examples set by the early Christians, (2) a "pacifism" based on the conviction that no modern war can meet the conditions of a just war, and (3) that a particular war fails to meet one or more of these conditions.[16]

Regarding the first kind of pacifism, the committee explained that the early Christians, until the time of Constantine, believed that Christians should not participate in any kind of war. According to the second kind, no state should go to war under contemporary conditions. Thus the members of the Dougherty Committee found a place for the total pacifism described previously; they believed it should be respected under the teachings of the Church. The committee also reaffirmed that the just war theory was an acceptable Catholic position and should be taught by the Church. But it did not explain how the Church could retain two contradictory teachings. According to the just war theory, a state may go to war in certain cases; and under one of the types of pacifism the committee accepted as a Catholic position, no state may ever go to war.

Perhaps the contradiction is easily resolved. In no statement issued by the bishops have they taught as acceptable Catholic doctrine the principle that the state may never go to war. The bishops teach that *individuals* may be pacifists and that states may legitimately defend themselves under certain conditions. This is a consistent position. The Dougherty Committee, representing the bishops, misrepresented their teaching.

The Reverend Joseph Komonchak of the Dougherty Committee addressed the obligations of those exempted from military service.

According to him, priests and other religious were exempted from military service throughout the Middle Ages because in this way "they served Christ more fully, more perfectly."[17] They abstained from secular affairs, especially war, in order to dedicate themselves to God and their fellow men. Thomas Aquinas remarked, "Although to wage wars may be meritorious, it is rendered illicit for clerics because they are deputed to carry out even more meritorious works. . . ."[18] This exemption was extended to certain groups of laymen such as members of the Third Order of St. Francis, "who made special commitments or sought to serve the Gospel in a more complete way."[19] Professor Komonchak regarded this pacifist position as a higher calling that should be taught as such by the Church. He implied that the Church should teach that a special kind of life goes along with being a pacifist—that is, a greater than average dedication to the highest level of perfection demanded by the Gospel.

In their 1971 statement, the bishops said nothing about any extra obligation of the conscientious objector. They did say that the selective conscientious objector should provide some service to the community if the Selective Service Act were modified to allow people to refuse to serve in wars they consider unjust.

Nuclear Strategy

In their 1968 pastoral letter "Human Life in Our Day," the American bishops reiterated the teaching of the Second Vatican Council that it is a crime against God and man to use weapons that indiscriminately destroy whole cities or vast areas and their inhabitants. This statement was reaffirmed in January 1976 by Archbishop Peter Gerety of Newark, testifying before the Senate Foreign Relations Committee. Archbishop Gerety restated the principles regarding nuclear weapons laid down in Vatican II's *Gaudium et Spes*:

First, use of these weapons against cities and populated areas is prohibited in a special way because of their destructive capacity; second, while use is prohibited, the possession of these weapons for deterrence may possibly be legitimated as the lesser of two evils; third, even deterrence is questionable unless it is conceived as an interim expedient accompanied by extraordinary efforts to negotiate their limitation and reduction.[20]

In light of these principles, Gerety criticized the present U.S. policy of being prepared to use nuclear weapons against cities. He did tacitly sanction possession of a nuclear deterrent targeted against cities as long as the United States intended never to use the weapons. But he said nothing about the continuous and persuasive deception that this strategy requires: in order for it to work, the Soviet Union must believe we are willing to use the deterrent if necessary.

In November 1976 the NCCB added significantly to its teaching on nuclear weapons in "To Live in Christ Jesus: A Pastoral Reflection on the Moral Life." The bishops asserted that not only the *use* of strategic nuclear weapons but also the *declared intent* to use them is wrong:

> As possessors of a vast nuclear arsenal, we must also be aware that not only is it wrong to attack civilian populations, but it is also wrong to threaten to attack them as part of a "strategy of deterrence."[21]

The bishops did not say it is wrong to *possess* nuclear weapons but seemed to distinguish between the intent to use and possession. The question naturally arises whether the very possession of nuclear weapons constitutes a declared intent to use them.

In September 1979, the bishops further elaborated their thinking on nuclear weapons through testimony before the Senate Foreign Relations Committee delivered by John Cardinal Krol. They explicitly argued that they would be willing to tolerate the possession of nuclear weapons for deterrence as the lesser of two evils, as long as negotiations proceeded toward "the phasing out altogether of nuclear deterrence and the threat of mutually assured destruction." If the hope for negotiations disappeared, "the moral attitude of the Catholic Church would almost certainly have to shift to one of uncompromising condemnation of both use and possession of such weapons." In this statement the bishops reaffirmed their view that "the declared intent to use [strategic nuclear weapons] involved in our deterrence policy is wrong."[22]

In testimony before the House Armed Services Committee in March 1980, the Reverend J. Bryan Hehir, director of the USCC's Office of International Justice and Peace, interpreted Cardinal Krol's testimony to mean that the U.S. bishops do tolerate the threat to use nuclear weapons. Hehir explained:

> The American bishops in a pastoral letter of 1976 highlighted the moral problem of ever threatening to use these weapons against civilian centers. Cardinal Krol's testimony sought to address directly the relationship of use and threat. He argued that the deterrent could be tolerated (not approved) as a "lesser evil" than use, since it still seemed that deterrence was a barrier against any use of the weapons.[23]

If the use of nuclear weapons against a civilian population is always immoral, what about a nuclear strategy that targets enemy forces (i.e., the strategy of counterforce)? Hehir presented the USCC's position on counterforce in congressional testimony in which he argued against adopting the counterforce strategy on the grounds that it might increase the possibility of using nuclear weapons.

A 1976 paper presented by Hehir to the American Society of Christian Ethics helps to clarify the USCC position on nuclear deterrence and the actual use of nuclear weapons.[24] We can best understand Hehir's position by comparing it with what he said about the positions of Paul Ramsey, a professor of religion at Princeton University, and Walter Stein, a British scholar.

Ramsey, said Hehir, holds that recourse to nuclear weapons is legitimate within the limits imposed by the principle of discrimination (that civilians are to be distinguished from soldiers) and the principle of proportionality (that the amount of force used should be proportionate to the objective):

> Such a position consists of an absolute prohibition against any countercity use of nuclear weapons [principle of discrimination] supplemented by a complex calculus regulating the use of nuclear weapons against legitimate military targets for limited political purposes [principle of proportionality].[25]

Ramsey would unconditionally prohibit the use of nuclear weapons against cities because it necessarily requires the indiscriminate killing of innocent civilians. However, the tactical use of nuclear weapons against military targets is permitted "to stop an invasion across a clearly defined boundary, our own or one we are pledged to defend by treaty."[26] Ramsey's position leads to acceptance of a counterforce (i.e., against enemy forces) rather than a countercity strategy. Any nuclear deterrent is acceptable to Ramsey only if it does not require the intention to use, or the actual use of, nuclear weapons against civilians. On these grounds, he regards the countercity strategy as morally unacceptable.

Walter Stein, said Hehir, holds that there can never be a legitimate use of nuclear weapons. Any use would violate the principle of proportionality because of the enormous damage it would cause. Since deterrence rests in part upon the willingness to do what one threatens, the mere *possession* of nuclear deterrents is immoral. Stein's position can be called nuclear pacifism.

Hehir drew upon the positions of Ramsey and Stein to form his own "mixed model." Like Stein, Hehir said that nuclear weapons should not be used for any reason. Unlike Stein, however, he did not base this decision upon the principles of discrimination and proportionality. He pointed out that some nuclear weapons have less firepower than some large conventional weapons. Hence, in certain circumstances, some nuclear weapons may cause less damage than conventional types.

In order to maintain an absolute ban on nuclear weapons, Hehir proposed to supplement the principles of proportionality and discrimination, which constitute only "physical criteria," with "psychological criteria." The purpose of the latter would be to solidify in people's minds the dangers of crossing the gap between conventional and nuclear weapons. According to Hehir, nuclear weapons should be proscribed "not solely because of their size, but because they establish an order and style of combat for which we have no precedents or experience to control its conduct. Our best safeguard is not to initiate combat on this level."[27]

Hehir agreed with Ramsey in supporting nuclear deterrence as a legitimate option for policymakers. Unlike Ramsey, he approved of the countercity deterrent strategy. Yet Hehir held that the United States should never *use* a nuclear weapon on an enemy city, even if the enemy were to attack the territory of the United States. Nuclear weapons exist "to be not used; their purpose is to threaten, not to strike." According to Hehir, it is morally legitimate to threaten the mass killing of innocent civilians as a means of maintaining the balance of terror. This position admittedly depends on convincing other nations that "the determination to use nuclear weapons is beyond question."[28] In other words, various forms of deception are necessary to make this an effective policy.

The ongoing public debate about supplementing the countercity nuclear capability of the United States with a counterforce nuclear strategy prompted Hehir to raise the following question: "Does the principle of discrimination decisively point toward a counterforce deterrent as morally superior to the MAD [Mutually Assured Destruction—the countercity use of nuclear weapons] strategy?" If counterforce *replaced* countercity instead of merely supplementing it, civilian populations would no longer be threatened with direct attack. Consequently, statesmen would no longer have to intend mass killing or to pretend to intend it. But counterforce strategy could increase the chance of nuclear exchange because, in theory, the damage could be limited to acceptable levels.

After weighing the consequences of moving to a counterforce strategy, especially the increased danger of nuclear exchange, Hehir concluded that there is more of a chance of preserving the psychological barrier against nuclear use by retaining the countercity strategy. Since in his mind the principle of discrimination does not need to be treated as an absolute, he concluded that it does not require the adoption of only one nuclear strategy. The principle is an important one but should not be decisive in causing policymakers to choose one strategy over another.

Hehir was able to accept the countercity strategy, with its huge civilian casualties, because of his belief that it is morally legitimate to *threaten* what can never be *done* without moral guilt. In other words, Hehir could accept the countercity strategy as long as the United States intended never to fire any nuclear weapons. He could also accept the deception required to convince other nations that we *would* employ our nuclear arsenal if necessary. As we have seen, Hehir also argues that this is the position of the U.S. bishops.

SALT II

In testimony on behalf of the USCC before the House Armed Services Committee in April 1978, Hehir said that failure to ratify the Strategic Arms Limitation Treaty, known as SALT II, "must surely be judged as capricious and irresponsible" in light of the teaching of the Second Vatican Council and that of the American bishops.[29]

Testifying before the Senate Foreign Relations Committee on behalf of the USCC in September 1979, John Cardinal Krol argued strongly in favor of ratifying SALT II, even though he conceded the limited nature of the agreement. Of great interest in Cardinal Krol's testimony are the political convictions that led the USCC to discount the argument that SALT II fails to protect U.S. security. He argued that the United States need not worry even if the treaty permitted the Soviet Union to achieve a first-strike capability against our land-based ICBMs. Even with this capability, "would not the leaders of the Soviet Union be insane to start, or threaten to start, a nuclear war?" Besides, "is it not clear that the other legs of the triad [the sea-based and air-based defense, nuclear submarines and B-52 bombers] will continue to deter a Soviet first strike, if indeed that were the Soviets' intention?" Cardinal Krol also expressed skepticism that the global political balance would be altered if the nations of the world perceived the Soviet Union as having a first-strike capability:

> I do not pose as a political or technical expert, but I must ask whether in the nuclear age it can be argued that an increment in strategic power can be translated into an effective instrument of political influence.[30]

In 1980 the USCC, through its spokesman J. Bryan Hehir, reaffirmed its support for the ratification of SALT II before the House Armed Services Committee.[31] Hehir said the Krol testimony was the most complete expression of the USCC position on nuclear strategy and was based on three principles. First, it is a moral imperative to prevent any use of nuclear weapons. Adherence to this principle leads the USCC to oppose the neutron warhead and the nuclear strategy known as counterforce, both of which would make nuclear war more thinkable. Second, the USCC accepts the strategy of nuclear deterrence, which threatens to inflict massive damage on civilians, but this raises the problem "whether it is possible to accept a threat whose execution could never be approved." The third principle places a limitation on the acceptance of deterrence: the USCC will continue to give moral approval to deterrence if the United States makes serious efforts to achieve arms control and disarmament. Because of these three principles, the USCC, according to Hehir, must support the SALT II agreements.

In defense of SALT II, Hehir also discussed the relation of military to political power. Like Cardinal Krol, he argued for the limited political usefulness of military power. The holding of American hostages in Iran, Hehir argued, "is not an example of American impotency, but of the limits on using the power we have." More military power would not have made it easier or less risky to secure the release of the hostages. As for the Soviet invasion of Afghanistan, Hehir said no rational case could be made for the use of military power that would have thwarted the invasion or dislodged the Soviets afterwards.

Hehir did recognize the possibility that the Soviet Union could be trying to change the balance of power in the Middle East. Not wanting the United States to use nuclear weapons to repel a Soviet advance, he argued that the United States should possess "the capability of fighting a conventional war if necessary." Presumably, the USCC would support U.S. military action against the Soviets if motivated by concern for the defense of legitimate national interests.

HUMAN RIGHTS

The bishops have been most consistent in denouncing human rights violations in Latin America, southern Africa, South Korea, and the Philippines. In 1977 they did, after a twenty-year silence on the matter, criticize Eastern European states for suppressing the religious liberty of their citizens, mentioning in particular Lithuania and the Ukraine (which are part of the Soviet Union), Albania, Poland, and Czechoslovakia. The USCC once urged the U.S. Senate to deny the Soviet Union most-favored-nation trade status because of Soviet restrictions on religious worship and Jewish emigration. The bishops have been silent about human rights violations in black Africa (e.g., Uganda, Zaire, Mozambique, Angola), the People's Republic of China, Cuba, and Cambodia (now Kampuchea). They have not addressed human rights violations by the Soviet Union in a major statement, though in a November 1980 "Pastoral Letter on Marxist Communism" they said they were "not blind to the horrendous violations of human rights perpetrated in the name of communism or the invasions of the territorial integrity of sovereign nations."[32]

In April 1976 Bishop James S. Rausch, then general secretary of the NCCB/USCC, explained in a letter to Secretary of State Henry Kissinger why the USCC addressed human rights violations only in Rhodesia and South Africa and not in other African countries. First, he said, almost all nations of the world have condemned the Republic of South Africa and Rhodesia on moral grounds. Second, African nations give high priority to the liberation of black majorities in the Republic of South Africa, Rhodesia, and Namibia; hence future U.S. relations with African nations may depend on our position on this issue. Third, the United States "has the possibility of regaining respect and leadership in the non-aligned nations, if it were to support efforts toward freedom."[33]

Although the U.S. bishops are not unconcerned about human rights violations in Communist countries (see "To Live in Christ Jesus," NCCB, 1976), for moral and practical reasons they have focused upon rightist regimes. Hehir argues that the USCC points out violations in those countries upon which the United States can exert influence through economic or military assistance. In the USCC's perception, these are mainly dictatorial governments on the right. Hehir defends this policy as a special obligation of the Catholic Church in the United States because of its ability to influence the formulation of U.S. policy. In Hehir's view it is quite natural and even a moral imperative that the USCC concentrate on human rights violations in rightist regimes.[34]

THE DEVELOPING NATIONS

As an example of the bishops' approach to development, I will examine their June 1973 testimony on "Proposed Reforms of U.S. Overseas Investment and Trade Policies for the 1970s," given by Bishop James Rausch. Bishop Rausch prefaced his specific remarks on investment and trade policies with some general comments on the international economic situation. He reiterated an observation found in the Vatican II statement *Gaudium et Spes*, that there is an ever-widening gap between the rich and poor nations. The wealthy nations "because of their own cupidity and waste" are in large measure responsible for the poverty in Third World nations, said Rausch. To come to the relief of these nations is a humanitarian goal "closely linked to the message of the Christian Gospel" and a duty of rich nations.[35] These nations have an obligation to structure their investment and trade policies so that the poor nations may eventually develop.

Rausch quoted Pius XI's *Quadragesimo Anno*, Vatican II's *Gaudium et Spes*, and Paul VI's *Populorum Progressio* to show that the Catholic Church has consistently refused to canonize the Western free enterprise system and its companion rule of free trade. The Church has never, according to Rausch, considered the right to property as absolute; it is always a right that must be balanced against the needs of society as a whole. Therefore it is wholly proper, according to church teaching, for the Church to ask the state to regulate the activity of corporations.

In fact, the USCC went farther than simply requesting state regulation of corporations. Bishop Rausch cited Paul VI's remarks on multinational corporations in *Populorum Progressio* and *Octogesima Adveniens* as a basis for his own call for international regulation of such corporations. However, since no international body exists to regulate these organizations, Rausch proposed to the U.S. Congress that it, in the name of justice, regulate American overseas investments by instituting the following three control mechanisms. First, he suggested canceling government subsidies to multinational corporations and instituting a special tax on these corporations, the revenues from which would be used for economic and human development of Third World countries. The rationale behind this proposal is that those who benefit from investment in the Third World should contribute to its development. Second, he recommended imposing penalties on multinational corporations that intervene in the political and economic affairs of Third World nations. Third, he proposed legislation to limit profit-taking in the Third World in order to offset the unequal bargaining power of poor nations in relation to rich ones.

The bishop further suggested that "excess profits" from investments in developing nations not be put into the U.S. treasury but be rebated through some multinational agency to the countries from which they came. He applauded as a "hopeful phenomenon" the formation of what he called "effective and socially responsible coalitions by which poor nations can act in consort to demand better prices for natural resources needed by wealthy consumer nations." An example of such a coalition given by Rausch in this 1973 testimony was OPEC, the Organization of Petroleum Exporting Countries.[36]

The greatest obstacle to growth in developing countries, according to Bishop Rausch, is the restrictive trade policies imposed by wealthy nations. The rich fix prices of products that do not compete with their own, and they impose tariff and nontariff barriers, such as import quotas, to restrict the sale of competing products. For example, rich countries not only close their own doors to developing countries' agricultural products that compete with their own but also use agricultural policies to reduce the sale of these goods in the world market, keeping prices and profits low for the small amount poor countries do succeed in selling.

Rausch called for fairer prices for raw materials. Specifically, he urged the United States to conclude multilateral commodity agreements between producing and consuming nations. These agreements should give producing nations a majority vote, or at least an equal vote, in determining the prices of commodities, and should provide for remuneration to producing nations in case of crop failure.

Rausch also reiterated a recommendation the USCC made in 1972 that preferential treatment be given to developing nations for their manufactured goods. In 1968, the nations of the world at a United Nations Conference on Trade Agreements for Development had issued a call for a system of generalized preferences for the poor countries. As of June 1973, said Rausch, the United States and Canada were the only rich nations of the world that had failed to act on a general system of preferences. In fact, the U.S. trade policy is more favorable to rich nations than to poor:

> The average American trade barrier against manufactured imports from rich countries was a tariff of 6.8 per cent; while the average post-Kennedy Round tariff for manufactured imports from poor countries was a disproportionate 12.4 per cent.[37]

On the basis of these facts, Bishop Rausch concluded:

> *Global justice* demands generalized preferences for Third World countries to enable them to counteract in some measure the innumerable handicaps and economic disadvantages they now experience in trying to gain access to the open markets of the rich [emphasis added].[38]

According to Rausch, justice also requires the participation of the poor countries in trade negotiations. Congress should require such participation if it decides to give the President authority to negotiate new agreements on tariff and non-tariff barriers to trade. Finally, Bishop Rausch expressed his opinion that granting trade preferences to poor countries is in the interest of the United States because of its growing interdependence with the Third World, which not only supplies it with great amounts of fuel and raw materials but also buys one-third of U.S. exports and actually gives it a trade surplus.

Bishop Rausch acknowledged in his testimony that organized labor would balk at his recommendations on trade with poor countries because they would have adverse effects on the salaries and jobs of many American workers. To avoid making the poor of the Third World the enemy of the American worker, Rausch urged Congress to provide domestic economic development, accelerated public works, expanded public-service employment, stronger minimum-wage laws, and adequate funding of manpower-training programs. For the worker who loses his job because of import policies, Rausch urged adequate compensation in the form of either another job for which he would be trained or continuation of his prior salary and benefits until another suitable job was available.

Rausch also expressed concern for the small farmers and farm workers who might be adversely affected by changes in trade policy. Small producers with large capital investments in the production of a given commodity could face tremendous hardship if they lost their markets to foreign imports. Hence Rausch suggested a congressional program to protect small producers from losses resulting from a drop in market prices.

Bishop Rausch concluded his testimony to the House subcommittee by stating his belief that the restructuring of world trade so that it was more favorable to Third World countries was possible "because people are becoming more aware of the profound reality that all persons are united in one human family."[39] He also expressed the belief that corporate greed and narrow self-interest could be restrained by the establishment of new community standards—that is, a new public morality. Regrettably, he did not describe the precise content of this morality or explain how it could be taught and implemented.

In August 1974 the USCC Department of Social Development and World Peace issued "Development-Dependency: The Role of Multinational Corporations." This statement described the U.S. role in the international economic system and the impact of multinational corporations on our domestic economy, and suggested that the Church play a role in alleviating economic injustice around the world.

The statement was extremely critical of multinational corporations and expressed the conviction that "the concentrated power in the hands of a relatively few multinational corporations and banks inhibits international development and deters the process of achieving justice here and abroad."[40] It cited Anthony Sampson's book *The Sovereign State of I.T.T.* as evidence that ITT acted wrongly in Nazi Germany and Chile. It also drew upon a study, submitted to the U.S. Senate Judiciary Subcommittee on Antitrust and Monopoly, documenting unjust activities on the part of Ford and General Motors in Nazi Germany. These and other corporations were motivated by the desire to augment profits all over the world, the statement said. This motivation "leads to the development and control of international market strategy which is of primary benefit to the controlling power and not the development of peoples."[41] The statement expressed agreement with a comment of Pope Paul VI:

> Multinational enterprises . . . can conduct autonomous strategies which are largely independent of the national political powers and therefore not subject to control from the point of view of the common good.[42]

As evidence, the statement quoted a U.S. Senate report dated March 1974:

> Oil companies deal with foreign nations regarding oil supply and cost. Pipeline companies deal with the Soviet Union for natural gas. . . . Milling companies and the Soviet Union arrange grain sales which sharply affect domestic price, supply, transportation, and storage. These are momentous public issues in which Federal officials play a minor role, much of it after basic decisions have been agreed upon by American companies and foreign governments.[43]

In addition to being virtually independent of government supervision, the statement said, multinational corporations are at times significantly assisted by U.S. government policies. One primary objective of U.S. foreign policy is to facilitate and protect American overseas investments. To support this point, the statement quoted Richard Nixon's second inaugural address: "We will act to defend our interests whenever and wherever they are threatened, any place in the world."

And so, in the eyes of the USCC Department of Social Development and World Peace, the practices of multinational corporations and the foreign policy of the United States work together to keep Third World countries dependent and underdeveloped.

The conclusion of this statement on multinational corporations can be seen as a summary of the American hierarchy's attitude toward international economic injustice. The statement urged Catholics to question the existence and motivation of multinational corporations and the concentration of so much power in so few hands. Catholics should be committed to self-determination and economic development in all nations. Furthermore, Catholics have a special role to play in the campaign for economic justice— that of "a religious prophetic people who stand apart from the powers which possess dominant control in society" and who "pronounce God's judgment on the side of [the] powerless."[44]

CONCLUSION

To what extent do the bishops' foreign policy statements serve an educational purpose? On a general level, they surely teach that addressing issues of war and peace, development, and human rights flows from the Church's mission to evangelize, and that the Christian faith has reverberations on social, political, and economic levels. Since many Catholics do not understand that their faith should lead them to take an interest in American foreign policy, the bishops' statements are instructive at this general level.

But these statements do not communicate the fullness of Catholic social teaching (as contained in papal social encyclicals and the documents of the Second Vatican Council) on war and peace, human rights, and development. For example, they provide no serious explanation of Catholic teaching on the relation between rights and duties, or the dangers of materialism.

Nor do the foreign policy statements furnish enough information about the issues under discussion. This is particularly true of the statements on development and human rights, which provide little help in learning to think deeply about the political and theological aspects of these matters. The bishops' statements are written in a summary fashion and focus on delivering a policy proposal; consequently, they have little educational value. Imagine, if you will, what the individual members of a Catholic parish would learn about American foreign policy and Catholic social teaching if the pastor distributed the bishops' statements on development and human rights.

Lastly, the bishops' foreign policy statements are mostly political statements framed for a particular occasion. Consequently, the emphasis is on persuading people to adopt a particular policy rather than on elaborating general principles that would inspire and guide people to choose policies in the light of their faith. It is true that in stating their policy positions, the bishops often provide a *summary* statement of some Catholic principles. But none of the policy statements issued since the founding of the USCC could be regarded as an outstanding exposition of Catholic teaching on international policy. There is nothing comparable to a papal encyclical or to the enlightening speeches Pope John Paul II has delivered at the U.N., at UNESCO in Paris, to the Latin American bishops at Puebla, Mexico, and elsewhere.

CHAPTER FOUR

Domestic Policies

STATEMENTS BY THE USCC are prepared for the guidance both of individual citizens and of legislators and other policymakers. In their statements on domestic issues, the American bishops have argued primarily for social justice, meaning especially economic and social equality. The stress on a more equal distribution of material resources is seen in the USCC's testimony in 1980 before the Democratic and Republican platform committees. Speaking for the USCC, Bishop Thomas Kelly, then NCCB/USCC general secretary, made this revealing remark:

> The primary responsibility of the state is to serve the *common good*. It has to adopt economic policies to ensure that the essential needs of all its people are met. These needs include adequate income, employment, food, shelter, health care, education, and access to the necessary social services. All persons have a right to these basic necessities; and the government, as the provider of last resort, has the responsibility to ensure that they be made available to all [emphasis added].[1]

Bishop Kelly implied that the attainment of the common good depends on the proper distribution of economic resources.

To promote *economic* justice, the bishops have issued detailed policy statements on the economy, housing, welfare reform, national health insurance, and rural issues. They have also testified extensively before Congress on economic matters. These statements usually endorse specific legislative proposals without necessarily designating legislation by name.

To promote *social* equality, the bishops have denounced racism and appealed for better treatment of farm workers, the elderly, American Indians, the handicapped, and immigrants, especially illegal aliens. Generally, these statements do not call upon the government to take very specific policy measures. Except for the statements on illegal aliens and farm workers, policy recommendations remain on a general level. These statements also attempt to educate individuals and groups about how to promote the welfare of the minorities mentioned.

Other areas of social justice upon which the bishops have taken stands are capital punishment, handgun control, prison reform, and crime. And they have devoted considerable attention to abortion and financial aid to parochial schools, the two domestic issues that the public usually associates with the Catholic Church. The bishops have denounced abortion since 1968, and with more frequency and intensity since the 1973 Supreme Court abortion decisions. They have also argued that it is constitutionally sound, as well as good policy, for the government to aid parochial schools, but their arguments have not been especially visible. In statements distributed to the general public, requests for aid have recently been three-line statements or a paragraph placed within a larger context. Fully developed arguments can only be found in transcripts of hearings conducted by congressional committees. The American bishops believe that their opposition to abortion and support of government aid to parochial schools serve the common good of the nation and not simply the interests of the Catholic Church.

The bishops began to give serious attention to the family in "To Live in Christ Jesus: A Pastoral Reflection on the Moral Life" (NCCB, November 1976).[2] This was followed by "The Plan of Pastoral Action for Family Ministry: A Vision and Strategy" (NCCB and USCC, 1978), which committed the Church to serious consideration of family life throughout the 1980s.[3]

The USCC Department of Social Development and World Peace prepares most of the bishops' economic and social statements. A special NCCB committee does the staff work on abortion statements, while the USCC Department of Education has the primary responsibility for statements on Catholic schools. The USCC Office of Government Liaison assists all departments in presenting the bishops' positions to Congress.

The Economy

A prominent theme in the bishops' statements is economic justice, with an emphasis on the just distribution of national resources. In November 1975 the USCC made a major statement on the U.S. economy entitled "The Economy: Human Dimensions."[4] In the early part of the statement the bishops said they would address not "technical, fiscal matters, particular economic theories or political programs" but the moral, human, and social aspects of the economic crisis from the perspective of social justice and human rights.

Unemployment, inflation, and the unequal distribution of wealth were the economic problems that the bishops pointed to in this statement as the most serious. Rejecting the view that low unemployment and high inflation are necessarily related, they said it was unjust to fight inflation by tolerating unemployment.

To bring about a more equal distribution of goods, the USCC offered these policy proposals: an effective national commitment to full employment; improvement of the unemployment-compensation systems; adequate assistance for victims of recession; an income policy for the sick, old, and disabled; better use of land to insure more employment; and the preservation of small family farms. They called upon both the public and the private sector to promote fairness in taxation, to halt the bad effects of inflation, and to distribute more evenly the burdens and opportunities of society. They concluded by indicting the entire economic system for being largely based upon unlimited and unrestrained competition.

In later congressional testimony, the USCC expressed support for the 1976 Full Employment and Balanced Growth Act but said it did not go far enough by setting a target of 3 per cent unemployment within four years.[5] In "Welfare Reform in the 1970s" (USCC Department of Social Development and World Peace, February

1977)[6] the bishops called for the following: full employment; for those who cannot work, a guaranteed annual income not substantially lower than the median family income; participation by the poor in welfare policymaking boards; replacement of food stamps and other non-cash benefits with "an adequate income"; continuance of low-income housing; and programs for rehabilitation and housing maintenance.

Housing

The bishops' teaching on housing in the United States was set forth in a major statement entitled "The Right to a Decent Home: A Pastoral Response to the Crisis in Housing" (USCC, November 1975).[7] The statement presented *five approaches* the Catholic community could take to help resolve the housing problem:

First: Make people aware of the crisis. The bishops urged parishes and other organizations to promote understanding of housing problems and the role citizens can play in meeting housing needs. They also urged Catholics to join and support organizations that have shown effective concern for the nation's housing needs. The bishops promised "to educate people regarding the demands of justice in the area of housing and suggest principles upon which proposals for change might be based."[8]

Second: Analyze housing needs in the light of the Gospel and then advocate various policies before appropriate governmental bodies. As in their statement on the economy, the bishops stressed their interest in the moral dimensions of the issue. They promised support for action that:

1. Affirms and advances the realization of the national housing policy of "a decent home and suitable living environment for all American families."

2. Provides a variety of programmatic tools and sufficient resources to meet the housing needs of low- and moderate-income families, including the continued participation of non-profit, community-based housing corporations.

3. Focuses programs and resources on the special needs of the following: low-income people, rural Americans, the elderly, farm workers, Native Americans, and the handicapped.

4. Adapts our housing delivery system to meet the economic realities of inflation, recession, and unemployment.

5. Recognizes the central role of the neighborhood in the survival of viable urban areas by encouraging rehabilitation and reinvestment in central cities.

6. Encourages land use policies that provide for adequate planning and effective controls on unreasonable and wasteful development and speculation.

7. Encourages a monetary policy and credit allocation system that provides a sustained supply of affordable credit for housing production.

8. Encourages the integral participation of housing consumers and tenants in decisions regarding housing at local, regional, and national levels.

9. Encourages equal housing opportunity, within a framework of cultural pluralisms, through voluntary compliance and, where necessary, legal remedies.[9]

The first goal, decent housing for all, simply reaffirmed the national housing goal established in 1949 by the U.S. Congress. One means the USCC suggested was for government to establish policies encouraging maintenance of older homes.

In support of the fifth goal, revitalizing neighborhoods, the USCC suggested: effective use of revenue-sharing and development funds; the abolition of "red-lining," by which banks and other financial institutions restrict or deny mortgage and home-improvement loans in certain areas; disclosure of lending patterns by banks and loan associations; and the encouragement of just lending policies on the part of financial institutions by those who patronize them, including those responsible for church funds.

To accomplish the sixth goal, better land use, the bishops suggested more attached dwellings and planned unit developments, zoning policies and building codes that do not keep the less affluent out of suburban communities, control of land speculation, and more public participation in land-use decisions.

Third: Provide various kinds of housing services. The bishops especially encouraged dioceses, Catholic social agencies, and parishes to continue sponsoring the construction of housing for low-income people and the elderly as well as rehabilitation programs. Between 1964 and 1974, they said, 25,000 units were constructed under Catholic sponsorship. As other services that Catholic organizations and individuals could provide they mentioned housing management, education in tenant rights and responsibilities, financial and personal counseling, housing rehabilitation, and maintenance assistance. The bishops also encouraged providers of housing services under church auspices to involve tenants and the local community.

Fourth: Exercise more responsible stewardship over the Church's property. For example, the bishops said that some church real estate might better be used to provide adequate shelter for those without it. They also suggested better use of their own economic and personal resources, as well as investment policies, to assist those in need of housing.

Fifth: Develop a ministry of "community building." The bishops said that parishes should point out the problems, participate in community life, and encourage their members to get involved in community affairs and housing issues. The bishops stressed the role of the parish since historically neighborhoods tended to develop side by side with local parishes.

National Health Insurance

In the summer of 1974, the USCC, together with the Catholic Hospital Association and the National Conference of Catholic Charities, testified on national health insurance before the House Ways and Means Committee. These three organizations, claiming to represent the Catholic Church's concern for adequate health care in America, argued for the "moral necessity" of establishing a program of national health insurance. "The question . . . is not whether we should have a national program; it is how such a program should be developed and implemented."[10] The principle on which they based their reasoning about health care was that "every person has the right to life, to bodily integrity and the means which are necessary and suitable to the development of life."[11] In their minds, this meant that health care should be available to all without impediments, and the responsibility for making it available should fall primarily upon the federal government.

The rest of the fourteen-page statement explained how a national health-insurance program should be structured. Every U.S. citizen, resident, and alien should be covered. The package of benefits should include the following:

> ... preventive services, all physician services and all inpatient, outpatient, and medical services. This is intended to include coverage for all catastrophic illnesses, all prescription drugs, post-hospital extended care, nursing home care, medical home health services, rehabilitation services, care for the developmentally disabled, dental care including orthodontic, therapeutic devices, prosthetic devices including hearing aids and eyeglasses, health-oriented social services, mental health services, and necessary medical transportation.[12]

The statement favored folding Medicaid and Medicare into a national program with no deductibles and no coinsurance (i.e., no portion paid by the recipient). It strongly recommended health-education programs and preventive medicine as means of preventing illness, reducing unnecessary hospitalizations, and cutting medical costs.

To finance a national health-insurance program, the Catholic groups suggested reliance on general federal revenues as well as taxes on employers and the self-employed. They recommended the creation of a national trust fund within the Social Security Administration to disburse and collect health-insurance funds. While favoring a strong fiscal role for the federal government, the Catholic organizations urged state involvement in regulatory activities. They saw private insurance companies supplying supplemental insurance and operating health-maintenance organizations at reasonable prices. Further, they recommended funding of professional-standards review organizations to provide peer medical review of the quantity and quality of medical services rendered, particularly to the aged and poor. Finally, the statement argued that consumers should participate in making and reviewing policy for any national health-insurance program. It stated strong disapproval of the inclusion of funds for sterilization and abortion within such a program.

The USCC reaffirmed its support for comprehensive national health insurance in a 1979 statement by its Administrative Board entitled "Political Responsibility: Choices for the 1980s" and in 1980 testimony before the Republican and Democratic platform committess.

The Family Farm

The bishops' major statement on rural issues is "The Family Farm," published in 1979 by the USCC Committee on Social Development and World Peace.[13] The statement went into extensive detail about why family farms should be preserved and how to do it. More than half of it consisted of specific recommendations that the Church, farmers, and government could adopt to promote this goal.

The statement said that preservation of the family farm promotes individual, family, and national growth. Farm life brings people into close contact with the rhythms of nature and "encourages the development of patience, self-reliance, a simplicity of outlook, and the particular bond that comes when father and mother and children join in earning their common bread."[14] Farm life is conducive to promoting virtue and strengthening family life. The statement also argued that the widespread ownership of private property, such as family farms, was "one of the strongest guarantees of human dignity and of democratic freedoms."[15] Furthermore, the family farmer is more likely than an absentee owner to take good care of the land. Finally, the statement noted that corporate farm practices have caused a decline in nutrition and taste. One example: the hard tomato, bred to withstand machine harvesting.

In this statement the USCC committee discussed government's role in preserving the family farm only after discussing the roles of the Church and the farmer. In so doing it was following the principle of subsidiarity enunciated by Pope Pius XI and reaffirmed by Pope John XXIII. The statement explained the principle in this way:

> In order to preserve citizen liberties, action to promote social justice should be taken at the lowest practical level within a society. Functions properly performed by individuals should not

be given over to groups, functions properly performed by small groups should not be given over to large groups, and government should act only when it alone is competent to achieve the desired end.[16]

This is a very significant point in view of the USCC's tendency in its statements to give priority to recommending specific policies to the national government. In fact, most of the major USCC statements on domestic questions published after this one on the family farm were primarily addressed to persons and groups within the Church rather than to the government.

Farm Labor

November 1968 brought the first formal statement on farm labor ("Farm Labor," NCCB).[17] The bishops expressed great sympathy for workers who were receiving low wages and no assistance from social legislation. They were especially desirous that farm workers receive "legislative protection for their natural rights to organize for purposes of collective bargaining."[18] They urged Congress to include farm workers under the National Labor Relations Act as well as under a national employment-insurance program and a national minimum wage.

In addition to supporting the cause of farm workers, the bishops also expressed sympathy for small growers who were willing but unable to pay higher wages. The NCCB said it would encourage dialogue between growers and workers "by helping to create an atmosphere of charity and justice."[19]

In July 1972, the USCC Committee on Social Development and World Peace issued "The Farm Workers' Lettuce Boycott," urging support for the boycott begun by farm workers as a means of bringing about collective bargaining.[20] The United Farm Workers (UFW) union decided to resort to boycott when growers in two areas of California refused to bargain with them even though they represented a majority of the farm workers in those areas.

The following year the same USCC committee issued another statement in support of the UFW ("Resolution on Farm Labor," May 1973).[21] The provocation was "union busting" by the International Brotherhood of Teamsters, which signed contracts with grape-growers who had been under contract with the UFW for three years. To remedy this injustice, the USCC committee called on the Teamsters and growers to accept the UFW request for a secret-ballot election in which the farm workers could choose which union they preferred. The resolution asserted that "the right of farm workers to organize and join a legitimate organization of their own choosing is the 'dominant moral issue' in this dispute."[22] It urged continued support of the boycott of table grapes and iceberg lettuce until the growers agreed to collective bargaining with the union preferred by the farm workers.

In November 1974 the NCCB Bishops' Committee on Farm Labor called for legislation, at either the national or the state level, to assure farm workers the right to choose a union by secret ballot.[23]

Finally, in November 1975 the NCCB issued a "Resolution on Farm Labor" in response to passage of the California Agricultural Labor Relations Act, which guaranteed the right of farm workers to decide by secret ballot which union if any they wanted to represent them at the bargaining table.[24] The bishops called the legislation a historic step toward resolution of the farm labor problem and expressed their willingness to work with all parties for an era of peace and justice in the agricultural industry.

Support for the rights of workers to organize and bargain collectively is not new in the Catholic Church; Pope Leo XIII vigorously defended this right in the first of the modern social encyclicals, his 1891 *Rerum Novarum*. In their 1968 statement on farm labor, the bishops pointed out that the Second Vatican Council had reaffirmed the traditional teaching of the Church on this matter in *Gaudium et Spes*, from which the bishops quoted a section that reads in part:

> Among the basic rights of the human person must be counted the right of freely founding labor unions. These unions should be truly able to represent the workers and to contribute to the proper arrangement of economic life.[25]

The bishops did not begin their involvement in the farm-labor issue by taking sides. At first they remained neutral in the dispute between the growers and the UFW, and they actually sent a team of bishops with Monsignor George Higgins to California to act as mediators. Not until it became clear that the Teamsters were intent on destroying the UFW did the bishops abandon their neutral stance and support the UFW. Many would say that the bishops' firm support of the UFW and the farm workers paved the way for passage of the California law that gave farm workers the right to bargain collectively through a union of their choice.

Racial Justice

The American bishops issued two pastoral letters on race, one in 1968 and the other in 1979. In the first, "The National Race Crisis" (NCCB, April 1968), the bishops described the racial problem in a very grave tone.[26] They began by congratulating American religious leaders for their efforts to secure racial justice for minorities.

> The 1963 National Conference on Religion and Race became a landmark of ecumenical social action. There is reassuring evidence that the ensuing religious involvement contributed greatly to the passage of national civil-rights legislation in 1964 and 1965.[27]

Then they admitted their own failure to do enough over the previous ten years. The bishops affirmed the judgment by the National Advisory Commission on Civil Disorders that "white racism was a key factor in creating and maintaining the explosive ghettoes of our cities."[28] That judgment also proved how much remained to be done. In response to this need, the bishops directed USCC departments to set up an Urban Task Force "to coordinate all Catholic activities and to relate them to those of others working for the common goal of society, based on truth, justice, and love."[29] They urged Catholics to join civic and religious groups working to end discrimination, and asked government and the private sector to pay special attention to education, job opportunities, housing, and welfare assistance. Finally, they themselves pledged to work with other groups for racial justice.

In the second statement, "Brothers and Sisters to Us: A Pastoral

Letter on Racism" (NCCB, November 1979), the bishops noted the persistence of the sin of racism in American society and in the Church.[30] They said racism is a sin because it is an affront to the dignity of the human person. The bishops called attention to evidence of racism in the United States: high unemployment among minorities; violent resistance to attempts to achieve racial balance in education (through busing) and housing; segregated housing patterns in major cities and suburbs; the disproportionate number of minority members in prisons and on welfare; the low income of non-white families; and opposition to affirmative-action programs (quotas are not explicitly mentioned but seem to be implied).

To alleviate racism, the bishops did not suggest any specific government action but urged the Church to proclaim that racism is a sin, called for affirmative-action programs in every diocese and religious institution, and stressed the importance of maintaining the commitment to Catholic education in minority neighborhoods. They recommended examining church investment portfolios to determine "whether racist institutions and policies are inadvertently being supported," and they pressed Catholic institutions not to do business with industries or agencies "which refuse to take affirmative action to achieve equal opportunity."[31] In addition, the bishops urged individuals both to teach others, especially their children, to avoid racial bias and to take appropriate political action against racial discrimination in cooperation with members of other religious groups. Finally, the bishops observed that the ultimate remedy for racism lies not solely in human efforts but in re-creation of the human being according to the image revealed by Jesus Christ.

Other Disadvantaged Groups

On immigration, the bishops made five policy recommendations in the "Resolution on the Pastoral Concern of the Church for People on the Move" (NCCB, November 1976), including amnesty for illegal aliens.[32]

The bishops have issued one statement each on the elderly, American Indians, and the handicapped. They spoke out about these three "minority" groups not only to promote greater social respect for their dignity but also to improve their economic condition. In statements on the elderly ("Society and the Aged: Toward Reconciliation," USCC, May 1976) and American Indians ("Statement of the U.S. Catholic Bishops on American Indians," USCC, May 1977), they urged individuals and private groups within the Church to do their part and made some general policy recommendations.[33]

The bishops' "Pastoral Statement on the Handicapped" (USCC, November 1978) acknowledged the Church's failure to respond adequately to the needs of handicapped people.[34] The bishops urged members and leaders of the Catholic Church to welcome the handicapped into their communities and to educate themselves "to appreciate fully the contribution handicapped people can make to the Church's spiritual life." The handicapped have special insights into the meaning of life, said the bishops, because they live more than most in the shadow of the cross. The bishops concluded by designating ministry to the handicapped as a special focus for the NCCB and the USCC.

Capital Punishment

In November 1974 the USCC declared its opposition to the reinstitution of capital punishment in a one-line statement.[35] Three years later Archbishop Joseph Bernardin, then president of the NCCB and USCC, issued his own statement.[36] He recalled the USCC's 1974 action and pointed out that, since then, individual bishops, state Catholic conferences, and other Catholic organizations had expressed opposition to the death penalty.

Archbishop Bernardin's position was two-sided. He acknowledged the need for swift and certain punishment for criminal offenses but expressed doubt about the death penalty as a wise course of action in a society already sadly lacking in respect for human life. Bernardin advocated instead penal methods more consistent with respect for life and the gospel message of God's healing love. In February 1978 the USCC's Committee on Social Development and World Peace reaffirmed its opposition to capital punishment in "Community and Crime"; its reasons were essentially the same as Archbishop Bernardin's.[37]

The following year the USCC Administrative Board ("Political Responsibility: Choices for the 1980s," October 1979) confirmed the bishops' opposition to the reinstitution of capital punishment and pointed out that the application of the death penalty in the past had been discriminatory toward the poor and racial minorities.[38] The board said it was not questioning society's right to punish lawbreakers but was urging society to seek methods of dealing with violent crime that are more consistent with the teaching of Christ. The statement did not show, however, how Christ's teaching serves as a basis for opposition to capital punishment.

Finally, in November 1980 the entire body of bishops issued a comprehensive "Statement on Capital Punishment" in which they told why they opposed reinstitution of the death penalty.[39] They admitted, however, that support for capital punishment is not incompatible with Catholic teaching. They expressed concern for victims of crime and for law-enforcement officers who are more likely to suffer from the persistence and increase of violent crime. They even called upon governments to cooperate in stopping terrorists.

The greater part of the 1980 statement was devoted to the rationale behind punishing criminals. Punishment, the bishops argued, is traditionally defended on three grounds: reform, deterrence, and retribution. *Reform* does not justify capital punishment, since the executed criminal never has the opportunity to begin a new way of life. As for *deterrence*, empirical studies do not show that capital punishment deters criminals from committing murder. Finally, *retribution* or restoration of the order of violated justice, the bishops claimed, requires punishment but is not best served by taking the life of the criminal. The bishops did not really argue this point except to say that Jesus urged forbearance in the face of evil and forgiveness of enemies.

The bishops asserted that abolition of the death penalty would promote four Christian values. It would: (1) show that we can break the cycle of violence characteristic of modern society; (2) manifest belief in the dignity of all human beings, who have great worth because they are created in the image of God; (3) testify to the Judeo-Christian and Islamic belief that God is the Lord of life and strengthen the defense of all life, including that of the unborn, the aged, and the infirm; and (4) be most consonant with the teaching and example of Jesus, who practiced forgiveness.

The statements on capital punishment and abortion (and also nuclear deterrence) show a close link between the bishops' theological positions and the policies they propose. Fidelity to Catholic teaching requires the Church to be against abortion. One of the strategies by which the Church in the United States has opposed abortion—e.g., by proposing a constitutional amendment—is a question of political prudence and not theological dogma. The bishops' opposition to capital punishment stems from theological convictions about the dignity of life and the Christian doctrine of forgiveness. Nevertheless, they readily concede the existence of a strong tradition of Catholic teaching that allows the state to use capital punishment.

It is interesting that the bishops have been gradually increasing their opposition to the taking of life. They have always opposed abortion; however, in the 1970s they not only began to oppose capital punishment but also, as we saw in chapter three, qualified their toleration of nuclear deterrence.

Prison Reform

The basic view presented in "The Reform of Correctional Institutions in the 1970s" (USCC, November 1973) is that rehabilitation, not punishment, should be the primary concern.[40] The bishops also argued that a system should be worked out to compensate victims of crime or their survivors. They recommended higher wages and realistic safety provisions for prison staff and urged society to accept released offenders with compassion so they would not become repeat offenders.

After a discussion of problems within correctional institutions, the USCC offered twenty-two recommendations for reform. These are so extensive and detailed that a short summary would be inadequate; consequently, the full statement is reprinted in appendix B. The USCC's objective in speaking out in such detail on this subject was "to insure protection for all the civil rights of confined offenders in an atmosphere of human compassion conducive to reconciliation and rehabilitation."[41]

Causes of Crime

A comprehensive statement entitled "Community and Crime" (USCC Committee on Social Development and World Peace, February 1978) discussed the causes of crime, community-based alternatives to prisons, "white-collar" and youth crime, reform of the criminal justice system, victim compensation, research on the problem of crime, handgun control, and capital punishment.[42] (In September 1975 the committee had issued a separate statement on handgun control.) On each of these points the statement suggested both a role for the Church and government policy initiatives. I will focus on what was said about the first point, the causes of crime.

The committee discerned four major causes of crime in the United States: (1) acceptance of false values; (2) social injustice; (3) the breakdown of families and neighborhoods; and (4) lack of moral leadership from society's major institutions. By "false values" the committee meant materialism, excessive individualism, acceptance of violence, and loss of respect for human life. "Social injustice" refers to social and economic deprivation, which includes inadequate employment, housing, health care, education, and food. Victims of this deprivation are "the weak and unfortunate, the poor, the aged, the young, minorities and women."

In all racial, economic, cultural, and social groups the committee saw signs of "family breakdown": rising divorce rates, irresponsible parenting, child and spouse abuse, social and economic deprivation, alcoholism and drug abuse. Recognizing family breakdown as the most significant cause of crime, the committee said:

> We have to work more diligently to strengthen the stability of the American family and restore it to a role of importance in our society, for it is in the family that we learn to respect one another and to harmonize our personal needs with those of others.[43]

The committee did not make clear what it meant by "neighborhood breakdown" except to say that this breakdown brings disintegration of mutual concern and community support.

The fourth cause of crime, "lack of moral leadership," is evident in government, business, labor, medicine, education, the social-service professions, the entertainment and news media, and even among religious leaders. The statement mentioned abuses of power in government; the pursuit of profit by business to the extent that it overwhelms concern for the environment, for worker safety, and for service to customers; corrupt practices of labor leaders; and misuse of Medicare and Medicaid by some members of the medical profession. It argued further that educational institutions have not yet eliminated discrimination and have not provided "the ethical training and example which are needed to preserve a just and moral society." It criticized the media for appearing to condone materialism, violence, and greed and for supporting and condoning indecency, pornography, and the exploitation of sex. Finally, the committee criticized religious leaders for insufficiently stressing personal responsibility, moral formation, and social concern.

The committee suggested twenty-two initiatives that local churches could adopt in response to crime. The first was to foster "Christian values through education, liturgy and the media." This is significant, since the USCC rarely links its pursuit of social justice with moral formation through Christian education. Other suggestions included establishing "block patrols" and special protection for elderly people in high-crime areas, finding suitable work for young people and parolees, encouraging research and discussion on crime and its prevention, and sponsoring programs and institutions to attend to battered spouses and children, alcohol and drug abuse, and rehabilitation of prisoners outside traditional prisons.

The committee made eleven recommendations for public policy initiatives. First on the list was legislation that addresses the socioeconomic causes of crime; second, legislation that deals effectively with "white-collar" crime. The committee said nothing about encouraging public schools to provide any kind of moral formation, or about the role the government could play in strengthening families and neighborhoods.

Abortion

In response to the growing pressure to "liberalize" abortion laws, the NCCB expressed its strong opposition in 1968, in 1969, and twice in 1970. After the Supreme Court's landmark January 1973 decision that legalized abortion, the NCCB issued five statements highly critical of the decision. The statements called for a constitutional amendment to protect the life of fetuses.

In 1974, the NCCB and the USCC issued *Documentation on the Right to Life and Abortion*, a collection of statements on abortion made by members of the American hierarchy between November 1968 and March 1974 plus short excerpts from the Vatican II *Pastoral Constitution on the Church in the Modern World (Gaudium et Spes)*.[44]

The bishops' anti-abortion activity reached a high point in the USCC's March 1974 testimony before the Senate Subcommittee on Constitutional Amendments. That testimony expressed the crux of the Church's opposition to abortion. It stated the grounds for this opposition:

1. The right to life is a basic human right which should be protected by law.
2. Abortion, the deliberate destruction of an unborn human being, is contrary to the law of God and is a morally evil act.[45]

The first argument implied that human reason, unaided by revelation, can discover the right to life as a human or natural right, which has standing whether or not it is supported by law. But the testimony pointed out that the Declaration of Independence, the Constitution of the United States, and the United Nations Declaration of Human Rights all assert that the right to life is a basic human right.

The second argument indicated that Catholic moral teaching is based on faith in a transcendent God; in other words, revelation provides standards in addition to human reason by which to judge abortion. This point was made in the February 1973 "Pastoral Message" (NCCB Administrative Committee) on the decision of the Supreme Court the previous month. "Human life is valuable from conception to death because God is the Creator of each human being, and because mankind has been redeemed by Jesus

Christ."[46] Certainly it is known only through faith in divine revelation that Jesus Christ has redeemed all men.

The bishops' opposition to abortion is, the statements show, based on philosophical, legal, and theological grounds. However, the USCC's March 1974 argument before the Senate Subcommittee on Constitutional Amendments was based neither on *philosophical* views of human or natural rights nor on *theological* knowledge derived from revelation, but rather on the protection given to the life of the unborn in *legal* documents. First, the USCC marshalled scientific evidence to show that human life begins at fertilization, and that therefore the unborn child possesses human dignity. Then it cited the appropriate provisions of the legal documents: the Declaration of Independence states that "all men are created equal, that they are endowed by their Creator with certain inalienable rights, that among these are life, liberty, and the pursuit of happiness"; the Fourteenth Amendment to the Constitution provides that no person shall be deprived of life without due process; and the U.N. Declaration of Human Rights affirms that "everyone has the right to life, liberty and security of person."[47]

The bishops firmly asserted that the Supreme Court misinterpreted the Constitution in *Roe* v. *Wade*, the decision that in effect created the constitutional right to abortion on demand for the whole nine months of pregnancy. After explaining why it considered the Court's decision erroneous and dangerous, the USCC proposed a constitutional amendment to protect the unborn, beginning with the moment of conception. It also urged that the following services be made available to women and children as a matter of right: nutritional, prenatal, childbirth, and post-natal care for the mother, and nutritional and pediatric care for the child through the first year of life, as well as counseling services, adoption facilities, and financial assistance.

In November 1975 the NCCB issued a "Pastoral Plan for Pro-Life Activities" outlining the Church's plan to undertake three major efforts in the defense of life.[48] The *first* was a *public information and education* program. The Church planned to inform the general public both of the threat to human dignity posed by a permissive abortion policy and of the need to establish legal safeguards for the protection of life. A more intensive, long-range aspect of this educational effort was to present scientific information on the humanity of the unborn child; to make medical, sociological, legal, and, especially, moral and theological arguments in favor of societal protection of the child at every stage of its existence; and to point out the problems women face during pregnancy as well as humane and morally acceptable solutions to these problems. The bishops called upon priests, religious, and all Church-sponsored or identifiably Catholic organizations on the parochial, diocesan, regional, and national levels, such as schools, social services, and health agencies, to help in this program of information and education.

The Church's *second* major effort in defense of life was to be in *pastoral care*. The intention was to provide a moral perspective on abortion, which includes "accurate information regarding the nature of the act, its effects and far-reaching consequences, and [evidence] that abortion is a violation of God's laws of charity and justice."[49] Another aspect of pastoral care was to provide programs and care for pregnant women, including:

—adequate education and material sustenance for women so that they may choose motherhood responsibly and freely in accord with a basic commitment to the sanctity of life;

—nutritional, pre-natal, childbirth, and post-natal care for the mother, and nutritional and pediatric care for the child throughout the first year of life;

—intensified scientific investigation into the causes and cures of maternal disease and/or fetal abnormality;

—continued development of genetic counseling and gene therapy centers and neo-natal intensive care facilities;

—extension of adoption and foster care facilities to those who need them;

—pregnancy counseling centers that provide advice, encouragement, and support for every woman who faces difficulties related to pregnancy;

—counseling services and opportunities for continuation of education for unwed mothers;

—special understanding, encouragement, and support for victims of rape;

—continued efforts to remove the social stigma that is visited on the woman who is pregnant out of wedlock and on her child.[50]

Another kind of pastoral care was called "reconciliation": the Church "reconciles men and women to God" and "pursues the task of reconciling [them] with one another and the entire community." The bishops believe reconciliation is necessary because they regard abortion as a grave sin.

The *third* major effort in defense of life concerned *public policy*. The legislative agenda of the Church included:

(a) passage of a constitutional amendment providing protection for the unborn child to the maximum degree possible;

(b) passage of federal and state laws and adoption of administrative policies that will restrict the practice of abortion as much as possible;

(c) continual research into and refinement and precise interpretation of *Roe* and *Doe* and subsequent court decisions [*Roe* v. *Wade* and *Doe* v. *Bolton* were the two cases in which the Supreme Court made its landmark 1973 abortion decisions];

(d) support for legislation that provides alternatives to abortion.[51]

In order to promote respect for life through legislation, the bishops proposed coordinated efforts by Catholic and non-Catholic citizens at the national, state, and local levels. In particular they planned to rely on a coordinating committee in each state composed of the director of the state Catholic conference and the diocesan pro-life coordinators, diocesan and parish pro-life committees, and the pro-life effort in each congressional district.

In March 1976 the USCC testified before the House Subcommittee on Civil and Constitutional Rights (Committee on the Judiciary).[52] It summarized its pastoral plan for pro-life activities and then discussed aspects of abortion not covered in previous statements.

Not a few critics raise the issue of religious freedom in response to the bishops' campaign against abortion. They argue that the Catholic Church violates the religious freedom guaranteed by the First Amendment by pressing for a constitutional amendment to protect the unborn. Some say it would violate the First Amendment establishment clause to give public recognition to the view that human life begins at conception, since this is a religious belief of the Catholic Church.

In their March 1976 testimony the bishops responded as follows: the Declaration of Independence, the U.S. Constitution, and the U.N. Declaration of Human Rights all affirm the right to life as a basic human right. According to data available from the sciences of genetics, biology, and fetology, human life begins at conception. Hence the bishops did not think they were violating the First Amendment by arguing for a constitutional amendment to protect unborn life. In fact, they felt they were simply being faithful to the high ideals upon which the nation was founded. They admitted they had religious reasons for quoting these legal documents and for supporting the proposed constitutional amendment, for they hold that human dignity and human rights are rooted in God's creation of each human being. But their religious motivation was not unconstitutional unless it had been agreed that the proposal of any constitutional amendment or any law must proceed from wholly secular reasons.

As a matter of fact, the American people, the bishops contended, have willingly accepted the religious teaching of the Church in support of social justice and human rights, especially religiously motivated arguments against racism and poverty. The bishops threw the ball back at their critics by asking whether state support and funding of abortion did not violate the consciences of those who oppose abortion.

The bishops contended not only that they were not violating the First Amendment by pressing for a constitutional amendment but also that it was wholly reasonable for them to do so, since opposition to abortion was not limited to Catholics and support for an amendment was growing among the electorate. In other words, if the bishops attain widespread support, there can be no question of imposing the morality of one church on the American public. Another indication that it was reasonable to amend the Constitution, according to the bishops, was the criticism of the legal methodology of *Roe* and *Doe* by constitutional scholars.

Not only is abortion a grave evil in itself, said the bishops in this March 1976 testimony, but also the rationale supporting abortion leads to other evils. For example, the theory behind *Roe* and *Doe* "creates a prejudice against protecting the lives of newborn infants and sick children." The bishops mentioned Dr. Kenneth Edelin's reported remarks to a Boston jury that in sound medical practice abortion presupposed the death of the fetus; hence there was no responsibility on the part of a doctor to maintain the life of an aborted fetus. The bishops cited an article in the *New England Journal of Medicine* reporting that in Yale–New Haven Hospital, forty-three infants were allowed to die instead of being given necessary medical treatment. Furthermore, said the bishops, the Supreme Court's assertion that a fetus must have the "capacity for meaningful life" in order to be eligible for constitutional protection was a principle that could have far-reaching, frightening effects. The bishops did not elaborate on possible consequences of a wider application of that principle, such as the attempt to justify voluntary or compulsory euthanasia.

Aid to Parochial Schools

In November 1971 the USCC issued a "Statement on Parental Rights and the Free Exercise of Religion."[53] This was the only statement by the bishops in the last decade dealing entirely with financial aid to parochial schools. It argued that the Supreme Court's interpretation of the Constitution gives parents a constitutional right to send children to non-public schools. Inflation, taxation, and rising governmental costs, however, often prevent the exercise of this constitutional right. Consequently, the bishops claimed, government has an obligation to assist parents financially so that they will, indeed, have the freedom to choose private education for their children. (Ironically, the bishops' reasoning here bears a striking similarity to the argument that government should economically assist women who cannot afford to take advantage of the constitutional right to abortion.)

The only other statement in which there was any extended argument for aid to parochial schools was the USCC's "Teach Them," a short 1976 reflection by the bishops on the condition of Catholic schools. They promised to pursue and publicize every possible constitutional means of attaining government aid. Then the bishops made this forceful statement:

We urge that the entire nation realistically acknowledge the contributions which Catholic and other non-public schools make to the total educational enterprise in our country. . . . It is a deplorable fact that courts have often overturned [legislation to assist non-public school children] for reasons we and others consider tenuous and at times offensive.[54]

The USCC Administrative Board's two statements on political responsibility ("Political Responsibility: Reflections on an Election Year," February 1976, and "Political Responsibility: Choices for the 1980s," October 1979) listed five policy positions on education supported by the bishops. The fifth was: "Equitable tax support for the education of pupils in public and non-public schools to implement parental freedom in the education of their children."[55]

In "To Teach as Jesus Did: A Pastoral Message on Catholic Education" (NCCB, 1973), the bishops clearly stated their belief that Catholic schools make an important contribution to society:

Most important, the commitment of Catholic schools to Christian values and the Christian moral code renders a profound service to society, which depends on spiritual values and good moral conduct for its survival.[56]

Prayer in Public Schools

In 1973 the USCC Administrative Board made a "Statement on Prayer and Religious Instruction in Public Schools" in which it called for a constitutional amendment to permit religious instruction and prayer in public schools. It proposed this wording:

Section 1. Nothing in this constitution shall be construed to (i) forbid prayer in public places or in institutions of the several states or of the United States, including schools; (ii) forbid religious instruction in public places or in institutions of the several states or of the United States, including schools, if such instruction is provided under private auspices whether or not religious. *Section 2.* The right of the people to participate or not to participate in prayer or religious instruction shall never be infringed by the several states or the United States.[57]

The Administrative Board justified its proposal in two ways. First, the amendment would protect the religious liberty of parents and children. The freedom to learn the truths of his faith within the setting of formal education would help the child understand the importance of religion in his life. Second, if religion was not taught in schools there was a danger that the religious heritage of the nation would be supplanted by a pervasive secularism. (It should be noted that the bishops have not reiterated their call for a prayer amendment.)

Family Life

In 1978 the USCC issued "The Plan of Pastoral Action for Family Ministry: A Vision and Strategy." The bishops designated 1980 the Year of the Family and committed the Church to a decade of research on family life and ministry. They cited the Second Vatican Council's *Gaudium et Spes*, which said: "The well-being of the individual person and of human and Christian society is intimately linked with the healthy condition of that community produced by marriage and family."[58]

The bishops expressed their awareness that the Catholic family was suffering from many difficulties and that the mission of the Church depended very much on the strengthening of family life. But they were much less clear about the importance of the family for the general well-being of the nation. They did say that the "social mission of the family is a key dimension" of their plan. Families have social responsibilities, they said. For example, they should contribute to parish and neighborhood renewal and to the overcoming of "injustices experienced by the poor or by cultural, ethnic, and racial minorities." In the *National Catechetical Directory* (NCCB, 1977) the bishops expressed their belief that "the home is the critical educational institution."[59]

One way in which the bishops have tried to protect family life is to criticize TV programming. For the first time in eighteen years, the bishops spoke about censorship in a September 1975 "Statement on the Introduction of the Family Viewing Period During Prime-Time by the Television Networks," prepared by the USCC Administrative Board.[60] The board was responding to new guidelines created by the networks: they would show material suitable for families during prime time and the immediately preceding hour; if a program shown in this "family viewing" period was unsuitable for younger family members, a "viewer advisory" would precede it; these advisories would also be used at other times if a program might contain material offensive to a significant proportion of the viewing audience.

The bishops said the family viewing policy was an act of self-regulation by the networks that they basically supported. However, they argued that even self-regulation must be an open, accountable, and cooperative process. They said the networks did not seriously consult either local broadcasters or the public about programming. In fact, neither group was asked its opinion about introducing a distinction between family and adult programming. Effective self-regulation was thwarted because the broadcast industry was dominated by commercial interests. "American television is essentially concerned with the sale of consumers to advertisers."[61] The networks presented those shows that attracted the most viewers and therefore the most profits. Hence the main components of programming were "smart comedy," crime, violence, and sex.

Further objections to the family viewing period were based on lessons learned from the Motion Picture Code and Rating Program. The code's standards rule out, among other things, offensive presentations of violence and sex. But, said the bishops, it never worked. In fact, violence and obscenity had increased since it was put into effect. The bishops feared that television would undergo the same moral decline if a code and rating system were introduced.

The establishment of a family viewing period, then, with the strong possibility of an ensuing decline in the moral quality of programs, would add to the burden on parents and family life, in the bishops' opinion. Since television's influence is so pervasive in the American home (the bishops called it "the single most formative influence in shaping people's attitudes and values"), parents would have even more difficulty attending to the well-being of their children and preserving the quality of family life.

To counteract the commercialism dominating the broadcast industry, the bishops urged viewers to convince local station managers that they really wanted better programming. In particular, the bishops encouraged all Catholics to cooperate with their fellow citizens in pursuing this objective.

In August 1977 the USCC's Department of Communication argued that "Soap," ABC's "adult" situation comedy, should be removed from family television entertainment.[62] Its fundamental argument was that the program's manner of dealing with sex "debases not only the television medium but the humanity of the viewers." Furthermore, the introduction of "Soap" was inconsistent with a resolution passed by the National Association of Broadcasters that "calls on the Television Code Review Board to take positive, visible, affirmative steps to encourage industry and public awareness of both the spirit and letter of the code."

Another episcopal reflection on a family-life issue was the November 1966 NCCB statement "The Government and Birth Control," which criticized government for persuading and even coercing the underprivileged to practice birth control. This activity not only was unfair to the group targeted by government policy but also portended ominous consequences for society as a whole, said the bishops:

> History has shown that as a people lose respect for any life and a positive and generous attitude toward new life, they move fatally to inhuman infanticide, abortion, sterilization, and euthanasia.[63]

The American hierarchy also forcefully argued that the government should not make the reception of foreign aid dependent upon acceptance of birth-control programs.

The bishops expressed their belief that "the good of the individual person and that of human society are intimately bound up with the stability of the family,"[64] and that the well-being of the family depends upon freedom from external coercion. Therefore, said the bishops, they must publicly oppose the imposition of birth-control programs.

Conclusion

Most of the bishops' statements on domestic issues stress specific policy proposals. In the statements on the aged and American

Indians, policy recommendations remain on a general level. A good number of statements—particularly those on housing, the community and crime, the family farm, racism, abortion, immigrants, American Indians, the aged, the handicapped, and television programming—reflect fidelity to the principle of subsidiarity. In these statements the bishops suggest ways in which the Church, individuals, and groups can help to solve public problems.

Only a few statements—those on abortion, the community and crime, the family farm, and racism—lay out the principles of Catholic social teaching in such a manner as to be truly educational. The other statements do refer to Catholic social principles, but in summary fashion. The bishops have put their greatest effort into explaining Catholic teaching on abortion.

All the statements provide some factual information about the issues under discussion. Of all the bishops' statements on domestic issues between 1966 and 1980, the ones on the family farm, community and crime, and abortion are the most informative.

PART THREE

Toward the Recovery of Catholic Political Wisdom

CHAPTER FIVE

An Evaluation of the Bishops' Quest for Justice

THE FOLLOWING ARE SOME **general characteristics of the bishops' statements** revealed by my study:

First, the bishops tend to separate evangelization from the pursuit of justice. In fact, their quest for justice has become an activity parallel to evangelization instead of an integral part of it. While the bishops are certainly committed to evangelization, they do not stress that it is the most effective means for the Church to seek justice. Instead, the USCC has stressed the quest for justice through policy statements. In neglecting to seek justice through evangelization, the bishops are unwittingly failing to appropriate an essential aspect of papal social teaching that has been very clearly reiterated by Pope John Paul II.

Second, with the stress on proposing their own policy initiatives, the bishops have unwittingly failed to communicate the very rich tradition of Catholic social thought to Catholics—not to mention non-Catholics. Official Catholic teaching on political and social matters remains largely unknown despite the many political statements issued by the American hierarchy.

A good deal of material in the papal social encyclicals and in the teaching of the Second Vatican Council merits careful explanation. For example, it would be helpful for the bishops to explain basic concepts of Catholic social thought such as the dignity of the human person, the social nature of man, the purpose of politics, war and peace, the common good, social justice, human rights, the relation of rights to duties, the duties of individuals toward one another and toward society, the principle of subsidiarity, the value of work, the right to a living wage, the right to private property, the right to development, and the role of the family. The Pontifical Commission *Iustitia et Pax* has begun to issue booklets that explain the social teaching of Pope John Paul II and also collect his speeches and writings under specific headings.[1] The United States bishops could do the same, or at least distribute the material prepared by the Pontifical Commission

Between 1966 and 1980, the bishops issued two major documents that did explain some aspects of Catholic social teaching. These are the pastoral letters we looked at in chapter two, "Human Life in Our Day" (1968) and "To Live in Christ Jesus" (1976).[2] The second part of "Human Life in Our Day" briefly explains the teaching of *Gaudium et Spes* under the title "The Fostering of Peace and the Promotion of a Community of Nations." The bishops should prepare many more commentaries of this sort. The second pastoral, "To Live in Christ Jesus," touches on a wide range of issues under the heading "Moral Life in the Family, the Nation, and the Community." This letter is not a commentary on papal or conciliar teaching but does draw upon Catholic social thought to present the bishops' own vision of the moral life and their perception of many critical issues of the day. Although the pastoral may be too brief and sketchy to be an effective educational tool, it is a step toward integrating evangelization, education, and the quest for justice.

The bishops' failure to integrate their evangelical and educational activities with their quest for justice not only presents an obstacle to the renewal of the Catholic Church but also deprives U.S. citizens and policymakers of valuable guidance in the nation's pursuit of justice.

A *third* characteristic of the bishops' quest for justice follows from the first two: they do not instruct and involve the laity adequately. A number of insightful Catholics have pointed out that an evangelical and educated laity could infuse a Christian spirit into all levels of society—family, work, and leisure—and into all aspects of participation in public life. The bishops' 1980 statement entitled "Called and Gifted" shows they are aware of the laity's great potential.[3] To be faithful to their own views, the bishops must find a way to be effective teachers of Catholic social doctrine. This cannot be done through the conventional policy statement.

Fourth, the bishops have adopted a quasi-partisan approach to politics by placing on their political agenda mainly "liberal" issues, such as economic and social equality, and human rights violations by rightist regimes. (Abortion and federal aid for Catholic schools are the main exceptions.) While these are, indeed, important issues that the bishops should address, other topics deserve similar attention. So far, the bishops have not addressed as *public* problems a number of cultural issues suggested by Catholic social teaching. Among these are the decline of serious religious belief, especially among the educated; the spread of individualism and materialism; the breakdown of community and fraternity in all levels of society; decline of the work ethic and loss of pride in one's work, resulting in shoddy craftsmanship and unprofessional behavior; widespread ignorance of public affairs in the body politic; hedonism, moral permissiveness, and pornography; the increasing rate of suicide among the young; and the grave problems besetting the nation's schools, namely, abuse of drugs and alcohol, violence, and low academic achievement. Further, many young people are growing up without roots, or spiritual depth, and even without sufficient literacy to enable them to take their places in society.

While arguing sporadically that the practice of religion brings political and social benefits to society, the bishops have not made any sustained argument on this subject. Nor have they expressed their views on current intellectual movements such as positivism, historicism, and moral relativism.[4] (In November 1980 the bishops issued a pastoral letter on Marxism, and at the same time they promised one on capitalism.) Moral relativism has had a significant impact on the great arbiter of public morality in the United States, the Supreme Court. While the bishops may not be competent to discuss the legal aspects of Supreme Court decisions, they could and should discuss the philosophy undergirding them.

Although the bishops' economic statements reveal compassion for the poor, they do not effectively communicate Catholic teaching on property. Considerable explanation is needed to show the great differences among the Lockean, the Marxist, and the Catholic views of property.[5] Not many Catholics could explain why the Church defends both a relative right to private property and the duty to avoid waste and to share one's resources. In his 1981 encyclical, *On Human Work (Laborem Exercens)*, John Paul II discusses church teaching on ownership and on the right to private property in this enlightening paragraph:

> The Church's teaching . . . diverges radically from the program of collectivism as proclaimed by Marxism and put into practice in various countries in the decades following the time of Leo XIII's encyclical [i.e., *Rerum Novarum*]. At the same time it differs from the program of capitalism practiced by liberalism and by the political systems inspired by it. In the latter case, the difference consists in the way the right to ownership or property is understood. Christian tradition has never upheld this right as absolute and untouchable. On the contrary, it has always understood this right within the broader context of the right common to all to use the goods of the whole of creation: *the right to private property is subordinated to the right to common use,* to the fact that goods are meant for everyone.[6]

As this brief statement reveals, the Catholic position on property is nuanced and therefore needs considerable explanation to be understood by American Catholics.

Moreover, the bishops have not systematically elaborated the Catholic view of the common good or public morality. On the basis of the bishops' political statements, one would infer that they believe the common good to consist mainly in the protection of rights and a more equal distribution of material goods. This view is, of course, only partially true according to Catholic social teaching.

In the area of foreign policy, the bishops have not treated the questions of human rights and development in a comprehensive manner. Not only have the bishops failed to offer an adequate theoretical analysis of international human rights and the Church's role in promoting them, but they have also tended not to address human rights violations carried out in leftist countries. Statements on development fail to address the relation of economic well-being to the moral, intellectual, and spiritual development of the human person. This omission stands in contrast to the fuller treatment of development by Pope Paul VI in *Populorum Progressio*. On the subject of war and especially nuclear morality, a fuller treatment is needed. Despite some important statements on nuclear weapons, the bishops have yet to provide an in-depth discussion of all the issues pertaining to the possession and use of nuclear weapons. A committee established by the bishops has been studying these questions since the beginning of 1981.

Fifth, since the bishops emphasize federal action, it is not surprising that they have not attended to all the lessons to be drawn from the principle of subsidiarity. Pope Pius XI stated the principle this way:

> Just as it is wrong to withdraw from the individual and commit to a group what private industry and enterprise can accomplish, so too it is an injustice, a grave evil and a disturbance of right order, for a larger and higher association to arrogate to itself functions which can be performed efficiently by smaller and lower societies. This is a fundamental principle of social philosophy, unshaken and unchangeable. Of its nature the true aim of all social activity should be to help members of the social body, but never to destroy or absorb them.[7]

This principle is a clear repudiation of collectivist, especially totalitarian, forms of government, but it clearly does not mean that the state should not intervene in the political order. The state should not arrogate to itself any functions that can be performed as well or better by individuals or groups; nor should a larger governmental entity take over duties that can be carried out by smaller government bodies. When government should intervene is a determination of political prudence. In some circumstances and in some historical settings, the principle of subsidiarity could require a good deal of government action on a national level. Further, matters should be so arranged that "whenever the state does intervene, it does so to help individuals and lesser societies . . ., whence its name: *Subsidium afferre* (to bring aid)."[8] Oswald von Nell Breuning says subsidiarity demands that social groups "give their members generous help, especially help to self help." [9]

Recently the USCC has said that its statements adhere to the principle of subsidiarity; however, an analysis of the statements does not reveal a consistent pattern of fidelity to that principle. Statements issued in the mid-to-late seventies do point out the contribution that individual groups and the Church can make to the resolution of public problems; nevertheless, the stress has been on proposals for federal legislation.

Sixth, very significant staff influence is characteristic of the bishops' statements. Most bishops do not actually participate in the development of statements. It also seems that many bishops do not carefully study the statements before their publication. A good number of bishops feel ill at ease issuing specific statements on complicated issues with which they are not fully conversant.

The staff of the USCC's Department of Social Development and World Peace, which prepares most of the bishops' statements on political issues (with the notable exceptions of abortion and federal aid to parochial schools), has very limited theological competence, and no political diversity. That the bishops have addressed mainly liberal issues can be explained largely by the political bias of the staff of the Department of Social Development and World Peace. The theological and political outlook of that staff is also a contributing cause to the separation of evangelization and education from the pursuit of justice. The staff thinks it is more important to issue partisan policy statements than to communicate the principles of Catholic social doctrine.

One could object to the distinction I make between issuing policy statements and working for justice through evangelization and education. Some argue that policy statements can be a valuable instrument both of evangelization and of education, for if they are well done, they lead people to view specific issues through the prism of Catholic teaching and demonstrate the Church's commitment to solving the specific problems of our age. The bishops evangelize and educate to a *limited* extent in their policy statements, but not nearly enough. Even Catholic college graduates need a much fuller discussion of issues than that provided by the bishops. Furthermore, the policy statement is not the best forum for evangelization and education. Legislators are not particularly interested in hearing theological treatises. The bishops need something beside the conventional policy statement in order to pursue justice through evangelization and education.

Unquestionably, the suggestions made in this book put added burdens on the bishops. For one thing, they would have to place more emphasis on their role as teachers than as administrators. Greater reliance on evangelizing and educating as means of seeking justice will demand a deeper, broader involvement of the bishops in American political and social life than that required to draw up policy statements. Communicating all aspects of Catholic social teaching to American Catholics, not to mention non-Catholics, requires a prodigious effort. The bishops will need much cooperation in this work, especially from seminaries, the clergy, and the universities.

In May 1978 the American bishops established a five-year plan of action in response to a 1976 consultation on social justice.[10] The first part of that plan, "Education for Justice," suggests various programs that would make Catholic social thought better known to both clergy and laity.

Education for justice can be carried out in different ways. It can be genuine education in the rich tradition of Catholic social thought, or it can be consciousness-raising, indoctrination in the "correct" solutions to the nation's political problems. The bishops surely desire the first kind of education, but it is unlikely to occur unless some long-range steps are taken. One thing the bishops could do is to make sure that seminarians receive a sound philosophical education so that they will be better prepared to study and understand Catholic social thought.

The USCC's approach to political and social reform stands in contrast to the teaching of Pope John Paul II. The Pope, while recognizing the necessity of structural changes and government intervention, still maintains that bishops and priests make their best contribution to the political order by renewing the spiritual foundations of society:

> Ministers of the Church—bishops and priests—will be aware that their best and most effective participation in this social apostolate does not consist in becoming involved in party struggles or in options of groups and systems but in being true "educators in faith," reliable guides, spiritual stimulators.[11]

> The Church claims as her own right and duty the practice of the social apostolate, not along the line of a purely temporal project,

but as the formation and guidance of consciences, with her specific means, so that society may become more just. And the Church must do the same, bishops must do the same in the various countries of the world and in the various systems that exist in the world.[12]

The first service that the Church must render to the cause of justice and peace is to call upon men to open up to Jesus Christ.[13]

Pope John Paul's conviction that the Church should seek justice through evangelization and education, or what he in the middle quotation above called "the formation and guidance of consciences," is not readily understood today. This is largely attributable to widespread ignorance of the tradition of political philosophy that links politics with character formation, a tradition represented by Plato, Aristotle, Augustine, and Thomas More. A better understanding of ancient and medieval philosophers would help modern students of religion and politics understand the nuances of John Paul's approach.[14]

JUSTICE THROUGH THE POLICY STATEMENT

The bishops' pursuit of justice through the policy statement is open to a number of criticisms. First, there is the question whether the bishops are competent enough to propose concrete solutions to so many complex policy issues. Archbishop Joseph Bernardin chose to highlight this in a kind of farewell speech he delivered to the entire body of bishops just before he stepped down as president of the USCC/NCCB in 1977:

The mode in which we teach . . . demands a realistic awareness of the limits of our competence as bishops. . . . We cannot claim to have any special expertise concerning the concrete social, economic, and political solutions to the problems we seek to address from a moral and spiritual—an essentially evangelical—perspective. Devising and proposing these is perhaps better left to competent specialists. We should not hesitate to apply Christ's teaching to specific current issues. But we should also engage in a continuing effort to strike a balance between being too specific in these matters and being too general. Our credibility suffers when we err in either direction.[15]

This concern was relatively new to the USCC and the NCCB. Only at a general meeting in the spring of 1976, after ten politically active years, had the bishops begun to examine their own competence in making statements on American public policy. This self-examination came after two detailed statements issued in November 1975, one on the economy and the other on housing, had generated some uneasiness among the bishops. The following fall, after the bishops had passed a resolution calling on the United States to negotiate a new treaty with Panama, John Cardinal Carberry of St. Louis was quoted in the *New York Times Magazine* as saying that "he knew 'nothing at all' about Panama and it seemed silly to him to vote for or against a resolution on such an important matter." [16]

The bishops do well to question their own competence. Despite the fact that over the past fifteen years they have taken positions on many major public policy issues, they have by their own admission no expertise in these areas. How do the bishops do it?

In large measure they rely on the USCC staff, especially the Department of Social Development and World Peace. This department consists of eight professionals, a comparatively small group for the number and variety of statements they prepare each year. They are, of course, assisted by contacts in other episcopal conferences around the world, and they also rely on experts outside the conference.

None of this, however, solves the problem of addressing complex political and economic issues. Reliance on a staff does not provide instant competence. Lacking sufficient political and economic knowledge, the bishops are bound to have difficulty distinguishing good from better, or worse, advice. And the staff itself, being small, cannot possibly do all the research or engage in the reflection necessary to prepare so many statements covering such a diversity of subjects. It must therefore rely on selected experts, and choosing these requires keen political judgment.

Furthermore, even if the bishops had an expert and large enough staff (which is not possible because of budgetary constraints), this would still not overcome the problem of bias unless different points of view were represented on the staff. The present staff of the

Department of Social Development and World Peace, for example, does not include representatives of traditional conservative or even neo-conservative viewpoints. Since not all significant political points of view are represented, the recommendations received by the bishops are unlikely to have the refinement that often comes from healthy debate. Furthermore, with the exception of the Reverend J. Bryan Hehir, the staff of the Department of Social Development and World Peace possesses little or no theological expertise.

Given the limitations of a small staff with no political diversity and only one theologian, it is not surprising to find weaknesses in the statements prepared for the bishops—especially careless argumentation and incomplete treatment. And a number of important topics are conspicuous by their absence.

In the introduction to their 1975 statement on the economy, the bishops said they would address only the moral, human, and social aspects of the economic crisis and the impact of the economy on individuals and families—not "technical, fiscal matters, particular economic theories or political programs" (see page 64). Their general perspective was that "economic life must reflect broad values of social justice and human rights." By emphasizing the moral dimensions of the economy, the bishops implied that their remarks would, in a sense, be metapolitical or above partisanship. But immediately after saying that they would not endorse political theories or programs, the bishops went on to make a host of policy recommendations, such as improvement of the unemployment-compensation systems and the preservation of small family farms.

By presenting specific policy recommendations after disclaiming any intention of doing so, do the bishops not open themselves to charges—however unjustified—of misleading the public? (At the time the statement was issued, most bishops, I am sure, were unaware of the discrepancies in their reflections.) And by claiming to separate the moral dimension of economic programs from politics and economic theories, do they not encourage criticisms of political naïveté and incompetence? It is indeed possible to address the moral dimensions of the economy without opting for particular political programs, but this clearly is not what the USCC did.

An appendix to this statement on the economy contained policy suggestions made in a 1919 statement entitled "The Bishops' Program for Social Reconstruction." The bishops called attention to this old statement as evidence of the longstanding concern in the Catholic community for economic justice.

But there is an important difference between the statements of 1919 and 1975. The 1919 statement concluded its specific recommendations by reiterating Pope Leo XII's counsel that society can be healed only by a return to Christian life and institutions:

> Changes in our economic and political systems will have only partial and feeble efficiency if they be not reinforced by the Christian view of work and wealth. Neither the moderate reforms advocated in this paper nor any other program of betterment or reconstruction will prove reasonably effective without a reform in the spirit of both labor and capital.[17]

In other words, individuals must undergo a change of heart and be educated to Christian virtue before they will be just toward one another. The bishops of 1919 did not rely on structural changes alone to effect lasting reform. This emphasis on personal virtue as the most important element of social reform was characteristic of the bishops' approach to economic justice until the establishment of the USCC in 1966.

The USCC's 1974 congressional testimony on national health insurance was also poorly prepared (see page 67). The bishops argued for the "moral necessity" of establishing a program of national health insurance, expressly ruling out the usefulness of any debate on the advisability of a national health insurance program. They based this position on a principle, enunciated in papal teaching, that everyone has the right to health care. Perhaps national health insurance is the best way to deliver health services; however, it is inconsistent with Catholic social teaching to be dogmatic about the way to implement a particular right. There may be other equally good, or better, ways of providing health care. In an area as complex as this one, the bishops exceed the bounds of ethical discourse about politics in asserting the "moral necessity" of national health insurance.

In their 1979 statement opposing the death penalty, the bishops said they were not questioning society's right to punish lawbreakers but encouraging society to seek methods more consistent with the general vision of respect for life and Christ's message of healing love (see page 75). Yet they did not show *how* Christ's teaching serves as a basis for their opposition to capital punishment, nor did they support their position with any argumentation. In 1980 the bishops finally issued a statement explaining their reasons for opposing capital punishment; even then they did not explain how belief in Jesus' teaching about forgiveness will necessarily lead one to oppose capital punishment.

In their statements on abortion, the bishops have not discussed the moral harm people do to themselves by having or performing abortions. They have stressed the right to life of the fetus rather than the duty to avoid doing evil. Although the two approaches may have the same result, there is something missing from Catholic teaching if a stress on rights leads to neglect of an exhortation to virtue.

The bishops rightly reasserted a Catholic's right to be a conscientious objector (see page 43); however, they did not argue that a conscientious objector has an obligation to the state comparable to or greater than that of a soldier who fights for his country in a just war. As René Coste pointed out, conscientious objection is a special kind of prophetic calling (see page 44). It therefore, in my opinion, requires a special commitment to the Gospel. Making pacifism an "easy" option will detract from personal excellence and the common good.

The bishops also failed to argue adequately for *selective* conscientious objection (see page 42). In urging its legalization, they did not discuss in any detail the political and legal problems— much less possible solutions—that selective conscientious objection poses. For example, they could have addressed the problem of devising legal criteria for determining sincerity. They simply argued that selective conscientious objection is a moral option in the Catholic tradition and should therefore be made legal.

In a 1980 statement, "Registration and the Draft," the USCC Administrative Board opposed conscription, except in the case of a national defense emergency, and the concept of national service (i.e., that every citizen owes the state some service) because of "its compulsory character." [18] They hesitated to draw out the implications of their own principles. Man is a social animal and therefore has duties toward society and the state. Perhaps the idea of national service is not the best way to get the citizen to fulfill these duties, but that is surely not because of its "compulsory character." (The bishops, of course, support many other governmental measures despite their compulsory character.)

The 1977 statement on religious liberty in Eastern Europe (see page 53) signified an effort to be less one-sided in policy statements on human rights. It is striking that the USCC had not previously addressed human rights violations perpetrated by the left. And it is indeed extraordinary that not until the USCC had been in operation for more than a decade did it speak out on religious liberty in the world. Without religious liberty, the Church is inhibited from carrying out its fundamental mission—evangelization. Besides, there is a link between religious liberty and the other liberties (civil, political, and socio-economic), a point made forcefully by Pope John Paul II:

> Freedom of conscience and religion . . . is . . . a primary and inalienable right of the person; far more, to the extent it touches upon the most intimate sphere of the spirit, one can even say that it underlies the raison d'être of the other freedoms.[19]

As we saw in chapter three, one explanation for the relative neglect of religious liberty in the bishops' statements on human rights is the influence of the Reverend J. Bryan Hehir, who thinks the bishops should concentrate on addressing human rights violations in countries where the United States can exercise leverage. These, in Hehir's judgment, are mostly rightist regimes, whereas the most systematic denial of religious liberty has occurred in leftist regimes.[20]

I am not convinced that the bishops as a body are deliberately selective in their human rights statements. In 1975, Bishop James Rausch, then the general secretary of the USCC, told me he was unaware that there was a selective pattern to the USCC statements on human rights. If the operational head of the USCC was ignorant of conference policy, surely many other bishops shared his ignorance.

Even if Hehir is correct in arguing that the USCC *policy* statements should focus on rightist regimes, there are other methods of expounding Catholic social teaching. Should not the USCC find a way to communicate Catholic views on human rights violations in leftist regimes?

In the bishops' statements on development, considered as a whole, they blame the rich nations of the world for the poverty in developing nations. This is probably part of the truth, but it is surely not the whole. As the history of the industrialized West shows, development requires time. Also, injustice *within* developing nations presents a formidable obstacle to development. Moreover, the bishops in their political statements do not make a point of relating development to man's spiritual needs, nor do they point out the corruptive potential of affluence or the disadvantages of revolution. To do this would seem to be of great importance for a body that tries to look at political issues from a religious and moral point of view.

In his encyclical on development, *Populorum Progressio,* Pope Paul VI stressed that development must include the whole man. It must attend to man's moral, intellectual, and spiritual life. In other words, development must be characterized by an integral humanism (a concept derived from the thought of Jacques Maritain), one that considers, not only the needs of the body, but those of the mind and soul. "But a form of humanism circumscribed by narrower limits, divorced from spiritual values and God . . . can be more important only superficially," said Pope Paul.[21] This emphasis on integral humanism is not found in the bishops' statements on development.

It is also most interesting to note Pope Paul's cautions about development. Revolution begets new injustice and new inequalities. The Pope viewed industrialization not as good in itself but as good when it took into account the situation in the developing nation; "too rapid industrialization can throw institutions still needed into disorder and prepare the way for social ills and, indeed, retard men's progress."[22] Excessive nationalism, said Pope Paul, prevents the developing nations from accepting outside help. The racism of tribes endangers civil peace and welfare. Finally, the Pope saw material development itself as a possible obstacle to man's spiritual development:

> Modern civilization, not of itself but by reason of its excessive entanglement in things of the earth, can frequently make approach to God more difficult. . . . If a greater number of techni-

cians is necessary for the further progress of development, there is far greater need of wise men with keen minds to investigate a new *humanism* by which modern man, accepting the far-surpassing blessings of love, friendship, prayer, and contemplation, will be able, so to say, to find himself.[23]

This concern that spiritual blessings may be compromised by development, though never set forth by the American bishops in their political statements, is mentioned in the 1971 NCCB "Statement on the Missions."[24]

Although the American bishops surely share all Pope Paul VI's views on development, they apparently do not see USCC policy statements as the proper forum for discussing them. There is no reason why the USCC cannot formulate the kind of statements that would be the proper forum for presenting papal social teaching on development in all its richness and complexity.

While the list of topics on which the USCC has produced statements is long and impressive, the topics missing from the list are also striking. The reason why such topics as those mentioned earlier in this chapter (see page 95) have not been seriously addressed is that the bishops have unwittingly allowed the secular world to set their political agenda. With the notable exception of abortion, the topics of their statements on domestic and international issues are those that are taken most seriously by secular liberals. It is, of course, proper and necessary to address the social justice issues that secular leaders consider important; Catholic social thought counsels Catholics not to neglect any significant matter of public interest. However, this means also that they should not neglect those aspects of Catholic thought that are *not* fashionable in secular circles. From the list of issues addressed by the bishops (not their specific positions) one wonders if their political agenda is a little too influenced by the desire to be visibly relevant.

Some may criticize the bishops for taking liberal positions on public policy issues. But from a deeper perspective, this is not so noteworthy. As Pope Paul VI said, reasonable Christians legitimately arrive at conservative and liberal solutions to matters of public policy.

More significant is the fact that the bishops, under the influence of the Department of Social Development and World Peace, have tailored their political agenda almost exclusively to the "liberal" issues. This results not only in the neglect of other important issues but also in the adoption of a political philosophy that reduces the purpose of politics to the protection of rights and the equitable distribution of material goods. This reductionism neglects that tradition of political wisdom—of which Catholic social thought is a part—which links politics with character formation. As Thomas Aquinas put it:

> But the object for which a community is gathered together is to live a virtuous life. For men consort together that they may thus attain a fullness of life which would not be possible to each living singly, and the full life is one which is lived according to virtue. Thus the object of human society is a virtuous life.[25]

Another problem with the bishops' policy statements is their stress on moral imperatives and the "moral issue." The prominence of the "moral issue" in episcopal statements can be explained in several ways. First, it gives a satisfying justification for venturing into thorny political issues. Second, some contemporary theologians and many Catholic social activists have stressed that the clergy and religious are especially qualified to be the guardians of conscience in the political arena. For example, in an article entitled "Religious Organizations and International Affairs: Analysis and Reflections," the Reverend J. Bryan Hehir argues that religions are not political parties or research organizations but are equipped to form a "constituency of conscience" on key foreign policy issues:

> The dynamics of the model, as I see it, involve the religious institutions taking specific policy positions and then going to their constituencies with the position to see if they can garner support.[26]

Another view of the "moral issue" is given by Garry Wills in his book *Bare Ruined Choirs*. Wills argues that Catholic liberals in the late fifties and early sixties wholeheartedly endorsed the maxims of John Kennedy's speech at Houston:

I believe in an America . . . where no Catholic prelate would tell the President, should he be Catholic, how to act . . . where no religious body seeks to impose its will directly or indirectly upon the general populace or the public acts of its officials.[27]

Catholic liberals, according to Wills, accepted the autonomy of the secular sphere. Later, when President Kennedy summoned religious leaders to the White House to ask them to support his civil rights bill by creating a religious constituency in key states, they had to justify their participation in the political order. "Thus was the 'moral issue' born—something neither partisan nor political, but overriding all such considerations," says Wills.[28] Representatives of the three major faiths did their work, and the Civil Rights Act of 1964 was passed. Buoyed by this success, religious leaders pushed for a voting rights bill, also as a "moral issue," and then became involved in the government's war on poverty. Wills comments: "[The churches] . . . assumed a regular bargaining position on what now seemed an established permanent floating 'moral issue' . . . a thing above politics." [29] Wills reports that the discovery of the "moral issue" was sharply criticized by Edward Marciniak:

> Marciniak attacked clerical activism as an encroachment on the role of the layman who is the secular insider, the initiate of an expertise quite different from the clergyman's. If conscience is to mediate between moral teaching and politics while preserving the wall of separation, laymen must be mediators. The clergy speak too directly of moral imperatives, making churchly claims too little negotiable, too unyielding for the pluralistic marketplace.[30]

In my judgment, as all political issues have moral dimensions, one cannot justify addressing a particular political question because there is a moral issue at stake.

A further point about the bishops' policy statements is that they are relatively ineffective. Few people, including the Catholic clergy, are conversant with or even aware of them. Exceptions are the statements on abortion and, more recently, on nuclear weapons and El Salvador; the media have given a lot of coverage to these, though little or none to others. The bishops themselves are partly responsible for the lack of attention to their policy positions.

The statements are issued in pamphlets that are not readily available; the only sure way to receive them is to subscribe to the USCC's standing-order service. Without access to periodicals like *Origins* (a documentary service of the National Catholic News Service) and *Catholic Mind,* it is next to impossible to find copies of USCC statements. (Those from 1966-80 are now available, of course, in the *Compendium* frequently cited in this book.)

The USCC may have some effect as a lobby in Washington, but I have found no evidence that this effect is in any way substantial. An effective lobby limits its scope; no lobby can claim expertise on a host of issues. The American bishops would have to concentrate on a few issues to gain the respect of legislators and their staffs that is essential for effective lobbying.

Another problem with policy statements is that Catholics who disagree with them might reject the bishops' specifically religious teaching also. Alexis de Tocqueville foresaw this problem in *Democracy in America:*

> In seeking to extend their power beyond religious matters, [clergy] incur a risk of not being believed at all. I am so much alive to the almost inevitable dangers which beset religious belief whenever the clergy take part in political affairs, and I am so convinced that Christianity must be maintained at any cost in the bosom of modern democracies, that I had rather shut up the priesthood within the sanctuary than allow them to step beyond it.[31]

Tocqueville believed that both religion and democracy would decline if American clergy were to lose spiritual influence by becoming involved in politics. In his mind, religion is needed to counteract the excessive materialism and individualism that are inevitable results of the increasing equality of conditions in America.

Although Tocqueville's desire to confine the clergy to the sanctuary is extreme, his belief that partisanship by the clergy could weaken their influence is not. This is not to say that the clergy have no proper political role. On the contrary, if the clergy could resist the urge to act as if they were just like any other interest group, they might have a very special role.

The American Catholic bishops, organized as the USCC, should not rely on the conventional policy statement—which calls for specific legislation—as their principal contribution to the political

order. While formulating policy positions should be a USCC function, this should not take precedence over other means available to
the bishops' conference. Catholic social teaching suggests that the
bishops should stress the pursuit of justice through evangelization, through reliance on the laity, and through education.

This does not at all rule out the treating of particular issues. But
the bishops need not make a conventional policy statement every
time they address an issue. Their "Reflections on the Energy
Crisis" (USCC, April 1981) clearly shows that they can provide
information about a particular question, expound general principles of Catholic social teaching, and inform the consciences of
American citizens without offering specific policy proposals.
("Reflections on the Energy Crisis" is printed in this volume as
appendix C.)

This statement lays out the moral dimensions of energy policy
according to Catholic social teaching but, in its own words, "offers
no solutions to the controversies that surround the formation of
energy policy. It constitutes an invitation, not a pronouncement—an invitation to further study, to conscientious judgment,
to prudent action at all levels." In addition to stating Catholic
social principles, which are necessarily general, the statement
provides information about the present sources of energy as well as
the possibilities of developing new forms. This statement shows
that while addressing a particular issue, the bishops can take the
time to evangelize and to educate. I believe it should be a model for
most of the bishops' statements on both domestic and foreign
policy matters.

This does not preclude the use of the conventional policy statement in certain circumstances. However, I suggest that such statements should meet the following standards.

First, before making specific legislative proposals, the bishops
should look at all sides of an issue. To do this they need a politically
balanced staff, all or most of whom are well acquainted with
Catholic social thought. As I said earlier, there is currently no real
diversity in the staff of the Department of Social Development and
World Peace. Every influential voice in the department is committed to liberal solutions to most political problems. Such a staff is
appropriate for Americans for Democratic Action or the Ameri-

can Civil Liberties Union; it is not appropriate for the bishops' conference. A wholly conservative staff would be no more appropriate. The ideal staff would be composed of people who are not wedded to ideologies of either the left or the right and who are thoroughly conversant with Catholic social thought. Friendly but spirited staff debate would refine the USCC statements.

Second, if the bishops, after hearing both sides of an issue on which reasonable Christians could disagree, think they should recommend a specific policy, they should avoid behaving like an ordinary interest group. Something ought to distinguish the bishops' mode of taking a position from that of secular groups.

The bishops should primarily be agents of reconciliation and unity. John Paul II explained it like this:

> Pastors, having to devote themselves to unity, will strip themselves of all politico-party ideology. In this way they will be free to evangelize the political scene following the example of Christ starting from a Gospel without party bias or ideologization.[32]

> Serving the cause of justice, the Church does not intend to produce or deepen divisions, intensify conflicts or spread them. On the contrary, with the power of the Gospel the Church helps to see and respect a brother in every man, she invites persons, groups, and peoples to *dialogue,* in order that justice may be safeguarded and unity preserved. Under certain circumstances, she may even act as a *mediator.* This, too, is a prophetic service.[33]

But the USCC will not be able to act as an agent of reconciliation and unity in the political arena without a change of attitude in the Department of Social Development and World Peace. The staff leaders there are highly committed to their political opinions and tend in all sincerity to regard these opinions as indistinguishable from Catholic social thought. They cannot take the distance from their political opinions necessary for reasonable discussion.[34]

Third, the bishops should not allow secular trends to have undue influence on their political agenda. As we have seen, the USCC has neglected to address a number of important topics suggested by Catholic social thought but frowned upon by secular opinion. In my judgment, these issues would generally be best addressed in statements that avoid specific legislative proposals.

Fourth, the bishops will be more effective if they adhere to the principle of subsidiarity, as they promised in their 1979 statement on the family farm (see page 69). This principle requires the bishops not to seek governmental intervention as the first course of action. "In order to preserve citizen liberties, action to promote social justice should be taken at the lowest practical level within a society," explains this statement.[35] Individuals and groups, including the Church, should do whatever is feasible for them; government should act "only when it alone is competent to achieve the desired end."[36] Note that the principle of subsidiarity allows for as much government intervention as is necessary. Reasonable Christians will always disagree among themselves about the desirability of this or that form of state action.

Fifth, it is almost superfluous to add that the bishops should be much less hesitant to point out clear evils than to propose specific solutions to complex policy issues. As a matter of political prudence, the bishops should not attempt to make as many partisan policy statements as they have in the past. They cannot possibly demonstrate or acquire the expertise required to gain the respect of thoughtful people or the attention of the nation's lawmakers.

Sixth, would it not be advisable to make a clear separation between the political dimension of the NCCB, a canonical body, and that of the USCC, a civil body? The NCCB could focus on promoting justice through evangelization and education, that is, through the exposition of Catholic political and social teaching. The USCC could apply Catholic political principles to particular issues. Another possibility would be to find a way of making the policymaking process of the USCC's Department of Social Development and World Peace representative of Catholic political opinion in the United States. (This latter proposal, of course, raises many difficulties, perhaps insuperable. For one thing, it might divert attention from the main task of the bishops in the political and social order.)

THE ROLE OF THE LAITY

The recovery of an emphasis on evangelization and education as the Church's primary means of pursuing justice with a subtlety appropriate to the present age would necessarily stress the important role of the laity. It is ironic that in the period following the

Second Vatican Council, clergy and religious have tended to bypass the laity. A declaration by a group of Catholics in Chicago in 1977 expressed a widespread feeling:

> During the last decade especially, many priests have acted as if the primary responsibility in the Church for uprooting injustice, ending wars, and defending human rights rested with them as ordained ministers. As a result, they bypassed the laity to pursue social causes on their own rather than enabling lay Christians to shoulder their own responsibility. These priests and religious have sought to impose their own agendas for the world upon the laity. Indeed, if in the past the Church has suffered from a tendency to clericalism on the right, it may now face the threat of revived clericalism on the left.[37]

Certainly the bishops have not actively decided to impose their views on the laity. However, by making policy statements on particular issues, such as housing, human rights, and the Panama Canal Treaty, they are implicitly setting an agenda in the sense that they obviously want the laity to direct their attention to these issues.

The Chicago "Declaration of Concern" notes another way in which the clergy's activism tends to devalue the role of the laity:

> We also note with concern the steady depreciation, during the past decade, of the ordinary social roles through which the laity serve and act upon the world. The impression is often created that one can work for justice and peace only by stepping outside of these ordinary roles as a businessman, as a mayor, as a factory worker, as a professional in the State Department, or as an active union member and thus one can change the system only as an "outsider" to the society and the system. Such ideas clearly depart from the mainstream of Catholic social thought, which regards the advance of social justice as essentially the service performed within one's professional and occupational milieu. The almost exclusive preoccupation with the role of the outsider as the model of social action can only distract the laity from the apostolic potential that lies at the core of their professional and occupational lives.[38]

By stressing the policy statement, the American bishops have effectively adopted the role of the outsider as the model of political action.

That the bishops have assumed responsibility for directing social reform is not without merit. Still, it is a question whether that approach should take precedence over the bishops' more traditional role of evangelizing laymen and encouraging them to promote justice in their professional milieus.

Although the main thrust of the bishops' social teaching is not to rely on the laity, they have urged laypeople to maintain the link between faith and politics by approaching questions of public policy "from positions grounded in moral conviction and religious belief." This call to action is not sufficient. At a time of widespread concern about the weakening of family life, the lowering of standards in public schools, the decline of the sense of neighborhood, and ethical laxity among businessmen, professionals, and working people, the bishops should do more to prepare laypeople to work on these pressing problems from their own neighborhoods and places of work.

The Chicago "Declaration" cites a passage from the Vatican II statement *Lumen Gentium* which indicates clearly that the laity, not the bishops, clergy, or religious, are primarily responsible for transforming political, economic, and social institutions:

> But the laity, by their special vocation, seek the kingdom of God by engaging in temporal affairs and by ordering them according to the plan of God. They live in the ordinary circumstances of family and social life, from which the very web of their existence is woven. Today they are called by God, that by exercising their proper function, and led by the spirit of the Gospel, they may work for the sanctification of the world from within as a leaven.[39]

By ignoring character formation as an important part of their political teaching, and by implicitly downplaying the laity's role in working for justice, the bishops are unwittingly failing to appropriate worthy elements of Catholic theological tradition.

Pope John Paul II has emphatically distinguished the role of the clergy from that of the laity in the work for justice. Speaking to the bishops in Brazil, the Pope said:

> Your vocation as bishops forbids you, quite clearly and without half measures, anything that resembles political party spirit or subjection to this or that ideology.[40]

Bishops and priests should avoid taking ideologies such as Marxism, socialism, and liberalism as norms for judgments on the political and social order. They should, of course, learn from these political doctrines, but they must not be imprisoned by them. What the Pope means by avoiding partisanship—"political party spirit"—is more difficult to explain. Pleas by popes and bishops to relieve poverty in underdeveloped areas or to respect human rights anywhere are not considered partisanship. Archbishop Marcos McGrath of Panama expressed the mind of the Pope when he said:

> Puebla establishes at once its key distinction between politics in the broad sense and "party politics." The Church must be very active in the former through the promotion of values that should inspire politics, while leaving partisan politics to groups of citizens who set out to obtain political power to resolve social questions according to their criteria and ideology.[41]

Pope John Paul II clearly wants bishops and priests to project a moral vision of a just social and political order. But he wants them to do this in a way that is supportive of the fundamental mission of the Church, evangelization.

> The social apostolate must keep its eyes open to *all injustices* and all violations of human rights, wherever they may be, in the field of both material and spiritual goods. If it should lack this fundamental perspective, it runs the risk of becoming an object of one-sided manipulation [emphasis added].[42]

Evangelization includes pointing out the political and social implications of Christian life. The manner in which bishops and priests should fulfill this duty was described by John Paul II in a letter to them:

> With great perspicacity we must seek, together with all men, truth and justice, the true and definitive dimension of which we can only find in the gospel or rather in Christ himself. Our task is to serve *truth and justice* in the dimensions of human "temporality," *but always in the perspective that is the perspective of eternal salvation.*[43]

Pope John Paul II wants the laity to be receptive to the spiritual service tendered by bishops and priests. After receiving a thorough formation of their individual and social consciences, the laity should take up as their proper task the renewal of the temporal

order. Without waiting for specific orders and directives from the
hierarchy, they should try to infuse a Christian spirit into their
professional lives and into the attitudes, customs, laws, and structures of the communities and nations in which they live. With their
secular competence, they will be able to do things from their places
of work or in legislative halls that are beyond the reach of the
clergy. It is, indeed, their obligation to work for justice in ways that
are not possible or proper for the clergy to adopt. For example, if
bishops point out that all people have a right to health care, it is up
to competent laypeople to find ways of providing health services to
all through either private or public funding.

John Paul II is intent on avoiding the clericalization of the
Church. He does not want the clergy to usurp functions that
properly belong to the laity.

> Let this be emphasized today in face of the manifold trends to
> secularize the priest's service, reducing it to a purely philan-
> thropical function. His service is not that of a doctor, the social
> worker, the politician or the trade unionist. In certain cases,
> perhaps, the priest will be able to carry out these services, though
> in a supplementary way, and, in the past, he carried them out
> excellently. But today they are adequately discharged by other
> members of society, while our service is specified more and more
> clearly as a spiritual service.[44]

All take part in building up the body of Christ, each with his own
ability. The Pope has such high expectations of laypeople that he
has said that "the action of a lay member of the People of God may
be more effective than that of a member of the hierarchy or of a
religious order."[45]

The quest for justice through evangelization and education requires personal excellence from each and every member of the
Church. Pope John Paul II believes that the dedication of even one
individual at a crucial stage can be decisive. In Ireland, the Pope
reminded a group of seminarians what the fidelity of St. Patrick
meant for Ireland and the world.[46] His thought runs counter to the
view that only big institutions or the vast, impersonal forces of
history can have significant effects.

If the life of one individual can mean so much, what would
happen if a nation of individuals took their faith seriously? Pope

CHAPTER SIX

Evangelization, Catholic Social Teaching, and Political Philosophy

UNLIKE THE OLD National Catholic Welfare Conference, the USCC does not stress individual conversion through evangelization or education to Christian life in the home, school, and Church as its principal means of working for justice. The bishops preach conversion, of course, but not in their political statements. In nearly every political statement issued by the NCWC, however, the bishops emphasized individual change of heart as a necessary element of lasting political reform. (For a brief description of the NCWC's approach to political and social reform, see appendix D.) In this the NCWC was simply following the lead given by Pope Leo XIII and Pope Pius XI in their social encyclicals. As Pius XI wrote in *Quadragesimo Anno:*

> "Wherefore," to use the words of our predecessor [Leo XIII], "if human society is to be healed, only a return to Christian life and institutions will heal it." For this alone can provide effective remedy for that excessive care for passing things that is the origin of all vices.[1]

Behind this approach lies the idea that evangelized, converted men and women infuse a Christian spirit into their work, their politics, their families—in short, into all areas of life. Converted laypersons work to bring about suitable structures in society. The strength of the Church, even in its social mission, lies in its ability to touch the hearts of human beings.

119

JUSTICE THROUGH EVANGELIZATION
AND EDUCATION

Since the beginning of his pontificate, Pope John Paul II has taught that the Church can make its best contribution to the political order through evangelization properly understood. "We shall reach man, we shall reach justice, through evangelization," he says. He believes that the Church can help modern civilization overcome its inadequate view of the human person and its injustices through evangelization, which is the essential mission, the distinctive vocation, and the deepest identity of the Church.

Evangelization requires above all the communication of the truth about Jesus Christ. "There is no true evangelization if the name, the teaching, the life, the promises, the Kingdom, and the mystery of Jesus of Nazareth, the Son of God, are not proclaimed," said Pope Paul VI.[2] The proclamation of Jesus Christ must include such truths as the following: the creation of man in God's image and his redemption by Jesus Christ, eternal salvation, hope in God's promises, God's love for man, brotherly love for all, the reality and mystery of evil, the necessity of searching for God through prayer, and communion with the Church of Jesus Christ. Evangelization also requires that the Gospel be applied to man's personal and social life. Hence evangelization includes teaching about rights and duties, family life, life in society, peace, development, and justice.

Pope John Paul II's thinking about man is based on two fundamental beliefs about human beings: they are created in God's image, and they are redeemed by Jesus Christ. Created in God's image, man has a spiritual dimension. He is free and has a capacity to know, to love, and to achieve his perfection by living according to the nature given him by God. He does not determine or create his own essence.

> The human person created in the image of God is not set beyond the confines of good and evil, as Nietzsche and other propounders of the absolute autonomy of man would have it.[3]

In Christian anthropology, existence does *not* precede essence. Man does not create his essence by absolutely free choices.

Redeemed by Jesus Christ, the human person is liberated from guilt, sin, and death and made capable of eternal life. Christ, the new Adam, who is the very revelation of the mystery of the Father and of the Father's love, *fully reveals man to himself* and brings to light man's highest calling. The life, death, and resurrection of Jesus reveal God's love for man, and thereby reveal to man his great worth. John Paul II wrote in *Redemptor Hominis:*

> How precious must man be in the eyes of the Creator, if he "gained so great a Redeemer," and if God "gave his only Son in order that man should not perish but have eternal life."[4]

Modern civilization can overcome its inadequate view of the human person by getting to know Christ.

The dignity of the human person—this truth about man is the bedrock for Pope John Paul's political and social teaching. Since all human beings are created by God and redeemed by Jesus Christ, they have not only *great* worth but also *equal* worth. All people deserve their due from the state, intermediary associations, and other human beings.

The doctrines of creation and redemption signify that man is a dependent creature who receives the gift of life and salvation from God. The human person is in no way self-sufficient: he is called to be "poor in spirit," which means willing to receive grace from God. The Pope argues that hearts open to God are more open to other human beings and much less susceptible to seduction by totalitarian ideologies or consumerism.

Seeking justice through evangelization presupposes a close relation between private lives and the public interest. Wilson Carey McWilliams offers this reflection:

> Public virtue germinates in "private life." Authority concerns parents and teachers as well as presidents and kings: justice before it is sought in courts and law books, is taught or mistaught in homes, workplaces, and playing fields. The art of politics is learned in the practice of daily life; private and public orders are parts of an inseparable whole.[5]

McWilliams believes that the private order "is increasingly fragmented and unstable and must be invigorated for the sake of public life." Political wisdom, he says, "counsels us to rebuild [the private order] . . . in ways that will enhance the virtues and minimize the vices of the older private order."[6] If there is a close relation between the private and the public order, then serious evangelization, which leads to the growth of the kingdom of God in the heart of man, has great political significance.

Modern papal social teaching has consistently stressed that man is a social and political being. This is also the teaching of Aristotle, Aquinas, Augustine, Thomas More, and others. John Paul II explains:

> Man is an intelligent and free being, ordained by natural purpose to realize the potentialities of his person in society. Expressions of this innate social character are the natural society based on marriage . . . such as is the family, and the free intermediary formations, the political community, of which the state in its various institutional articulations is the juridical form.[7]

The affirmation that man is a social and political being entails a teaching not only on rights but also on duties.

> A genuine and faithful Christian is also a genuine and good citizen. A Christian—in any country of the world—is faithful to God, but he also has a deep sense of duty and of love toward his native land and his own people.[8]

Pope John Paul II argues that the Church serves as a sign and safeguard of the transcendent dimension of the human person not only by defending human rights, but also by encouraging the fulfillment of duties and the right use of freedom. The Christian has duties because he is a social being and not a solitary one. In his major philosophical work *The Acting Person,* John Paul II discusses the duties incumbent upon the human person under the categories of solidarity and opposition, two necessary components of a true community. *Solidarity* simply means that a person should demonstrate concern for the welfare of his country. Those in *opposition* to the ruling power in the community draw attention to aspects of the common good that have been neglected.

Fulfillment of duties requires excellence from people. They are to love one another, conscientiously perform their duties in the workplace, and take an active part in public affairs. John Paul II eloquently expressed this thought when he spoke in Warsaw's Victory Square before the tomb of the unknown soldier:

I wish to kneel before this tomb to venerate every seed that falls into the earth and dies and thus bears fruit. It may be the seed of the blood of a soldier shed on the battlefield, or the sacrifice of martyrdom in concentration camps or in prisons. It may be the seed of hard daily toil, with the sweat of one's brow, in the fields, the workshop, the mine, the foundries, and the factories. It may be the seed of the love of parents who do not refuse to give life to a new human being and undertake the whole of the task of bringing him up. It may be the seed of creative work in the universities, the higher institutions, the libraries, and the places where the national culture is built. It may be the seed of prayer, of service of the sick, the suffering, the abandoned—"all that of which Poland is made."[9]

John Paul's argument is that society cannot be just unless people are just in their souls. This is the same as the teaching of Augustine that justice is primarily order in the individual soul. Augustine insists that justice exists only when the body is subject to the soul, and the passions are subject to reason. Furthermore, the soul can properly control the body, and reason, the passions, only when the soul serves God. There can be no justice, according to Augustine, in a community of persons who are not just individually. This teaching stands in contrast to a prevailing contemporary view, most clearly expressed by Kant, that justice is only a question of the good organization of the state. "Hard as it may sound, the problem of establishing the state [i.e., the just state] is soluble even for a nation of devils, provided they have sense." Even if individuals are self-seeking and wholly bad, justice is still possible, provided citizens are enlightened enough to secure for themselves the proper institutions and structures.[10]

John Paul II presents a variation on the argument that social justice first requires justice in individual souls. He asserts that this is a world not only of material values but also of spiritual values, and that there is an important relation between the two.

It is the spiritual values that are preeminent both on account of the nature of these values and also reasons concerning the good of man. The preeminence of the values of the spirit defines the proper sense of earthly material goods and the way to use them. *This preeminence is therefore at the basis of a just peace* [emphasis added].[11]

Spiritual goods are open to unlimited enjoyment by many people at the same time; they thus associate and unite people. Material goods, limited by their very nature, provoke divisions and often conflicts between the haves and the have-nots. The Pope fears that the present diminished sensitivity to the spiritual dimension of man will exacerbate quarrels over material things, since those things are regarded as the only real values in life. In order to overcome division over material goods, greater honor must be given, "before everyone's eyes in the sight of every society," to the spiritual dimension of existence.

What are these spiritual goods that give the proper attitude toward material things and thus lay the groundwork for a just peace? The answer lies primarily in the Pope's notion of culture.

> Yes, the future of mankind depends on culture. Yes, world peace depends on the primacy of the spirit. Yes, the peaceful future of humanity depends on love.[12]

"Culture is that which makes man ever more man; he 'has' more being and is able to 'become' more human."[13] Man serves as the artisan of his own culture by *being* in a certain way, not by having things. Culture, understood as being, is characteristic of human life. It is a spiritual value and, indeed, the most important aspect of civilization. The culture of individuals determines the social character of human existence in a nation. In other words, the social and political order is decisively affected by culture. "The nation exists 'by' culture and 'for' culture and it is thus the great educator of men so they may be 'more' in the community."[14]

Education is the main concern of culture, for it is through education, beginning in the family, that a person learns to *be* more and to *be* for others. A person learns to achieve more being by the cultivation of mind, heart, and will; and he learns that, as a social animal, he has obligations to others. A suitable education gives a human being the proper perspective on the use of goods, and on the pursuit of pleasure, honor, and power. The future depends on educating persons to *be* in a certain way.

> Consciences must be mobilized: the efforts of human consciousness must increase as the tension between good and evil, to which man is submitted at the close of the twentieth century,

grows. We must be convinced of the priority of the ethical over the technical, of the primacy of the human being over things, of the superiority of spirit over matter.[15]

Human beings need material things in adequate measure in order to acquire culture through education. "But we must distinguish very precisely that which is *only a condition* of a truly human life from that which decides that human life is truly such."[16] It is being or culture that determines whether human life is truly human; possessing material goods is important only as a means. John Paul II points out that the Second Vatican Council took up Gabriel Marcel's distinction between "being" and "having" and derived from it a fundamental principle: "Man is worth more for what he is than for what he has." In stressing being over having, Pope John Paul II is not minimizing the obligation to relieve poverty in the world. He merely asks if a danger more serious than deprivation does not exist "where the superabundance of what man has veils what man is and what he should be."[17]

At Shea Stadium in New York, Pope John Paul II asserted that a city needs a soul if it is to be a true home for human beings. It is the mode of being, or the culture of individual citizens, that provides that soul. "You, the people, must give it this soul. And how do you do this? By loving each other."[18] *Love* is the commandment of Jesus Christ and the *pinnacle of culture.*

In Poland, the Pope said of nations:

> The history of the nation deserves to be adequately appraised in the light of its contribution to the development of man and humanity, to intellect, heart, and conscience. This is the deepest stream of culture. It is culture's firmest support, its core, its strength. It is impossible without Christ to understand and appraise the contribution of the Polish nation to the development of man and his humanity in the past and its contribution today.[19]

The culture of Poland, which is inextricably linked with the Christian faith, enabled the Polish nation to remain spiritually independent and, in a way, to retain its sovereignty during one hundred years of political subjugation, from the end of the eighteenth century until the beginning of the twentieth—and, by implication, after World War II. While culture, then, has a very obvious political significance, it also makes a more subtle contribution to the political order by transforming the lives of individual citizens.

In addition to celebrating the presence of Christian culture in Poland, John Paul II also argues that Europe, from the Atlantic to the Urals, must seek its unity in Christianity, because that faith lies at the root of Europe's history.

> Christianity must commit itself anew to the formation of the spiritual unity of Europe. Economic and political reasons cannot do it. We must go deeper to ethical reasons.[20]

John Paul II believes that the spiritual tradition of Europe must be strengthened and that he is in a good position to provide leadership in this task.

> Is it not Christ's will, is it not what the Holy Spirit disposes, that this Polish Pope, this Slav Pope, should at this precise moment manifest the spiritual unity of Europe?[21]

Pope John Paul II's goals may be purely spiritual, but they have important political consequences. The revival of Christianity in Eastern Europe would surely strengthen the resistance to Communist rule. The Soviets must be concerned that a Slavic Pope presented, on Polish soil, a vision of a wider Europe, culturally and spiritually united, that would include all Slavs, even the Russians. Peter Hebblethwaite has commented:

> Like Aleksandr Solzhenitsyn, John Paul II appeared to believe that Soviet society corresponded less and less to what its people wanted and needed, and that there would be a disintegration of communist regimes, not through any pressure from outside but because their hollowness would become clear. Only a Slav could conceive such a vision; perhaps only a Pole could think it realizable.[22]

Few would deny that the faith of the Polish people has significant social and political consequences. John Paul's argument is that the serious revival of spiritual traditions anywhere on this planet will significantly affect political and social life. That is why evangelization and culture take on such importance in the Pope's political vision.

John Paul constantly speaks of building a "civilization of love," a phrase drawn from the writings of Pope Paul VI.[23] Love must supplement justice. Justice is the necessary but not the sufficient condition of a decent civilization.

> The equality brought by justice is limited to the realm of *objective and extrinsic* goods, while love and mercy bring it about that people meet one another in that value which is man himself, with the dignity that is proper to him.[24]

The exclusive stress on justice leads to "a world of cold and unfeeling justice in the name of which each person would claim his or her own rights vis-à-vis others."[25] John Paul II argues that the political and social order needs mercy, love, and forgiveness. In his mind, these virtues—seemingly very personal—have enormous political and social consequences. John Paul often reminds his hearers that Father Maximilian Kolbe offered his life in exchange for that of a Polish lay compatriot when they were imprisoned in Auschwitz. This act of mercy made life more bearable for other victims in the camp. Acts of mercy have an enduring value even in the midst of oppressive evil.

What can love do to overcome the great divisions present in the world today?

> The Church confesses with humility that only love which is more powerful than the weakness of human divisions *can definitively bring about that unity* which Christ implored from the Father and which the Spirit never ceases to beseech for us "with sighs too deep for words."[26]

Love or mercy is an elevating and unifying power,

> . . . an indispensable element for shaping mutual relationships between people in a spirit of deepest respect for what is human; and in a spirit of mutual brotherhood. It is impossible to establish this bond between people if they wish to regulate their mutual relationship solely according to the measure of justice.[27]

In every sphere of human relationship, justice has to be corrected, so to speak, by love.

John Paul II is fully aware that the world does not want to hear talk about the limits of justice and the importance of mercy. The latter is viewed as condescending, an affront to the equality of all human beings. "Hence the attempt to free interpersonal and social relationships from mercy and to base them solely on justice."[28]

Because mercy is so little understood and yet so important for life on all levels of society, the Church has a grave responsibility.

> The Church must consider it one of her principal duties—at every stage of history and especially in our modern age—*to proclaim and to introduce into life* the mystery of mercy, supremely revealed by Jesus Christ.[29]

The Church must strive to reveal this mystery of mercy, namely God himself, no matter how much human history resists.

This stress on evangelization, culture, and the "civilization of love" might seem utopian as a political strategy. Some would argue that it is unrealistic to expect Christian conversion and that attention should be focused on realistic solutions, i.e., systemic or structural change. But though not all people will have a change of heart, the conversion of even a few will have good effects.

In addition, structural, legal, and systemic changes in society through governmental intervention are not sufficient to bring about a just society. Institutional changes, such as various kinds of social insurance, may help, but they will not eliminate all the causes and effects of self-regarding, unjust behavior. It is utopian to expect a solution solely from new structures and new laws. This kind of expectation reveals an ignorance of the effect irreligion and immorality inexorably have on political and social life. It is a modern error to believe that equitable social arrangements can be worked out without attention to the moral conviction of citizens. Alexis de Tocqueville was correct in arguing in *Democracy in America* that, though church and state are separate in the United States, religion is the first of our political institutions because it teaches citizens how to use freedom properly, especially by moderating the pursuit of physical pleasure and material goods.

POLITICAL PHILOSOPHY IS INDISPENSABLE

In chapter one I suggested that a careful study of political philosophy would shed light on the contemporary tendency to downplay the political and social implications of evangelization and education. I also said that the works of Leo Strauss could conceivably help Catholics recover their tradition of political wisdom. For one thing, Strauss can teach students how to read carefully the great classics of the Western tradition.

Strauss reminded us that, for all classical political philosophers, the goal of political life is virtue. "The best regime is the order most conducive to the practice of virtue, and the actualization of the best regime depends on chance."[30] Modern political philosophy rejects the classical scheme as unrealistic. Machiavelli argued that the goal of political life must be lowered to suit what we actually desire; he even said chance could be conquered by the right institutions and methods. Leo Strauss briefly described the modern orientation initiated by Machiavelli in this most enlightening paragraph:

> The political problem becomes a technical problem. As Hobbes put it, "when commonwealths come to be dissolved by intestine discord, the fault is not in men as they are the matter but as they are the makers of them. "The matter is not corrupt or vicious; there is no evil in men which cannot be controlled; what is required is not divine grace, morality, nor formation of character, but institutions with teeth in them. Or, to quote Kant, the establishment of the right social order does not require, as people are in the habit of saying, a nation of angels: "Hard as it may sound, the problem of establishing the state [i.e., the just state] is soluble even for a nation of devils, provided they have sense," i.e., provided their selfishness is enlightened; the fundamental political problem is simply one of a "good organization of the state of which man is indeed capable."[31]

Modern political philosophy denigrates formation of character, or education to virtue, as a means of achieving sound political order. Instead there is a stress on institutional or structural changes.

Contrary to what one might think, Strauss was not advocating a simple return to the classical philosophers. He did not expect "that a fresh understanding of classical political philosophy will supply us with a recipe for today's use."

> The relative success of modern political philosophy has brought into being a kind of society in which the classical principles are not immediately applicable. Only we living today can possibly find a solution to the problems of today.[32]

Nevertheless, Strauss maintained that the solution to contemporary problems may depend upon study of the ancients.

> An adequate understanding of the principles, as elaborated by the classics, may be the indispensable starting point for an adequate analysis, to be achieved by us, of present-day society in its peculiar character, and for the wise application, to be achieved by us, of these principles to our task.[33]

One of the great contributions of Catholicism has been to oppose the revolution inaugurated by Machiavelli and continued in various forms by such philosophers as Hobbes, Locke, Rousseau, Kant, Marx, and Nietzsche. As Strauss said:

> Anyone who wishes to judge impartially of the legitimacy or the prospects of the great design of modern man to erect the City of Man on what appear to him to be the ruins of the City of God must familiarize himself with the teachings, and especially the political teachings, of the Catholic Church, which is the most powerful antagonist of that modern design.[34]

Catholic political teaching, for example, stresses the close connection between the formation of character and the quality of the political order; it opposes reducing the purpose of political life to comfortable self-preservation; it upholds the spiritual dimension of the human person and argues that there is genuine common good distinct from the sum of individual interests.

As Strauss was not narrowly traditionalist, neither is Catholic social thought. While drawing upon its classical and medieval heritage, contemporary Catholic social thought does not expect that heritage directly to supply solutions to our present predicament. Pope John Paul II and other Catholic scholars are still groping for more adequate ways of elaborating and developing Catholic political wisdom and relating it to current problems.

Catholic political and social teaching can continue to enlighten modern man if it is presented in all its richness and complexity. Pope John Paul II has made an auspicious beginning in expounding the political wisdom of the Catholic tradition. He still has much to offer, especially a more complete, systematic treatment of the common good. The United States Catholic bishops could add to their contribution by expounding thoroughly the political and social teaching of the Catholic Church both to Catholics and to non-Catholics. This is especially important because of the widespread lack of knowledge and interest in things political and because of the way the Christian faith is being misrepresented. As John Paul II said in addressing the Latin American bishops:

> The kingdom of God is emptied of its full content and is understood in a rather secularist sense: it is interpreted as being

reached not by faith and membership in the Church but by the mere changing of structures and social and political involvement and activity for justice. This is to forget that "the Church receives the mission to proclaim and to establish among all peoples the Kingdom of Christ and of God. She becomes on earth the seed and beginning of that Kingdom" (*Lumen Gentium, 5*).

In one of his beautiful catechetical instructions Pope John Paul I, speaking of the virtue of hope, warned that it is wrong to state that political, economic, and social liberation coincides with salvation in Jesus Christ, that the *Regnum Dei* is identified with the *Regnum hominis*.[35]

A competent presentation of Catholic social teaching would highlight this secularist understanding of the Kingdom of God that prevails in some Catholic circles, both on the right and on the left. Pope John Paul II even argues that bishops have the duty to clear up the confusion when theologians and other scholars deny or downplay any truths of the Catholic faith.

To increase their contribution to building a "civilization of love," a constant theme of both Paul VI and John Paul II, the Catholic bishops need to seek justice primarily through evangelization and education into the rich heritage of the Catholic social and political tradition. This will probably not take place without a significant theological renewal, including an intelligent rereading of the great Christian classics and the primary sources in the philosophical tradition, and especially a much deeper study of political philosophy. Both theologians and philosophers have an important role to play in this renewal.

OBSERVATIONS ON TEACHING CATHOLIC SOCIAL THOUGHT

To educate people in the Christian understanding of faith and justice, the Church must first have a very clear self-understanding. As Pope John Paul II has pointed out so well, there are two serious misinterpretations of the Christian teachings in the Catholic Church. These misinterpretations, which have become a kind of ideology, inhibit the Church from fulfilling its proper mission. On one side are the progressives, about whom John Paul II said:

> [They] are always impatient to adapt the content of faith, Christian ethics, liturgy, and the organization of the Church, to the changes in mentality, to the demands of the world, without sufficiently taking into account not only the common sense of the faithful who are troubled by these opinions, but also the essence of the faith—which has already been defined, since the beginnings of the Church—its age-long experience and the standards necessary for its fidelity, its unity, and its universality.

And on the other side are the traditionalists:

> [They] are shutting themselves up rigidly in a given period of the history of the Church, and at a given moment of theological formulation or liturgical expression which they have absolutized, without penetrating sufficiently the profound meaning, without considering history in its totality and its legitimate development, fearing new questions without admitting, in the long run, that the Holy Spirit is at work today in the Church with its pastors united around the successor of Peter.[36]

The Pope believes there is a tendency among progressives to "reshape" Christ and the Christian faith to suit the prevailing *zeitgeist*. He must be thinking, for example, of Hans Küng and those theologians who have argued in favor of suicide, contraception, and abortion.

Karl Barth made a strikingly similar criticism of nineteenth-century Protestant theology, which, he said, ascribed a normative character to the ideas of its environment. Acceptance of the prevailing philosophy or world view was the presupposition of theological investigation:

> The world views changed in the course of the century, but there were always theologians who went along more or less convinced, if not enthusiastic, and who started the theological task afresh within the new framework.[37]

Because of this approach, theologians compromised the integrity of the Christian faith. Pope John Paul believes there is a tendency in some quarters of the Catholic Church to repeat the errors Barth ascribed to nineteenth-century Protestant theologians. Even where Christ is accepted, there is opposition to the full truth of his Person and his Gospel. John Paul II explains:

There is a desire to "re-shape" him, to adapt him to suit mankind in this era of progress and make him fit in with the program of consumerism and not of transcendental ends . . . This opposition to Christ which goes hand-in-hand with paying him lip service is particularly symptomatic of our times.[38]

The Pope's quarrel with the traditionalists is that they lack the education necessary to understand the depths of Christianity as well as the new problems facing the modern world. The Pope argues very insistently that the Church needs people who have a deep knowledge of their own faith as well as a knowledge of the human disciplines, including the natural sciences, literature, and, especially, philosophy.

As in preceding ages, and perhaps more than in preceding ages, theologians and all men of learning in the Church are today called to unite faith with learning and wisdom, in order to help them unite with each other. . . . This task has grown enormously today because of the advance of human learning, its methodology, and the achievements in knowledge of the world and of man. This concerns both the exact sciences and the human sciences, as well as philosophy, which as the Second Vatican Council recalled, is closely linked with theology.[39]

Not surprisingly, he has said a lot about the education of students for the priesthood. "The full reconstitution of the life of the seminaries throughout the Church will be the best proof of the achievement of the renewal to which the Council directed the Church."[40] Seminarians must take very seriously not only the quest for holiness but also the pursuit of learning. Priests, too, says the Pope, must study assiduously, especially philosophy and theology.

This process of intellectual formation must last all one's life, especially in modern times, which are marked—at least in many parts of the world—by the widespread development of education and culture. To the people who enjoy the benefits of this development we must be witnesses to Jesus Christ, and properly qualified ones.[41]

Bishops have a special responsibility to be men of learning because their principal duty is to be "teachers of the truth," the whole truth about Jesus Christ.[42] This includes, of course, presentation of the Church's social teaching. In Puebla, Mexico, John Paul II spoke to the Latin American bishops of "the urgent need to make your faithful people aware of this social doctrine of the Church."[43] "[The Church] must preach, educate individuals and collectivities, form public opinion, and offer orientations to the leaders of the peoples," he said.[44] In the face of contemporary "rereadings of the Gospel," especially erroneous teachings about Christ, the Church, and man, the bishops have the duty "to point out these errors serenely and firmly and propose the truth in exact terms to the faithful."[45]

To perceive and refute deviations from the whole Christian message requires a great deal of theological and philosophical learning. Without a knowledge of philosophy, bishops will be hard pressed to realize when theologians are reshaping the Christian faith to conform to philosophical theories. The late French scholar Gaston Fessard, S.J., a man of uncommon philosophical depth, showed very clearly and convincingly in a 1979 book that the French bishops have failed to perceive the gradual infiltration and subversion of French Catholic thought by Marxist principles.[46] In fact, according to Fessard, the French bishops themselves have unwittingly compromised the Christian faith by incorporating certain Marxist principles into their social teaching.

In light of the situation described by Fessard, the reflections of Pope John Paul II on the rereading of the Gospel and the importance of learning have special relevance for France. While we Americans are not yet afflicted by the same problems as the French, we can learn much from the Pope's remarks.

· Many educators have observed that respect for the liberal arts among university students is declining. It is less widely known that many students for the priesthood in the United States share, to a great extent, the bias against the serious pursuit of the liberal arts, including theology and philosophy. The distaste for philosophy has become a special problem. One cannot expect the modern seminarian to become enthusiastic about Catholic social thought when he has very little interest in serious education. The American bishops, in collaboration with the rest of the Church, need to find ways to reawaken the love of learning in students for the priesthood.

Pope John Paul II is so concerned about seminary education that he has ordered a study to be done of every Catholic seminary in the United States. Less than a month after assuming the papacy, he made this revealing statement to the U.S. bishops:

> These hopes for the life of the Church—purity of doctrine and sound discipline—intimately depend on every new generation of priests, who with the generosity of love continue the Church's commitment to the Gospel. For this reason, Paul VI showed great wisdom in asking the American bishops "to fulfill with loving personal attention your great responsibility to your seminarians: *know the content of their courses,* encourage them to love the Word of God and never to be ashamed of the seeming folly of the Cross" (address of June 20, 1977), and this is my ardent desire today, that a new emphasis on the importance of doctrine and discipline will be the postconciliar contribution of your seminaries, so that "the word of the Lord may speed on and triumph" (2 Thes. 3:1) [emphasis added].[47]

While most bishops and priests have studied philosophy and theology more seriously than contemporary seminarians, their intellectual formation is, in most instances, not in conformity with the higher standards established by John Paul II. The philosopher-pope has presented an intellectual challenge to the American clergy and hierarchy that, if heeded, would cause a veritable revolution in American Catholicism. If bishops become more learned in philosophy and theology, they will be more capable of explaining and defending the Christian faith. If priests take a more serious interest in their studies, it is very likely that the laity will gradually learn more from homilies and catechism classes. Many have observed that young laypeople seem to know less and less about their faith and its implications for everyday life. As Margaret O'Brien Steinfels has said:

> The evangelization of adolescents and young adults has become a haphazard process that more often than not has produced large numbers of theological and religious illiterates who, though they remain practicants, have almost no knowledge about their tradition.[48]

As a result, the young fail to realize that they have a vocation to renew the temporal order as lay members of the Church. Bishops, priests, families, parishes, and schools must share the blame for this illiteracy.

The Catholic Church in the United States will not easily respond to the intellectual challenge of Pope John Paul II. There are very great obstacles to improving the education of seminarians, priests, and bishops. For example, at few U.S. universities and even fewer seminaries can a student be solidly educated in the tradition of political philosophy and in the basic principles of Catholic social thought. If it is true that Catholic social thought cannot be adequately understood without knowledge of political philosophy, as I would maintain, the prospects are not encouraging.

The American bishops have vividly affirmed that education, especially higher education, is important for the life of the Church. In a 1980 pastoral letter entitled "Catholic Higher Education and the Pastoral Mission of the Church," they expressed strong support for Catholic colleges and universities, urging them to maintain their Catholic identity and mission.[49] They stressed academic excellence, the importance of strengthening the teaching of the liberal arts, and the task of the Catholic university to show how theology and all other areas of human knowledge are related. They encouraged universities to gather together bishops, theologians, and other members of the Church and the academy for theological reflection. They stressed the study of ethics and justice. And they made this important assertion: "Without solid philosophical grounding, both teachers and students in all fields cannot avoid the risk of superficiality and fragmentation."[50]

It is indispensable for the mission of the Church, especially its social and political aspects, that Catholic universities successfully teach philosophy, theology, ethics, justice, and the other liberal arts. If the university fails at this, highly educated Catholics will be hard pressed to see how they can infuse a Christian spirit into their lives as workers, professionals, and citizens. As it stands now, many students focus their energies on career preparation with little enthusiasm for courses that teach them how to think and acquaint them with the culture of Western civilization.

The bishops need to take a more active role as educators of their flock if they are to be more effective "teachers of the truth." Our examination of their political and social statements has shown that the American Catholic bishops as a body have not explained Catholic social teaching in a comprehensive manner to Catholic clergy and laity—and certainly not to non-Catholics. The political and social thought of Pope John Paul II, of previous popes, and of the Second Vatican Council remains unknown to most Catholics. While policy statements have a value in certain circumstances, they cannot fulfill the bishops' clear duty to communicate Catholic social doctrine in all its richness.

To carry out this task of education, the bishops must have a good knowledge of papal social encyclicals and of the tradition of political philosophy; and they must investigate the relation between the two. Aristotle, Augustine, Thomas Aquinas, Locke, Marx, and others have influenced Catholic social thought. The bishops must know, for instance, the philosophical origins of human rights doctrines; the difference between the natural law doctrine of Thomas Aquinas and the natural or human rights theories elaborated by Hobbes and Locke; the difference between the Thomistic view of the common good and that espoused by the liberal state; and the difference between modern egalitarianism and Catholic teaching on equality.

The popes have argued against the fundamental political principles of both Marx and Locke. Without an understanding of these philosophers, Catholic social thought is apt to be misunderstood. For example, in a highly touted 1981 article, Professor John Coleman, S.J., looking at Leo XIII's *Rerum Novarum* in "historical context," noted how ironic it was that the great defender of Thomas Aquinas had a Lockean view of property.[51] In my judgment, a close study of Locke reveals that his position on property is opposed to that of Leo XIII.

The study of political philosophy reveals that the Catholic view of human rights is quite different from that of philosophical liberalism. The Second Vatican Council clearly indicated that the Catholic perspective on human rights is not divorced from duties and the *summum bonum,* as Hobbes and Locke argued.[52] In *Gaudium et Spes* the council said:

> Therefore, by virtue of the Gospel committed to her the Church proclaims the rights of man. She acknowledges and greatly esteems the dynamic movements of today by which these rights are

everywhere fostered. Yet these movements must be penetrated by the spirit of the Gospel and protected against any kind of *false autonomy*. For we are tempted to think that our personal rights are fully insured only when we are *exempt* from every require-ment of *divine law*. But this way lies not the maintenance of the dignity of the human person, but its annihilation.[53]

The divine law provides a standard for man in the exercise of his rights. To proclaim the rights of man without duties would be to proclaim a false autonomy. Pope Paul VI made the same point in his apostolic letter *Octogesima Adveniens*.[54] Pope John Paul II also insists on the close relation between rights and duties. For exam-ple, in a message to the Secretary General of the United Nations on the thirtieth anniversary of the U.N. Universal Declaration of Human Rights, he wrote:

> While insisting—and rightly so—on the vindication of human rights, one should not lose sight of the obligations and duties that go with these rights. Every individual has the obligation to exercise his basic rights in a responsible and ethically justified manner.[55]

An even more trenchant statement is found in an address by the Pope to the College of Cardinals:

> Very often, freedom of will and freedom of the person are understood as *the right to* do anything, as the right not to accept any norm or any duty that involves commitment also in the dimension of the whole of life; for example, the duties following from the marriage promises or from priestly freedom. *But Christ does not teach us such an interpretation and exercise of freedom.* The freedom of each individual creates duties, demands full respect for the hierarchy of values, and is potentially directed to the good without limits, to God. In Christ's eyes freedom is not first of all "freedom from" but "freedom for." The full enjoy-ment of freedom is love, in particular the love through which individuals give themselves. Man, in fact, as we read in *Gaudium et Spes*, *"cannot fully find himself except through a sincere gift of himself."*[56]

The climate in many academic and non-academic circles is not conducive to deep reflection on the major themes of political philosophy and Catholic social thought. As Peter Berger has noted, there are religious people on both the right and the left who identify their political opinions with God's will.[57] Catholic theologians, and especially the so-called social activists, are not immune to this attitude. Theoretical inquiry appears much less necessary if one believes his own political opinions are identical to Catholic social thought, rather than an always fallible application of principles to complex issues.

This ideological or dogmatic mentality makes it all the more necessary for the bishops to teach Catholic social doctrine. While all aspects require explanation, the spirit of the age requires special attention to the following themes: morality and nuclear weapons, the just war theory, international human rights, development and integral humanism, the common good, public morality, the equality of human beings, the relation between rights and duties, subsidiarity, the Catholic view of property, detachment from material goods, the social role of the family, the difference between historicism[58] and legitimate invocation of the "historical context," the difference between Baconian relief of man's estate and compassion for the poor, the tension between philosophical liberalism (to which a number of contemporary conservatives and liberals adhere) and Christianity, the influence of a regime on the character of its citizens, and the relation of evangelization to the pursuit of a just social order.

Concluding Note

In a brief but powerful speech on the "crisis of the West and Europe's spiritual task," Pope John Paul II argued that the threats which mankind faces today "arise ultimately from a crisis of culture, from collapse or fading of common values and generally binding ethical and religious principles." Europe, in John Paul's mind, contributed to this collapse and bears a special responsibility in overcoming the current crisis.

> But this requires that Europe itself undertake a profound spiritual and moral and political renewal through the power and according to the laws of its Christian origins. . . . As with the numerous renewal movements of history, so the necessary renewal of the mind of Europe has to begin in the hearts of individuals, above all in the hearts of Christians.[59]

The same could be said of the United States. The pursuit of a peaceful and just social order depends on affecting the hearts and minds of individuals through evangelization and education. This is the task of the whole Church and a special responsibility of the U.S. bishops.

The American hierarchy has not yet forged a close link between the pursuit of a peaceful and just social order and the affecting of individual hearts and minds through evangelization and education. To do so requires a thorough study and knowledge of Catholic social thought, especially that of Pope John Paul II. The bishops need help from the universities, especially from students of theology and philosophy. However, the bishops themselves will have to devote more time to study than to administration. We need more learned bishops, men who are highly qualified to speak and write not only *to* to the Church but also *for* the Church in the public arena.

To endure, the United States needs not only economic well-being but also a genuine culture and a high standard of morality, including a sense of community or fraternity. Abraham Lincoln expressed this thought dramatically by telling the following story at a Wisconsin state fair in 1859:

> It is said an Eastern monarch once charged his wise men to invent him a sentence, to be ever in view, and which should be true and appropriate in all times and situations. They presented him the words: *"And this, too, shall pass away."* How much it expresses! How chastening in the hour of pride!—how consoling in the depths of affliction! "And this, too, shall pass away." And yet let us hope it is not quite true. Let us hope, rather, that by the best cultivation of the physical world, beneath and around us, and the intellectual and moral world within us, we shall secure an individual, social, and political prosperity and happiness, whose course shall be onward and upward, and which, while the earth endures, shall not pass away.[60]

Commenting on this paragraph, George Will remarked:

> The United States has been . . . a prodigy of productivity in cultivating the physical world. It has been less energetic . . . at cultivating the intellectual and moral world within us.[61]

Much of contemporary political thought in the United States does not seem able to offer either moral guidance or an adequate understanding of things political. The Catholic political and social tradition, properly understood, could contribute greatly to preserving and promoting the knowledge and moral qualities that the nation needs if it is to endure.

APPENDIX A

How the Catholic Bishops
Make Policy Statements

THE NATIONAL CONFERENCE OF CATHOLIC BISHOPS (NCCB) is a canonical body (i.e., one established by church law). Like other bishops' conferences around the world, the NCCB finds its basis in the Second Vatican Council's *Decree on the Bishops' Pastoral Office in the Church.* It is concerned mainly with the internal life of the church; it works in such areas as liturgy, seminary education, and canon law. The NCCB is also active in pro-life matters and occasionally issues statements in other political and social areas. Its members are the Catholic bishops of the United States, who assemble annually for general meetings.

The United States Catholic Conference (USCC), a civil body incorporated in the District of Columbia, is the primary body through which the bishops address public issues. Like the NCCB, its members are the American bishops, but its policymaking structures include priests, religious, and laypersons also. The USCC is organized around three Departmental Committees and three corresponding Departments with the same names: Communication; Education; and Social Development and World Peace. The Departments have subdivisions; Social Development and World Peace, for instance, is divided into an Office of International Justice and Peace and an Office of Domestic Social Development.

The Office of International Justice and Peace has described its essential function in this way:

> To assist the Bishops of the United States in forming the consciences of American Catholics so that the message of the Gospel and the teachings of recent Popes, the Council, and Synod of Bishops concerning peace and justice for all nations and peoples may be accepted more fully; [and] . . . to represent the institutional Church vis-à-vis the Congress and the Executive, and the United Nations, under the direction of the General Secretary, on foreign policy questions judged to be of central concern to the Church's work for justice and peace ["1976 Plans and Programs," interoffice memorandum from the files of the Office of International Justice and Peace, p. 1].

To form the consciences of American Catholics, the Justice and Peace staff prepares curriculum material for use in diocesan schools and adult education programs, conducts diocesan leadership and continuing education programs, and writes articles for the Catholic press and journals. To represent the institutional

143

Church before the various branches of government, the staff maintains contact with government officials and presents oral and written testimony to government bodies.

The NCCB and the USCC have the same officers, the principal one being the President. A General Secretary serves as the chief operating officer.

Four types of statements emanate from the general membership of the NCCB/USCC (i.e., all American Catholic bishops): in order of authority and importance, they are (1) joint pastorals, (2) formal statements, (3) special messages, and (4) resolutions and other brief statements.

A *joint pastoral* is issued only by the NCCB; it can be initiated either by the general membership (the bishops) or by the NCCB Administrative Committee. The written draft is circulated to all bishops at least one month before a general meeting. A joint (or collective) pastoral must be approved by two-thirds of the NCCB members.

Formal statements of the NCCB or USCC that officially commit the organization to a particular position may be initiated by the general membership or by the NCCB Administrative Committee or the USCC Administrative Board. Drafts of NCCB formal statements need not be circulated a full month in advance of a general meeting but are given to the bishops prior to the meeting. Formal statements of the USCC can be issued if approved by two-thirds of the bishops *present* at the general meeting, not two-thirds of the entire membership.

Special messages and *resolutions and other brief statements* follow a similar procedure: they are discussed at a general meeting and must be approved by two-thirds of the bishops present.

Besides these four types of statements issued in the name of the whole body, various units of the organizations can issue statements in their own names, if they follow prescribed rules for consultation and authorization. In the NCCB, statements can come from the Executive Committee, the Administrative Committee, the President, and the General Secretary. Certain committees and committee officials may occasionally be authorized to issue statements also.

In the USCC, statements can be issued by the Executive Committee, the Administrative Board, the President, the General Secretary, a Departmental Committee (as mentioned, the USCC has three Departmental Committees and three corresponding Departments) or its chairman, and a Departmental secretary or other Departmental staff.

In November 1981, which is after the period examined in this study, the bishops adopted some new regulations dealing with statements. According to these, NCCB statements are generally to be issued by the whole body of bishops (though statements by units of the NCCB are not wholly ruled out), and USCC statements are generally to be issued at the Departmental Committee level (though exceptions are possible), with approval of the Administrative Board.

The Reform of Correctional Institutions in the 1970s

USCC, November 1973

"I was ill and you comforted me, in prison and you came to visit me." Then the just will ask him: "Lord . . . when did we visit you when you were ill or in prison?" The King will answer them: "I assure you, as often as you did it for one of my least brothers, you did it for me" (Matt. 25:36 ff.).

Introduction

In the preparation of this statement, more than a score of persons were consulted, both in their individual professional capacities and, in some instances, as representatives of particular groups. Included in this consultation were prison chaplains, minority group representatives, administrative and custodial personnel of correctional institutions and representatives of an ex-offender organization. Comments of the Federal Bureau of Prisons were helpful, particularly in verifying certain factual points and the feasibility of specific recommendations, without implying endorsement of this statement by the bureau.[1] To all who assisted us we are indebted for their contribution.

Concern

In recent years Americans have experienced deepening concern over the presence and nature of crime in our nation.[2] We share this concern. Fully adequate law enforcement and protection of law-abiding citizens are clear but unmet needs. We oppose violence, whether in defiance of law and order or under the cover of preserving law and order. We oppose both "crime in the streets" and "white collar crime." Dedicated people throughout the country are earnestly striving to identify and deal with the roots of crime.[3] Some, very properly, are questioning society's reaction to victimless crimes. Others are addressing themselves to the issues of law enforcement and the procedures of our criminal courts.

The Reform of Correctional Institutions in the 1970s, published November 1973 by the United States Catholic Conference, Washington, D.C., is used with permission.

Still others are concentrating their attention upon the manner in which suspects and convicted criminals are dealt with and provided for while incarcerated.

The numerous reports issued by representatives of this last group, coupled with incidents of violence in correctional institutions across the nation, have aroused many consciences. In a few instances, federal district court orders have dealt positively with abuses in local institutions of incarceration, because some of the constitutional rights of the resident offenders were being violated. We believe it is timely and urgent that we express ourselves on the moral problems involved in sentencing and incarcerating violators of the law.

We wish it clearly understood that most administrators, guards and other staff members of our correctional institutions are decent, dedicated public servants and that those confined—aside from those awaiting trial—are there because they have been found guilty of crimes or contempt of court.

Crime and punishment are pre-eminently moral issues.[4] Much of the amorality in society today arises from contemporary man's neglect or refusal to place his affairs ultimately in God's hands. In attempting to take control away from God one begins the process of losing control over himself. The immorality of crime results from disregard for the love and worship owed to God; from lack of consideration and esteem for one's neighbor; and from failures in self-knowledge and in self-discipline.

It behooves us to be aware that, despite well-publicized exceptions, prisons are largely filled with the poor, the disadvantaged minorities and the "losers" of our society. We need to examine whether we may not have a "poor man's" system of criminal justice. Often the petty thief—the shoplifter or the pickpocket—goes to jail while the clever embezzler, the glib swindler, the powerful racketeer, the polished profiteer may only undergo the litigation of the civil courts. In the case of the open "vices" prohibited by law, the "town drunk" is sentenced by a judge while the "country club alcoholic" is treated by a physician. We insist that punishment, in order to fulfill its proper purpose, must fit the nature of the crime; it must be considerate of the offender's human dignity; and, it must be tempered by mercy and constantly aimed at reconciliation.

In our response to the urging of Jesus, recorded in St. Matthew's Gospel, to "visit" those in prisons, it is necessary that we not only visit individuals confined in prison but "visit" the correctional system itself. Our concern for correctional institutions does not exist in isolation from other related issues. The injustices and inequities that plague our society affect both the incidence of crime and the administration of correctional institutions. The problems in these institutions are also intimately bound up with the inadequacies of our judicial system. These include unreasonably delayed trials, particularly aggravating when the accused is jailed; the lack both of quality and adequate quantity of legal counsel for the needy; difficulties with bail bonds; and widespread abuses of such useful expedients as plea bargaining.

What happens in the correctional institutions of this nation should not be considered apart from what is happening in the courts, in the executive offices of powerful corporations where major economic decisions affecting millions of people are often made, in the legislatures, in police stations, in employment offices, in schools, in homes and on the streets. Society's most serious failings—in the ugly and despicable forms of racism, disrespect for life, physical violence, political repression and corruption, erosion of individual and civil liberties, setting profit for the few over the necessities of the many, sexual perversion and materialistic inducements—all add explosive fuel to the smoldering problems in the field of correction.

Several broad issues of criminal justice are distinct from, but related to, conditions in correctional institutions. One is the general slowness and inadequacy of federal and state criminal judicial procedures. Delays and overloads by themselves raise serious questions of equity, most often adversely affecting the poor. The rights of the accused should be protected before and during trial. Before formal changes are made, adequate evidence should be an absolute requirement. Additional analyses and funding to reorganize the criminal justice system to accord with the best aspirations of all our people should be given urgent priority.

Recompense for the innocent victims of crime is a sensitive and painful problem. Society must share at least some of the responsibility for compensating innocent victims of crime. When a way is found to pay offenders a fair rate for the work they do in confinement, provisions should be made for regular court-determined payments as at least partial recompense to the victims, or the survivors of the victims of their crimes. This also could become a more personalized aspect of programs such as now exist in several states to compensate innocent victims of violent crimes.

Purpose of Correctional Institutions

Whether the penal system of the United States should not seek to deal with all except dangerous offenders outside of penal institutions is a question which merits much attention. This is a challenging concept clamoring for a fair chance to prove itself—a chance which society should give it forthwith. There is increasing and strongly convincing evidence that a large center of incarceration should *not* be the major instrument for dealing with convicted offenders. Bigger, better, more modern buildings are not the answer.

Smaller, community-based facilities are beginning to prove that they are more appropriate and effective. Half-way houses, work contracts and other alternatives need to be more fully explored. A sympathetic consideration of such approaches should precede any extensive remodeling of existing buildings or construction of contemplated new structures.

In the meantime, however, we must deal with the correctional system as it is. When one examines the situation of confined, convicted criminals, one finds an urgent need to clarify precisely what society is seeking to achieve through their incarceration. Is a correctional institution an instrument of punishment whereby a criminal "does time" in expiation for his misdeeds? Is it a place of custody where a dangerous citizen is detained in order to protect and restore order in society? Is it a means of retribution designed to deter the criminal himself and/or the populace at large from engaging in unlawful behavior? Is a correctional institution ultimately a place for rehabilitation in which a criminal is re-educated or reconciled to a lawful way of life? We feel it is, or ought to be, a composite of all of these, but that pre-eminently it is a place for rehabilitation.

Correctional institutions in fact do harm if they do not offer opportunity for rehabilitation. We are unequivocally committed to the view that rehabilitation should be their primary concern and will do all in our power to make this a reality. There are, however, limitations in this concept. The ideal of rehabilitation cannot, for example, justify investing members of the criminal justice system with excessive discretion to extend a prisoner's term of incarceration. Because of the very common practice of indeterminate sentencing and the frequently arbitrary decisions of overburdened parole boards, a criminal's confinement time can be unjustly and inhumanely extended beyond any reasonable criterion of retribution for his offense. There is need for a mechanism by which parole board decisions can be reviewed, with provision for judicial intervention if necessary.

Those engaged in motivating confined individuals should bear in mind that they are dealing with human beings, created in the image and likeness of God and endowed with free will. Rehabilitation cannot be imposed. The offender has to be convinced of its value and led freely to desire it. Moreover, methods of rehabilitation whose appropriateness can be called into question by reasonable persons should not be forced upon any and all indiscriminately. Certain kinds of group therapy or chemico-psychological treatments or experimentation should not be required of those unwilling or unable to make an intelligent and free decision to submit to them. Furthermore, when such unwillingness results in prolonging the term of incarceration or other discretionary penalties, basic freedoms of the incarcerated are affronted. "Hiring out" the sentenced, as is occasionally done with illegal immigrants in particular, is a wholly unacceptable practice. As the intention to rehabilitate does not exempt from the obligations of retributive justice, so retribution does not legitimatize assaults upon human dignity. Although we speak in the defense of rights of prisoners, we are not unaware of their responsibilities and obligations. They should obey reasonable regulations, serve the just sentences imposed, respect the staff and other residents of the institution and cooperate in the process of rehabilitation.

There is general agreement among qualified commentators that the correctional institutions of our land have, in most cases, failed in the matter of rehabilitation. The numbers of those who are re-incarcerated tend to prove this. Chief Justice Warren E. Burger recently argued the need to reform penal institutions and to develop processes to determine whether particular convicted persons should or should not be confined.[5] The widespread failure to rehabilitate, the Chief Justice observed, is demonstrated by the degree of recidivism. It is true, of course, that rehabilitation is not the only purpose of prisons and that their historic purpose has been to incarcerate. However, even the effectiveness of prisons in incarcerating is related to their effectiveness in rehabilitation. Certainly with regard to rehabilitation, they are, in general, not performing acceptably. All blame, however, for recidivism cannot be attributed to the institutions. Society's unwillingness to accept released offenders with compassion and understanding is a large factor in recidivism.

Operation of Correctional Institutions

Whatever the professed intentions of society may be, our correctional institutions are fundamentally places of custody, strongholds for the secure removal of certain citizens from our midst. Accordingly, the rehabilitative staff (psychologists, sociologists, chaplains, teachers, instructors, etc.) is regularly subordinated to the custodial staff (wardens, guards, etc.), not only on the organization chart of the institution's administration but also in regard to budget. In addition, correctional institutions are commonly located far from urban centers from which the majority of convicted criminals come and to which they are likely to return. Consequently, inmates have little opportunity gradually to learn or re-learn conventional societal living through controlled educational and social contacts or even through regular visits from relatives, friends or sympathetic volunteers. Distance from urban centers also greatly reduces the likeliness of recruiting a staff whose racial, ethnic and social backgrounds are similar to those of the inmates. Thus, alienation and lack of understanding between staff and residents are almost inevitable; and rehabilitation remains largely an abstract ideal rather than a concrete achievement.

Add to all of this in some cases such positive injustices as minimal opportunities for academic or vocational training, unsatisfying work experience with pay that is frequently demeaning, sexual assaults, inadequate diet, meager bathing and recreational facilities, insufficient psychological and medical care, fear, loneliness and shame, plus the all-too-common outrage of associating youthful first offenders with hardened criminals, and the result can be the very reverse of an institution of rehabilitation. It is instead an instrument of punishment or perhaps just a means of deterring the criminally inclined from engaging in unlawful behavior; it may also be a setting which generates further crimes in a spirit of vindictiveness.

Rights of Prisoners

The conditions which prevail in many of our correctional institutions cannot be defended on the grounds of either punishment or deterrence. Christian belief in the potential goodness of man and recognition of every human being's dignity as a child of God redeemed by Jesus Christ causes us to recoil from any form of punishment which is degrading or otherwise corrodes the human personality. Society has a right to protect itself against lawbreakers and even to exact just and measured retribution, but the limits of what is reasonable and just are far exceeded in too many penal institutions. Abuses cannot be justified on the basis of their effectiveness as deterrents to crime. The disturbing statistics of recidivism demonstrate that our correctional institutions have little deterrent effect. It is necessary in any case to raise serious moral objection to tormenting one man unjustly in order to instruct or caution another.

All these considerations bring us back to the primary purpose of houses of correction in the United States as commonly articulated in law and accepted by society. Correctional institutions should be institutions of rehabilitation. They should help men and women rebuild their lives so that, with few exceptions, they can return to society as considerate, free and law-abiding citizens. They are places of custody, but they are never to be only that. They are also instruments of retribution and in a measure strategies for deterrence. These purposes, nevertheless, are to be kept in balance with the need to safeguard the moral order in society while at the same time assisting in the rehabilitation of offending human beings who urgently need society's understanding and care.

Such an analysis clearly derives from a religious conception of man and commitment to the virtues of justice and charity. However, even apart from religious and humanitarian motivation, society's self-interest will best be served by adopting such a view of correctional institutions and working to make it a reality. Nothing whatever is gained by permitting correctional institutions to function as mere fortresses within which self-hatred and embitterment thrive. Confined offenders are not our "enemies." They are fellow human beings, most of whom will one day move freely in our midst, either better or worse for their prison experience. If worse, either they have failed themselves or we have failed both them and ourselves. If better, we have acted in righteousness before God and man; and we have also made an important, essentially positive, contribution to safety and tranquillity in society. In addition, we are ever mindful that each resident offender has individual needs. We emphasize this even as we urge that the correctional institutions develop a relationship—far closer than heretofore—to society in general.

Recommendations

With all this in mind, we offer the following suggestions for reform in the correctional institutions of the United States. Some of these proposals are already being implemented in various places. We add our own endorsement not as experts in penology but as concerned citizens and men of faith. There is no intent to coddle criminals or to harass administrators of correctional institutions. We speak with a view of motivating all those with responsibilities in the field of correction so that their efforts may render correctional facilities more efficacious instruments for the rehabilitation of offenders and for deterrence of further crime. In the prayerful hope of sustaining the best efforts of the often heroic men and women who staff correctional institutions and whose skill, patience, prudence, kindness and dedication are vital to the rehabilitative process, we strongly recommend a higher scale of remuneration with realistic provisions for safety and security in the performance of their duties. Our fundamental purpose remains throughout—to insure protection for all the civil rights of confined offenders in an atmosphere of human compassion conducive to reconciliation and rehabilitation.

1. Correctional institutions whose residents come mainly from urban centers should usually be located near these centers. This will facilitate such desirable things as visitation by relatives, friends and volunteers, recruitment of prison staffs from among members of racial, ethnic and social groups similar to those to which the residents belong, and even the gradual reintegration of the residents into free society.

2. Staffs should be recruited on the bases of ability, training and experience without reference to partisan politics.[6] The most modern sociological and psychological means should be used to screen and select the staff. Salaries should be competitive with those paid persons engaged in education and training activities in the private sector. The custodial and rehabilitative staffs should be integrated so that rehabilitation is furthered rather than subordinated to other purposes. Staff members should be encouraged to seek further training through courses in universities and colleges and through regular participation in "in-service" training programs. Advancement and salary increases should be determined at least in part by the extent of such continuing education.

3. In developing programs and facilities careful consideration to the varying needs of men and women is important. Male residents should be separated from female residents in different facilities; juveniles from adults; first offenders from repeaters; sexual offenders in specialized treatment centers. The emotionally disturbed should be treated in institutions designed for this purpose. The availability of educational training and any other appropriate programs for men and women together should be investigated. Extraordinary efforts should be made to rehabilitate juvenile offenders. Few, if any, offenders should be deprived of access to families and friends.

4. Discrimination because of race, religion or national or ethnic background is never tolerable. Inspectors should be especially alert to expressions of such discrimination in work assignments, the granting of privileges and the manner in which residents are addressed, responded to, given orders and corrected by members of the staff.

5. Free exercise of religion should be guaranteed in every institution. Religious services of various faiths and denominations should be regularly available; chaplains should be welcomed on a continuing or an occasion-by-occasion basis, as needed; and dietary laws should be respected. Residents should be free to consult their chaplains in private and at length. The chaplains should never be constrained to testify before parole boards or to share privileged information with members of the staff. Chaplains should not be required to serve on administrative boards which make decisions about discipline, parole or probation.

6. All residents should be given the regulations of the institution in writing. They should be advised of their rights and privileges, their responsibilities and obligations, punishments to which they are subject for infractions of regulations and established grievance procedures. When necessary, the regulations should be read to residents, in a language they understand. The regulations should be available not only to inspectors but also to the general public.

7. Residents should never be authorized to punish one another. Members of the staff should not inflict any punishments other than those stipulated in the regulations for a particular infraction. Whipping, shackling as a punishment and other penalties which are of their nature cruel or degrading are to be excluded. If solitary confinement is necessary as a last resort, the cell should be standard size, well lighted and ventilated, and the resident should be properly clothed. Adequate diet and facilities for bodily hygiene are to be provided together with regular visitation by a medical officer.

8. All residents should be afforded protection against all assaults, sexual or otherwise, even if this requires a transfer.

9. At least elementary and secondary education and vocational training that is truly useful in free society should be provided all residents who wish to take advantage of these opportunities. In vocational and apprentice training the wholehearted cooperation of industry and labor is indispensable and could very well become a key factor in personal readjustment for the residents.

10. The work to which a resident is assigned should be—and appear to be—worthwhile and compatible with the dignity of a human being. Nothing is so devastating to human aspirations as a work assignment which both parties know is really useless. National standards* should be adopted and promulgated regarding compensation for work. Enabling the residents to work at a fair wage may, among other things, help keep their families off the welfare rolls, either totally or partially. Much greater emphasis is needed on practical job training and post-release employment opportunity. Government agencies should make it their policy to purchase products produced in correctional institutions when possible.

11. National standards should be adopted and promulgated regarding residents' diets, the lighting and ventilation of their living and working environments, their access to toilet and bathing facilities, the extremes of temperature in which they are required to live and work, the quality and cleanliness of their clothing and the medical and psychiatric care available to them. Undue regimentation in clothing and grooming should be eliminated.

12. A resident should be free to refuse treatments, aimed at social rehabilitation, whose appropriateness can be called into question by reasonable persons in and outside the institution. No penalties of any kind should result from such refusal.

13. National standards should be adopted and promulgated regarding the residents' right to send and receive mail, censorship of mail (allowing for necessary inspection), access to printed literature within the institution and from without, and opportunities to listen to the radio and watch television. In developing these standards, it should be borne in mind that most resident offenders are preparing to return to free society, where their survival will depend largely upon

---

*Reference here and elsewhere to "national standards" implies the hope that states would voluntarily adhere to them. However, consideration should be given to make adherence a precondition of any federal grants to the state's criminal justice system.

the persons with whom they maintained contact during their confinement and their knowledge and understanding of current events and thinking.

14. Authorities should encourage visiting by residents' relatives, friends and acquaintances. The design and appointments of visiting rooms should create an atmosphere of dignity, warmth and as much privacy as possible. Where feasible, opportunity and facilities for conjugal visits should be provided for married residents and their spouses. Where possible, family celebrations, picnics and such events as "father-son" and "mother-daughter" days should be arranged. Furloughs should be more liberal, when this is prudent in order to strengthen family life. Furloughs can help offenders apply for jobs, visit sick relatives, attend funerals and maintain social ties useful toward rehabilitation. The experience can also be a helpful forerunner to parole. In some states this has proven to be a success.[7] Several states have developed the work-release system for felony offenders; happily, even more have done so with regard to residents of local county jails. Work-release programs should be extended as far as feasible. Obviously the above opportunities could be made available only to offenders who exhibit an interest in rehabilitation.

15. A national committee of lawyers, state and federal legislators, members of correctional staffs, offenders and ex-offenders and other knowledgeable citizens should be assigned the task of establishing a national code of civil rights for the incarcerated and the development of standardized grievance and due-process procedures as well as a bill of rights clearly defining the extent of duties and limits of obligations of the incarcerated. A similar committee should be assigned to develop a plan of self-governance in such areas as recreation, entertainment, and voluntary educational and vocational training.

16. National standards should be adopted and promulgated regarding the inspection of correctional institutions. Educational requirements for inspectors should be specified. All inspectors' reports should be required to follow a standardized form in order to facilitate comparison from year to year and between various areas of the nation and various institutions. These reports should be available to the general public.

17. No resident should be detained simply because employment is not available. If employment is a condition for release and no private employment is available, federal, state or local government should make every effort to assist the resident. Career counseling, testing, guidance and bonding—where applicable—should be offered all who are preparing to be released.

18. A resident should be informed of the date beyond which further detention demands another intervention of the court.

19. Parole is a vital function, both for the offender and for society. Consideration should be given to shifting the "burden of proof" by making a parole automatic after a definitely determined period of confinement unless there is sound reason against it.

20. Congress should investigate the feasibility of extending the Social Security Act (OASDI) coverage to residents of correctional institutions.

21. After release, ex-offenders, upon their resumption of life in society, should have their civil rights completely restored. Limiting the activities of an ex-offender in public life could undo what took years to build up. Individual and community acceptance of ex-offenders with love and understanding is absolutely necessary for their complete integration into normal community living. Community-based correctional efforts, therefore, should be high on the list of priorities.

22. The use and dissemination of arrest records should be strictly controlled. The revelation of arrest records, where there was no conviction, should be forbidden, as should the denial of employment for reason of an arrest without conviction. (There may, however, be some exceptions to these principles in the case of persons who have been committed for actions resulting from emotional disturbances, or where an inquiry can be demonstrated to be justified in terms of personal or community security. But care should be taken that the exceptions do not degenerate into abuses.)

Parole and Pre-Trial

Closely allied with concerns about correctional reform are two other issues: parole and conditions in jails for those awaiting trial. Both matters urgently need study and attention.

On every side, one hears of institutional case workers obliged to prepare recommendations for parole boards on the basis of meager records and little or no contact with the custodial or training staffs. Parole officers are commonly over-burdened with lengthy reports and unreasonable numbers of persons to serve. Parole boards themselves often include members who have only token preparation for their responsibility and who frequently do not have the time even to grant a hearing to those upon whose freedom they are to rule. The effect of all of this on morale is devastating.

In our nation a man is presumed innocent until proved guilty. Yet after arrest he may spend many months awaiting trial in jail under conditions that can only be described as penal. Usually it is the poor who suffer most under these circumstances. Deprived of freedom, forced to idleness, associating with persons who in many instances are dangerous, the accused may well wonder just how much value the legal presumption of innocence really has. The result all too often is that he grows angry, bitter and is started—or confirmed—in a life of crime. If the prisons of our nation need reform, so also do the jails—a great many of which are houses of terror.

Responsibility

We wish to bring all these matters to the attention of chief executives, legislators and judges and of the staffs of correctional institutions, for we believe that they have an obligation in law and in conscience to undertake or continue a thoroughgoing reform of the American criminal justice system. At the same time, we recognize our own duty to alert all the Catholic faithful and to call . . . the attention of all our fellow Christians and citizens of this nation to the need for such reform and to the part they can take in urging, supporting and participating in it. Significant achievement in the reform of our correctional system will benefit society more than it will benefit the reformed criminal. The replacement of just a small tile in a grand mosaic makes a noticeable difference in its composite beauty.

Suggested Action Steps

Among other appropriate actions, and with whatever modifications are appropriate and prudent, the following steps are indicated.

The United States Catholic Conference will undertake widespread distribution of this statement. In addition, under coordination of the Conference's Division for Urban Affairs, each staff office, department and division of the USCC and the committee secretariats of the National Conference of Catholic Bishops will be asked—as will the National Catholic Community Service, the National Conference of Catholic Charities, and the National Council of Catholic Laity—to develop programs furthering the purposes of this statement. The USCC will also consider joint ventures with other organizations in the field of correctional institution reform.

The state Catholic conferences should consider the many aspects of this problem which will require state legislation, interventions with the executive branches of the state government and—as appropriate—the filing of briefs *amicus curiae* in cases of special significance. State Catholic conferences may wish to develop more specific documents on reform, relating to conditions in their own states.

Dioceses will, we trust, continue or undertake a major role in fostering the concern of the clergy, religious and laity for the human rights of offenders. Diocesan newspapers and other programs of communication can highlight the moral considerations involved in correctional reform and urge action. As bishops we will make every effort to provide qualified chaplains to serve the offenders.

Parishes have a singular opportunity to serve by helping to improve local institutions within their boundaries. This will include support of the chaplains or providing such periodic services where there are no chaplains. In addition, parishes can maintain continuing contact with correctional institutions by committees or groups of concerned parishioners and can work to overcome neighborhood resistance to community-based institutions.

Religious orders, because of their dedication and knowledge in various disciplines, can bring special assistance to administrative and custodial officials, as well as to the residents in our correctional system. They can offer the People of God a greater understanding of the problems of our correctional system and of all of the people concerned with it. In addition, religious communities can literally "visit" those "in prison." Perhaps some will make service to confined offenders their special apostolate as counselors and educators.

College and university groups, including those engaged in campus ministry, can bring companionship and comfort to prisoners by visiting and otherwise assisting them. Visits to prisons by local groups of the National Council of Catholic Women have proven valuable. Various groups can offer special services to the families of prisoners such as providing transportation for visits to the prisoners.

Recognizing that accountability at every level is a major ingredient for making our nation's criminal justice system truly a system of justice, we urge specific methods for evaluation and reasonable community accountability of the work of criminal justice professionals. This applies at every level of the system to both custodial and treatment personnel, pre-sentence investigators, parole and probation officials and all other workers involved.

Finally, each of us should responsively recall that Christ our Lord was a prisoner and according to His living gospel is still present in the person of those who are prisoners today. His apostles knew the agonies of dark dungeons. Many of His original disciples experienced the inhuman cruelty of primitive jails. To this day—in many lands—many of His most dedicated followers find themselves in penal cells or isolated under house arrest.

May our contemplation of these facts inspire us to provide a humble human presence—touched with the sacred—for those accused and those convicted. Let our standing by them or walking with them reunite us as good neighbors and true friends worthy of sharing in the lasting joys of the only absolute unity, God our heavenly Father.

Conclusion

We ask for the prayers and support of all God-fearing people and all those of good will in a renewed effort to improve our criminal justice system; to bring law, order and justice to society; and to strengthen correctional institutions as places where human dignity will be protected and advanced by serious, innovative programs directed to rehabilitation. We ask God's blessing on such efforts and on all who take part in them.

Notes

1. Larry F. Taylor, Executive Assistant, Federal Bureau of Prisons, to John E. Cosgrove, 5 November 1973, Personal Files of John E. Cosgrove, Division of Urban Affairs, U.S. Catholic Conference, Washington, D.C.

2. Harry Fleischmann, "Crime" (to be published in the *Encyclopedia Yearbook 1973*), pp. 8-9.

3. Milton Rector, President, National Council on Crime and Delinquency, to John E. Cosgrove, 26 December 1972, Personal Files of John E. Cosgrove.

4. Archbishop Philip M. Hannan to John E. Cosgrove, 24 January 1973, Personal Files of John E. Cosgrove.

5. Warren E. Burger, Chief Justice of the United States, address to the National Conference of Christians and Jews Annual Dinner, Philadelphia, Pennsylvania, 16 November 1972, p. 3.

6. Joseph R. Rowan, Executive Director of the John Howard Association, to John E. Cosgrove, 20 December 1972, Personal Files of John E. Cosgrove.

7. Ibid.

APPENDIX C

Reflections on the Energy Crisis

USCC, April 1981

I. INTRODUCTION

The fading of the petroleum age disquiets the entire world. Cheap oil and natural gas not only powered the dramatic transformation of Western society in the twentieth century, they underlie much of the material progress developing countries have made. Now it is only a matter of time until oil and gas production peaks and starts to drop.[1] In the years ahead the nations of the earth, both rich and poor, must learn to conserve what supplies they can obtain. They must also find some way of switching over to dependence on alternative sources of energy without sinking into economic chaos.

The United States cannot ignore this imperative. Almost half the energy we use comes from oil and 40 per cent of this oil is imported.[2] The abrupt price surges of recent years, besides affecting consumers directly, have contributed heavily to inflation and unemployment. Middle-class families find their budgets increasingly tight, while the poor are faced with the terrible prospect of choosing between fuel and decent clothing, fuel and health care, even fuel and food. Clearly, energy costs will prove to be a growing burden to millions of our people.

Moreover, the America economy is frighteningly vulnerable to outright disruption. The embargo of 1973-1974 and the more recent war between Iran and Iraq demonstrate that the nation lacks reliable access to foreign petroleum. If the flow of oil from Africa and the Persian Gulf were suddenly cut off, the production of goods would shrink, jobs would disappear and the delivery of necessary services would be hampered.[3] Under such circumstances, those who have less would presumably suffer more. In a competition for scarce energy and for reduced goods and services only the wealthy could win.

Because of its economic and political power, the United States bears a responsibility to the international community as well as to its own citizens. There are few greater gifts we can offer the people of other lands than openhearted cooperation

157

in the effort to develop a global policy to bring about future energy security. This duty takes a special moral urgency from the fact that America is the leading energy consumer. A half-century of plentiful oil has made us careless; we waste what other countries need.

Our power can be as much a force for evil as for good. Should we fail to help the world toward security, we increase the chance that we will lead it to destruction. In the absence of well-developed alternative systems, what happens when the oil and gas run out? Even before the wells dry up, what happens as global supplies dwindle and prices soar? Even before supply problems become acute, what happens if there is another, longer embargo or if turmoil engulfs the OPEC nations? Early in 1980 the president of the United States asserted America's readiness to defend its vital energy interests with force. The black seed of the final holocaust may lie beneath the sands of the Middle East.

II. The Moral Dimensions of Energy Policy[4]

The threat of war, the danger that scarcity poses for the poor—such considerations are reason enough for the church to take part in the national discussion of energy. Further, energy is one of those touchstone issues like arms control or the limits of federal power whose resolution will profoundly affect society in the twenty-first century. Unless some new perspectives are brought to bear, decision makers will have little to rely on but the hard and rather narrow analytical tools that have guided energy development in the past. In his first encyclical, *Redemptor Hominis,* Pope John Paul II said: "The development of technology and the development of contemporary civilization, which is marked by the ascendancy of technology, demand a proportional development of morals and ethics. For the present this last development seems unfortunately to be always left behind" (n. 15).

The present statement offers no solutions to the swirling controversies that surround the formation of energy policy. It constitutes an invitation, not a pronouncement—an invitation to further study, to conscientious judgment, to prudent action at all levels. At the same time it seeks to situate energy issues in a moral context, to arouse sensitivity to human considerations which are often ignored. Catholic social teaching suggests certain clear principles that should be borne in mind as Americans, remembering their brothers and sisters in other nations, strive to adjust to a world where oil and natural gas are no longer readily available.

Moral Principles

1. Upholding the right to life: It is clear that no overall energy strategy is free from risk to human life. Claims that there is a completely safe option are illusory; the choice is not between black and white but among shades of gray. Furthermore, a given policy can threaten life in various ways. For example, developing energy

source A may consign miners or local residents to death, while failing to develop it may indirectly kill others if supply falls short of essential demand.

The church recognizes these sad facts. It is deeply committed to the defense of human life, however, and this commitment is uppermost in its approach to energy. Energy planners and those in authority must do all in their power to safeguard human life. They must especially avoid exposing people to danger without giving them the opportunity to accept or reject that danger. As the bishops gathered at the Second Vatican Council said:

"At the same time, however, there is a growing awareness of the exalted dignity proper to the human person, since he stands above all things and his rights and duties are universal and inviolable. Therefore, there must be available to all people everything necessary for leading a life truly human, (including) the right . . . to (required) information, (and) to activity in accord with the upright norm of one's own conscience. . . . Hence, the social order and its development must unceasingly work to the benefit of the human person if the disposition of affairs is to be subordinate to the personal realm and not contrariwise" *(Gaudium et Spes, 26)*.

2. Accepting an appropriate share of responsibility for the welfare of creation: Judeo-Christian tradition views human beings not in isolation but as part of a larger whole—as creatures in the midst of creation. This tradition counsels respect for the natural world, emphasizing that we have duties as well as rights in its use. Since we derive all our energy from nature, the relationship of humanity and environment has the broadest implications for energy policy.

In the religious community, this relationship is often described as "responsible stewardship"; we are stewards to whose care the Master has entrusted his creation. The technological strides we have made since World War II require a sharpening of that concept. The human race has the capacity to alter nature, even to destroy it, and the scope of our responsibility grows with the scope of our power. We are no longer called upon simply to tend the garden God has given us. It is now in our hands to determine whether our descendants will inherit an earth capable of sustaining them.

This awesome responsibility has led some analysts to advance the notion that humanity is an intruder in nature; they advocate extreme measures, including methods of population control that are destructive of liberty. There is no question that in our present state of knowledge we cannot obtain adequate energy supplies without imposing some costs on the environment. But surely our response should not be to alienate ourselves from nature, to spurn the gifts God has given us. Pope John Paul gave the context in which we should approach the task of designing an ecologically sound energy program when he declared that "exploitation of the earth . . . and the uncontrolled development of technology outside the framework of a long-range authentically humanistic plan often bring with them a threat to our natural environment . . . and remove us from nature. Yet it was the Creator's will that humanity should communicate with nature as an intelligent and noble master and guardian, and not as a heedless exploiter and destroyer" (*Redemptor Hominis,* 15).

3. Accepting limitation in a Christian spirit: When a certain young man questioned Jesus on what he should do to be saved, Jesus advised him to sell what he had, take up his cross and follow. The young man "went away sad, for his possessions were many" (Mt. 19:16-22). If preservation of the common good, both domestic and global, requires that we as individuals make sacrifices related to energy use, we should do so cheerfully. Americans have become used to the idea that rapid economic expansion is an unqualified, even inevitable good. Future resource restrictions may force us to rethink our expectations; they may even lead to substantial changes in our way of life. Insofar as these adjustments affect excess possessions, we should welcome them. They are a blessing.

Adopting this attitude will free us to face the energy situation with hope. God did not put us here to build up his kingdom only to strike the requisite tools from our hands. The problems that close us in can be solved if we will seek the right solutions. This means rising above a preoccupation with material gain.

4. Striving for a more just society: The energy debate is not about abstractions and statistics. It is about war and famine and suffering; its content is the struggle against cold, against dark, against isolation. The energy policies we choose must reflect a search after justice for all, not only on the level of individual rights but also with regard to the structures of society.

Catholic social teaching has touched on these themes time and again. *Gaudium et Spes* declares: "Meanwhile that conviction grows . . . that it devolves on humanity to establish a political, social and economic order which will increasingly serve people and help individuals as well as groups to affirm and develop the dignity proper to them" (n. 9). Pope John XXIII, in sounding a similar note, emphasized that every human being is spirit and body, multifaceted, born to pursue a varied perfection. His words in *Mater et Magistra* remind us that economic considerations impinge on the development of energy policy in more ways than one. The desire for economic justice must dominate.

" 'National wealth' — as our predecessor of happy memory, Pius XII, rightfully observed—'inasmuch as it is produced by the common efforts of the citizenry, has no other purpose than to secure without interruption those material conditions in which individuals are enabled to lead a full and perfect life. . . . For the system whereby both the common prosperity is achieved and individuals exercise their right to use material goods, conforms fully to norms laid down by God the Creator.' From this it follows that the economic prosperity of any people is to be assessed not so much from the sum total of goods and wealth possessed as from the distribution of goods according to norms of justice, so that everyone in the community can develop and perfect themselves. For this, after all, is the end toward which all economic activity of a community is by nature ordered" (n. 74).

Finally, Pope John Paul teaches in *Dives in Misericordia* that the spirit of justice must be perfected by the spirit of mercy. "Certainly, the Second Vatican Council also leads us in this direction when it speaks repeatedly of the need to make the world more human and says that the realization of this task is precisely the mission of the church in the modern world. Society can become ever more human only if we introduce into the many-sided setting of interpersonal and social relationships, not merely justice, but also that 'merciful love' which constitutes the messianic message of the Gospel" (n. 14).

Public discussion of energy policy has been sharply polarized. Too often advocates of a particular point of view refuse to even consider the arguments of those they oppose. It is difficult to see how these attitudes, the antithesis of fraternal charity, can help create a more just social order. The church would be false to its founder if it did not take up the cause of the oppressed. But it must also insist that justice is not to be meted out to some and denied to others. Just as utility companies should not raise rates above the level needed to ensure a fair return for honest and efficient service, for example, consumers should not demand that rates be held below the same level.

5. Giving special attention to the needs of the poor and members of minority groups: The first Letter of John asks: "If someone who has the riches of this world sees his brother in need and closes his heart to him, how does the love of God abide in him?" (1 Jn. 3:17). As noted above, poor people, especially those with fixed incomes, will feel the sting of rising energy prices more keenly than their affluent neighbors. Moreover, racist attitudes may affect both price and access to supply. In circumstances where energy is essential to the maintenance of life, health or human dignity, there is but one course to follow. Private agencies and federal, state and local authorities must take whatever steps are necessary to ensure an adequate supply to people whom poverty or discrimination places at a disadvantage. No energy policy is acceptable that fails to deal adequately with basic needs.

No one will quarrel with the proposition that Christians cannot stand idly by while people freeze in their homes for lack of fuel. The church goes further in its advocacy for the poor, however. In "A Call to Action," Pope Paul VI outlines the attitude we should adopt toward those who suffer deprivation. He also shows why the poor should be singled out for special attention in dealing with the energy crisis.

"In teaching us charity, the Gospel instructs us in the preferential respect due to the poor and the special situation they have in society: The more fortunate should renounce some of their rights so as to place their goods more generously at the service of others. If beyond legal rules there is really no deeper feeling of respect for and service to others, then even equality before the law can serve as an alibi for flagrant discrimination, continued exploitation and actual contempt" (n. 23).

Our concern for the poor must extend beyond America's borders. Domestic policy, far from imposing burdens on the economies of other nations, should be consistent with the goal of promoting sound development throughout the world.

6. Participating in the decision-making process: Fairness requires that groups and individuals representing a broad spectrum of opinion have an opportunity to take part in formulating energy policy. Even local energy decisions often involve danger to life and health, and national ones can have major economic effects and can help determine the patterns of power in society. The stakes are too high both

practically and morally for the ordinary citizen to ignore the processes through which such decisions are reached.

Given the inequalities that pervade American society, fairness may also require active assistance to those whose voice is rarely heard in policy discussions. Pope Paul's words in "Justice in the World" describe the situation well:

"Unless combated and overcome by social and political action, the influence of the new industrial and technological order favors the concentration of wealth, power and decision making in the hands of a small public or private controlling group. Economic justice and lack of social participation keep a person from attaining basic human and civil rights" (n. 9).

The principle of subsidiarity, as outlined in *Quadragesimo Anno* and reaffirmed in *Mater et Magistra*, is relevant to any discussion of citizen participation. In general terms the principle holds that social functions that can be performed by an individual should not be transferred to a group, and that functions that can be performed by a smaller "collectivity" (the local community, for example) should not be transferred to a larger "collectivity" (state or, at the next stage, federal government). Pope Pius XI gave the reason: "Inasmuch as every social activity should, by its very nature, prove a help to members of the body social, it should never destroy or absorb them" (quoted in *Mater et Magistra*, 53).

Commitment

These principles are offered as a framework for moral reflection and action regarding energy policy. They are lenses through which such policy can be examined, benchmarks by which it can be judged. However, the principles have their limitations. Because they are general, different people will reach different conclusions when applying them, say, to nuclear power or coal use. The element of informed individual judgment remains critical. In the same way the principles cannot move anyone to take Christian morality seriously in grappling with energy. That is a matter of faith, a matter of religious commitment.

Our redemption makes us capable of seeking just, generous and loving solutions to the problems we face. But we are too sinful, too given to selfishness, to pursue this difficult search without a conviction that all humanity is one in Christ. Pope John urged his readers in *Pacem in Terris* "in the light of their Christian faith and led by love, to ensure that the various institutions—whether economic, social, cultural or political in purpose—will be such as . . . to facilitate or render less arduous humanity's self-perfection in both the natural order and the supernatural" (n. 146). Jesus, in St. John's account, spoke more simply:

"As the Father has loved me, so I have loved you. Live on in my love. You will live in my love if you keep my commandments, even as I have kept my Father's commandments and live in his love. All this I tell you that my joy may be yours and your joy may be complete. This is my commandment: Love one another as I have loved you" (Jn. 15:9-12).

III. Making the Transition: Sources of Energy

As annoying as they may be, gas lines and temporary crimps in the supply pipeline are not the "energy crisis." Even our reliance on oil imports is only one element in the crisis. The fundamental problem, simply put, is the need to effect a transition from primary dependence on oil and natural gas to primary dependence on something else in the fairly near future.

From the moral perspective just presented, it makes a great deal of difference how this transition is handled and where it leads. Will the development of alternative sources of energy contribute to a just society in which access to the necessities of life is universal? Will it reduce the risk of self-destruction through war that competition for energy supplies now poses? Will it help balance the need for economic development with the need for environmental integrity? Can it be a creative force in shaping a more hopeful future than the world seems to face today? In the remaining years of this century the human community will answer these questions for better or worse.

Conventional Oil and Natural Gas

This nation will not wean itself overnight from oil and natural gas. Great disruptions would result if it tried. America moves on petroleum; with minor exceptions our entire transportation system is bound to it. Moreover, large-scale technologies cannot now use any substitute energy source except coal or nuclear fission, and conversion takes time and money.

Not only will the United States continue to burn conventional oil and gas, it will continue to trade on the world oil market. Ideally, this trade is good. If governed by fair cooperative arrangements between oil producers and importers, it serves as a reminder of the interdependence of nations and benefits all. As noted above, though, many considerations make a sharp decrease in our use of foreign oil desirable. Such a step can even be seen as an act of justice toward importing countries struggling to develop their economies.[5]

American imports have dropped significantly since 1977,[6] and there seems to be room for further improvement. Even though domestic oil production has apparently peaked, industry can contribute by searching for new strikes and employing new techniques for forcing more crude from old wells. Such efforts have clear value.

Given the certainty that our resources are finite, however, oil production should not be overemphasized. Why pursue a policy that guarantees the early exhaustion of domestic supplies, especially when oil has certain uses (in the production of pharmaceuticals, for instance) that would be very difficult to replace? Without ignoring the need to produce for today's demand, it is prudent to begin identifying an alternative or mix of alternatives immediately. As long as oil remains our primary fuel, we are on a collision course with nature.

Conservation

What to do in this dilemma? One response comes quickly to mind. Pope John Paul, in an address to the Pontifical Commission on Justice and Peace in 1978, said that "Christians will want to be in the vanguard in favoring ways of life that decisively break with a frenzy of consumerism, exhausting and joyless." Sadly, few Americans take such exhortations to heart and fewer still think of energy when they think of consumerism. Yet all people of good will do have a positive duty to conserve energy and to use energy efficiently under the conditions prevailing in the nation and the world. Those who have adopted simple styles of life deserve praise for their courage and commitment.

The duty to conserve will vary from individual to individual, depending on each one's health, economic status and other circumstances. For example, older people who set their thermostats too low run the risk of illness or death from a gradual decline in body temperature (accidental hypothermia). Those who live outside metropolitan areas do not have the option of switching to mass transit systems to get to work. Poor people are not in a position to weatherize their homes out of their own pockets. Conservation is a matter of judgment, informed by a lively conscience.

The recent downturn in gasoline sales and slowed growth in demand for electricity show that conservation has gained a certain momentum.[7] It is up to ordinary men and women to make sure that this movement remains strong. Most of us can take some of the small but important steps to save energy that citizens' groups, government agencies and others are constantly proposing. A striking statistic highlights the urgency of the need: More than 10 per cent of the oil the entire world produces each day vanishes into the tanks of American cars.[8]

Relatively minor adjustments in the way we live can have only a limited impact of course. There are opportunities for conservation throughout the economy. For example, much can be done in the industrial sector by "co-generating" electricity with process heat, recycling discarded materials, phasing in more energy-efficient equipment and procedures, and so on. State and federal governments can offer incentives for such innovations where sound economics does not dictate them. Government can also stimulate other wide-ranging improvements in America's use of energy. It can establish stringent performance standards for automobiles, buildings and other products; institute weatherization programs (thereby creating job opportunities as well); and, in general, guide the country in an orderly and sensible conservation effort.

Some shy away from conserving energy because it connotes sacrifice or because they suspect industry of exploiting the market for private gain. Such a response makes little practical sense. A barrel of oil that is not burned today is available for tomorrow; every act of conservation brightens our chances of making a smooth transition to reliance on alternative sources of energy. Conversely, a rejection of small sacrifices today could enforce large sacrifices tomorrow. It is not yet clear whether Americans will have to accept fundamental changes like abandoning inefficient suburban housing and shopping centers accessible only by car for efficient central-city apartments and stores that are served by mass transit. But such changes are certainly more likely to be necessary if we bury our heads in the sand.

Coal

Conservation only saves oil; it cannot replace it. Leaving aside the transportation sector, the leading alternative to oil is coal. About 75 per cent of the coal we now consume goes to make electricity, with most of the rest consigned to industry.[9] It is tempting to increase coal production. America has abundant reserves of the mineral,[10] and the technology surrounding its use is well developed. Coal could become the key transitional fuel, bridging the gap between petroleum and renewable energy sources.

However, the advantages of accelerated coal production must be evaluated in the light of some very serious disadvantages. As the Appalachian bishops' pastoral statement "This Land Is Home to Me" points out, the history of coal is a tale of sweat, of suffering, of bloody conflict, of disease, of early death. Even today miners lose their lives in accidents and black lung remains a crippling curse. New mining also threatens local residents. In Appalachia, it can lead to increased blasting, flooding and road damage. In the West, it can disrupt communities, turning them into overnight "boom towns." The economic and social health of some small towns and cities has already been shattered; these places are blazing a sad trail that many others may follow.

Environmental considerations loom large. First, strip mining has heavily damaged land and poisoned water supplies in the past; and recently enacted federal law has not yet effectively halted this devastation. Second, burning coal releases huge amounts of sulphur and nitrogen oxides and other pollutants into the atmosphere. The oxides can combine with water to create "acid rain," which is suspected of wiping out fish populations in lakes and damaging some crops.[11] More important, air pollution poses a danger to human health, killing thousands of people every year.[12]

The use of coal (and other fossil fuels as well) has been associated in recent scientific investigation with a darker, more shadowy threat than mining accidents or pollution. Combustion releases carbon dioxide and a buildup of this gas over time could affect temperatures worldwide in ways that are difficult to predict. Such a phenomenon could cause significant climatic changes, jeopardize food supplies by altering growing conditions in agricultural areas, perhaps even trigger catastrophic flooding by melting parts of the polar ice caps. No one is sure how great an increase in carbon dioxide levels would be necessary to produce such consequences or if they would happen at all. But it would be the height of folly to tamper in ignorance with the ecology of the entire planet.[13]

Unlike the question of conservation, the question of increased coal use does not present the Christian with a clear moral choice. As with many other issues related to energy, there are many gaps and uncertainties in the facts about coal. How great a risk does atmospheric carbon dioxide imply? What elements in air pollution are most toxic? How dangerous will contaminated rain be at higher levels of acidity? Moreover, the facts change over time. Until now neither voluntary compliance nor federal requirements for pollution abatement have been notably successful.[14] Coal's supporters note, however, that future power plants will be designed to conform to rigorous emission standards and that promising new techniques to remove sulphur during combustion are being developed. The basis for moral judgment will shift as our knowledge improves.

The present state of affairs certainly calls for caution in accepting a more prominent role for coal in America's future. The church cannot ignore the benefits coal offers; it is an energy "cushion" which the average person might one day be very glad to have. But neither can the church ignore the attendant dangers to human health and the environment. If a commitment to coal is made, it should be balanced by a simultaneous commitment to improved mine safety and strict ecological and community-protection standards. To act otherwise is to seek a just end through unjust means.

Nuclear Fission

Besides coal, the only developed and expandable alternative is nuclear fission. It is based on a domestic resource, uranium, and could provide power for a very long time if the breeder reactor were perfected on a commercial scale. America already has a functioning nuclear industry, with some seventy plants in operation and another ninety under construction or cleared for construction.[15] Since atomic energy produces about 12 per cent of our electricity nationwide,[16] the question is not whether to use it. Rather, we must decide whether to continue using it and, if so, whether to use more of it.

Nuclear power has been aptly described as standing at the center of an incomplete system.[17] The by-products of fission are hazardous radioactive wastes. These high-level wastes must be totally isolated from the environment for a very long time and scientists disagree on whether that is possible in all cases.[18] There are also unresolved safety questions in the operation of nuclear plants, as the 1979 accident at Three Mile Island forcefully demonstrated.[19] The effects of low-level radiation on uranium miners and others is the subject of intense and confusing debate. Finally, the spread of nuclear technology here and abroad raises the specter of nuclear arms proliferation.[20]

As everyone knows, atomic energy is fiercely controversial. Many uncertainties surround this complex technology and both pro- and anti-nuclear advocates seem prone to exaggerated claims, creating an atmosphere in which rational public discussion is difficult. Under these circumstances, it is hardly surprising that individuals disagree in good faith on the course national policy should follow. Some favor shutting down existing nuclear plants, others press for a moratorium on licensing or construction, still others want to build new reactors while working to solve the problems implicit in the fission fuel cycle.

This controversy, which has been conducted largely in moral terms, will persist. It should be dominated by a concern for human life, both now and in the future, and by a desire to mold a just society where everyone has access to the necessities. According to one viewpoint, these principles support the continued development of nuclear energy. Failure to pursue the technology could eventually put the United States at a disadvantage vis-à-vis other nations in supplying power to its people. Abandoning the nuclear option altogether creates more immediate risks. Those who would close plants or forbid new ones must concretely show how conservation and alternative energy sources can provide for essential services.[21]

Without discounting such arguments, we should be aware that nuclear power's share in electrical generation remains fairly small. Our commitment to atomic energy could still be reversed through careful planning. This possibility deserves careful consideration. While nuclear energy is not evil in itself, it can do great evil. The consequences of a core meltdown or an accident involving "hot" wastes could be catastrophic, far outweighing any good society derives from the electricity fission could supply. It may be unwise to cooperate in the spread of nuclear technology through the world, despite the fact that many nations seek this technology. Finally, the effect that hundreds of nuclear plants and their stored wastes may have on our descendants must be taken into account. If the defenders of nuclear power are to prevail, they must be able to demonstrate its safety beyond reasonable doubt.

Because of the risks involved, people's right to participate democratically in decisions that affect them deserves special emphasis where atomic energy is concerned. The average person has the opportunity to vote for government officials, to speak up at public hearings and the like. However, some states have turned to a more direct and potentially more inclusive instrument for registering citizen opinion on nuclear power: the referendum. Industry advocates presumably have a financial advantage in putting their position before the public, but this advantage can be nullified through spending limitations. If fair referenda were held on such questions as the operation of nuclear plants or the disposal of wastes, the outline of a national consensus might emerge. At the very least, responsible leaders of various persuasions would have the chance to educate people on the choices they faced, helping dispel the mythology and reduce the tensions that cloud the nuclear issue.[22]

Geothermal Energy

Geothermal generating plants have been suggested as another substitute for facilities that burn fossil fuels, since in theory geothermal energy reserves are very extensive. But the contribution steam and water from the earth can make to our energy supply is limited by the fact that they can be tapped only in certain locations. They also entail heavy economic and environmental costs. Research into the possibility of drawing on geopressurized zones and on hot dry rock and magma formations may expand the potential of geothermal in the next few decades.[23]

Synthetic Oil and Gas

Electricity, of course, is only one form of energy and it is not suited to all tasks. Our immediate fuel crisis is largely a liquid-fuel crisis centered on transportation. As a result, the federal government is giving considerable attention to synthetic oil and gas derived from coal, oil shale, biomass and other hydrocarbons. The United States has massive stores of raw materials from which synthetics can be made.[24] Furthermore, the corporations that trade in conventional oil and gas can both produce and market synthetic fuels, using techniques related to those they presently employ.

The major emphasis today is on products synthesized from coal and oil shale. Unfortunately most of the human and environmental problems associated with accelerated coal combustion apply in varying degrees to the liquefaction and gasification processes under consideration.[25] Manufacturing these substances also requires great quantities of water. In semi-arid Western states public officials would face some very hard choices between water for coal conversion and water for agriculture and home use.

Clearly, the moral concerns mentioned in connection with burning coal are relevant here as well. A serious disruption of our transportation system in the future could have a disastrous effect on millions of people and threaten the stability of the entire economy. However, the legitimate need to find a replacement liquid fuel should not make us less vigilant in protecting human life and environment. We will pay a price for fossil-derived synthetics, perhaps a heavy one. It would be irresponsible not to weigh the risks very seriously, and to examine any promising alternative technology before embarking on a massive "synfuels" program.

Proceeding with care should not cause excessive delay. At present the United States has no commercial synthetic-fuel plants. Although the practicality of several liquefaction and gasification technologies has been demonstrated on a relatively small scale, further research will be required to develop the most desirable methods and to make sure that large-scale production is feasible.[26] While these economic and technical questions are being settled, we should also study the social and environmental implications of synthetic-fuel production, both for America and other nations. We will probably discover that we can have a synthetics industry. We must then decide whether we should have one.

Solar Power

Given the severe difficulties they present, one cannot help viewing most energy sources with a touch of apprehension. By contrast, the general reaction to solar power is hope. (The term "solar power" includes energy from the sun; from wind, wave and falling water; and from biomass.) The sun is an inexhaustible fount of energy for a variety of purposes, with the probable exception of tasks requiring high heat—firing utility and industrial boilers, for example. Its effects on people and the environment are relatively benign.[27] Since some small solar applications are appropriate for use in poor as well as developed countries, we can render the whole human family a service by perfecting the relevant technology. Most important, solar power can help open the way to permanent energy security, pointing beyond the end of fossil fuels.

Hope centers on something yet to be realized. Hydroelectric generation is an established energy source and working solar units of various kinds are scattered throughout the country. But the rewards of solar power lie mainly in the future, partly for technical reasons and partly as a result of social, economic and institutional barriers. Moreover, since most solar technologies are still in an early stage of development, it is extremely difficult to predict their potential—or for that matter the unforeseen problems they may present. This accounts for much of the controversy surrounding energy from the sun. The value of pursuing the solar option is not in serious dispute. But analysts disagree vehemently on when various solar devices will come into general use and how strong a contribution they will make, individually and collectively, to our energy supply.[28]

The matter of timing is critical in a discussion of the transition period from primary dependence on oil and natural gas to alternative sources—roughly the next twenty or thirty years. Again, few would deny that the sun may provide a significant share of our power in the long run. Will it prove practical in the short run? The way different people answer this question helps determine their attitude not only toward solar but also toward the energy sources solar is intended to replace or supplement.

How quickly scientists and engineers can develop solar systems is a technical issue that does not invite moral reflection. However, two related considerations deserve stress. First, energy is a tool for fulfilling essential human needs. No energy policy is just which fails to meet these needs; that is the fundamental requirement. Those who question the near-term effectiveness of some solar devices, therefore, raise a legitimate concern. Second, solar energy, because it is renewable and generally benign, possesses key advantages over the rest of the field. It follows that energy planners, while making sure that essential needs are served, should favor the development of selected solar technologies, offering generous public incentives and attempting to remove the obstacles that impede rapid advance.

Active and passive systems for space and water heating, the leading direct solar applications, are the likeliest vehicle for ushering in a solar age.[29] In the present state of the art, solar heating remains beyond the reach of the poor and even affluent people will exercise care in purchasing equipment whose performance is relatively untried. However, the benefits of these systems will increase as the price of fossil fuels rises and they can provide a valuable buffer against interruptions in oil supply.

On the basis of continuing research, the prospects seem good for using solar radiation to produce other forms of energy besides heat. Photovoltaics, the direct conversion of sunlight into electricity with silicon cells, may be extremely important to a society so thoroughly electrified as ours is.[30] Mention has already been made of biomass (non-fossilized organic materials ranging from garbage to crop residues to trees to manure) as a feedstock for synthetic liquids and gases. If one or more of the conversion techniques under study proves successful on a commercial scale, the outlook for solving our transportation fuel problems could brighten considerably.[31]

Support for biomass conversion must be qualified, however. The creation of large "energy farms" featuring fast-growing plants destined for the factory could cause serious erosion and water pollution problems. Planning should include steps to minimize these effects. The well-established trend toward fermenting alcohol from grain for gasohol also bears watching. While it is true that the grain presently used for this purpose is surplus, the alcohol-fuels industry could become a powerful competitor in the world food market. Research into ways of deriving ethanol from materials without food value should be encouraged.

Perspectives

Although it is necessary for analytical purposes to separate one energy source from another, they are intertwined as closely as threads in a tapestry. Because oil and natural gas are such versatile fuels, replacing them requires broad adjustments across the entire energy spectrum. Moreover, changing the role one source plays in supplying America's energy has an impact on the role alternative sources play. Increasing the use of coal for electrical generation, for example, might well have any or all of the following consequences: decreasing the need for nuclear power; retarding the development of photovoltaics; retarding research on new ways to tap geothermal energy; and impeding (through production and transportation bottlenecks) the rapid establishment of a synthetic-fuels industry. When one adds to this the further complications associated with human health, the environment and world peace, the impossibility of isolating one aspect of the energy situation becomes clear. Wise decisions can only come from maintaining perspective on the whole.

Humility also has a particular value in the debate over energy sources. The hallmarks of the field seem to be uncertainty and change. Experts work with educated guesses as to demand, supply and the timing of both. Furthermore, we cannot see very clearly over the rim of the century. While a technology like nuclear fusion will have no immediate impact, it is the subject of intense research and development and holds considerable promise in the longer run. Breakthroughs in fusion or in such areas as hydrogen research or energy-storage capacity may shift the range of choices. While these considerations must not be allowed to paralyze energy planning, they should serve to keep it undogmatic.

The most valuable perspective of all, of course, comes from giving moral and ethical standards the attention they deserve. How shall we choose the energy sources we rely on, and how shall we handle them once chosen? The church must answer: "as creatures and as fellow creatures." The love of God and the love of humanity must guide us if we are not to injure ourselves in the search for energy security.

IV. Making the Transition: Energy Distribution and Control

The national debate is not exclusively a discussion of where our energy will come from. It also takes in the structures that control the flow of energy through American society and the uses to which energy is ultimately put. The church's interest in these topics is quite straightforward. To the extent that energy is necessary for human life and health, and for life with dignity, access to it is a matter of justice. Institutions and energy policies that fail to take human need sufficiently into account violate rights which the church must defend. In doing so it both espouses the common good and reaffirms its sense of identity with the poor.

The Distribution of Energy

Late in 1980, the Congress of the United States appropriated about $2 billion to help low-income people pay their fuel bills. Some question the adequacy of this funding. Others see the need for government aid as an indictment of the economic system that produced the need in the first place. Whatever its precise implications, the legislation makes a two-pronged statement about our society. It acknowledges the fact that the days of cheap and plentiful power are over. It also acknowledges society's responsibility to respond by making sure that the poor are not denied necessities. Just as food stamps are an attempt to deal with inequitable food distribution, this assistance is an attempt to deal with inequitable energy distribution.

If anything, the problem is likely to get worse. Our oil-supply system is so vulnerable to disruption that we must expect a series of spot shortages and-or price increases in the future.[32] The price of oil, in turn, will draw the price of other fuels upward, magnifying the effects of rising construction costs, high interest rates and general inflation. These conditions, devastating to the poor, will progressively squeeze other groups of Americans as well.

There are basically two ways to allocate energy among all its possible users and uses. The first is reliance on the marketplace tempered perhaps by the social conscience of individual companies. The value of such an approach is that it generally reflects the cost of energy to each individual and the economy as a whole and encourages conservation. Its primary disadvantage is that some people and some activities lose out in the competition for energy supplies. When money is the only consideration, affluent citizens can maintain even their most frivolous amusements while their less wealthy neighbors go without fuel for heating and cooking.

The second approach to energy allocation is through government fiat. Public officials, either alone or in cooperation with the private sector, choose the activities and classes of citizens that are to receive help in obtaining energy and decide what form this aid is to take. This method allows for comprehensive planning which protects the interests of all members of society. However, it involves a degree of government intervention in private decision making that many people find offensive.

The United States has chosen to combine elements of both these approaches in dealing with the energy situation. For instance, the federal government has decontrolled oil prices and is in the process of decontrolling natural gas prices. At the same time it is giving the poor some help and trying to spread part of the benefits of decontrol by means of the "windfall-profits tax."

Christians will differ on how to justly distribute energy supplies, but principle will lead them to agree on certain goals. Even as they offer a neighborly hand to distressed individuals in their own communities, they will back public energy assistance for all low-income people offered in a spirit of respect for the recipients' dignity. They will not be content, indeed, unless such aid completely offsets price increases attributable directly or indirectly to decontrol. It is manifestly unfair that the poor should have to spend an ever greater percentage of their meager income on necessary power as a result of measures aimed at cutting excess consumption.

Government assistance should take other forms besides simple payments. Money used for fuel is immediately helpful, but it does nothing to improve one's long-range situation. Substantial funding should also be invested in weatherizing the homes of low-income people and, where feasible, in installing solar heating equipment. Further, government should work with utility companies to bring about the adoption of rate structures that protect the interests of the poor.[33]

Steps must be taken to ensure that in times of shortage the essential functions of society do not falter for lack of fuel. Authorities on all levels should perfect contingency plans for supplying energy to farms, to health facilities, to basic transportation systems and to other elements in the social fabric that are most important for sustaining life and health. In the absence of such plans the disruption that a major crisis would cause could explode into chaos.

Concern for the poor and for essential services takes priority in designing strategies for energy distribution because they involve necessities. Beyond that the standard must be equity. To take a concrete example, there is nearly unanimous agreement that the United States should move to free itself from excessive dependence on imported oil. The common good this move would serve is the good of the whole human race, given the threat of nuclear war. Obviously, however, cutbacks in oil could have significant implications for energy distribution, both in terms of access and price. The burden of such a policy must be fairly shared.

The Control of Energy

The energy industry is dominated by very large companies, ranging from the oil "majors" to the utilities that supply electricity. Moreover, many of the strongest corporations have substantial interests in more than one energy source.[34] This concentration of economic power has become increasingly controversial.

Public discussion of the role of the great oil companies illustrates the point best. Undeniably, our rapid economic development has been based in large part on the availability of cheap energy. The argument can be made that industry concentration was necessary to achieve this end, that it would have been impossible to obtain the requisite supply of oil and natural gas from domestic and foreign wells, transport it, refine it, distribute it and sell it at low prices unless vast resources were invested in a few corporations. If this premise is granted, the companies plausibly claim some credit for America's well-being.

On the other hand, many stress the harm these firms have done. Concentration in the oil industry, critics say, has led to profiteering and monopolistic pricing policies, to the exploitation of people and of nature's gifts, and to the creation of a power structure that undermines democratic ideals. In this view, our material progress has been won at the expense of other nations, which have been denied fair access to humanity's common heritage, the riches of the earth.[35]

This debate, as it applies to the oil companies or to other components of the energy industry, involves enormous complexities that cannot be analyzed here. It is worth noting, however, that since the publication of *Rerum Novarum* in 1891 the Catholic church has warned against the dangers of unbridled capitalism.[36] Concentrated economic power is as much a threat to individual liberty as concentrated political power where necessities are concerned. In theory, any corporations that controlled the food supply or the clothing supply or the energy supply could, in the absence of regulation, do what they pleased with the consumer. Their decisions could mean life or death for those unable to pay the price.

In fact, no corporation has such power in America today, and many are run by good people who reject unethical practices. There have been serious abuses, however. In recent years people have suffered great hardships because the firms that supplied their heating fuel cut them off for failing to pay their bills.[37] While it is true that a business cannot continue to operate—cannot supply fuel to anyone—if customers default, cold-weather cutoffs are not a legitimate remedy. Companies should subordinate their economic rights to the higher right to life. Likewise, while the church fully recognizes the right to collective bargaining, workers should avoid strikes that force suspensions of service in winter.

The development of certain solar technologies offers a limited but real opportunity for counteracting the undesirable effects of concentration. Clearly the need for large, centralized, impersonal production and distribution facilities will not fade away. But if solar heating systems proliferate and other small-scale devices prove reliable and affordable, substantial decentralization could occur.[38] Movement in this direction would permit some people—even the poor if installation funds were available—to insulate themselves against complete reliance on outside sources of power. The homeowner with an array of solar cells on the roof of a passive solar house, the farmer with a windmill and equipment for distilling fuel alcohol from crop residues or waste, the tenant with a safe wood stove would have a species of control over their lives that most Americans now lack.

Decentralization through solar power could also have an important side benefit. While analysts disagree on the relationship between energy policy and employment,[39] the installation of small-scale solar devices in homes and businesses is by nature a labor-intensive activity. It should lead to the creation of new jobs, especially when combined with efforts to properly weatherize the buildings where solar power is used.

Prudent efforts to achieve some decentralization clearly deserve encouragement. At the same time there are more direct ways to guard against potential and actual abuses of power. One, of course, is government regulation. Another was briefly mentioned in the discussion of nuclear power: citizen participation in the decision-making process. Whether they are expressing their views on the risks associated with some energy source or helping ensure that corporate actions respect human needs, people have every right to intervene when energy policy is designed and implemented.

What form might such interventions take? With respect to energy companies themselves, they could range from orderly protests to testimony at public hearings to consumer representation on corporate boards. They could also include advocacy in the political arena aimed at influencing the content of legislation or regulation. The possibilities are as varied as the institutions that control energy in this country.

Generally speaking the smaller the entity responsible for a particular decision—individual rather than group, state rather than federal government, local distributor rather than multinational corporation—the better chance an informed citizenry has of affecting it. Some policies must be made on the highest levels; only Washington, for example, can commit the nation to greatly increased coal production. Nevertheless, those holding authority in the public and private sectors should be constantly looking for ways to center energy decision making as near the grass roots as possible. While adopting this course might lessen efficiency, it should produce results more satisfactory to the people and ultimately to the institutions that serve them.

The Problem of Systemic Evil

Most socioeconomic systems are established for worthy purposes. However, in a world made imperfect by sin problems inevitably arise in their application. Obeying some law of institutional inertia, these systems tend to perpetuate themselves and the evil they do is tolerated for the sake of the good. Partly for this reason the status quo never lacks defenders and reformers never lack zeal.

Certainly the control and distribution of energy in America today occasion as much structural sin as any major feature of our national life. Some corporations neglect or deny their social responsibilities, government sometimes acts without due regard for the common good and pressure groups relentlessly pursue their narrow goals in defiance of others' legitimate concerns.

People who seek justice must do their best to sort out the evil from the good and act on their perceptions. Obviously this will not end controversy; it may at times have the opposite effect. But by approaching the debate in a certain spirit—again as creatures and as fellow creatures—we elevate it. We also increase the likelihood that it will lead one day to a broad consensus, since sound conclusions flow from sound premises.

V. CONCLUSION

The world "energy" appears only a handful of times in papal or conciliar documents and even these scant references have little application to the current discussion in the United States. That is hardly surprising. Pope Paul VI, commenting on social justice in "A Call to Action," said: "There is of course a wide diversity among the situations in which Christians . . . find themselves according to regions, sociopolitical systems and cultures." Therefore, "it is up to these Christian communities . . . to discern the options and commitments which are called for in order to bring about the social, political and economic changes seen in many cases to be urgently needed" (n. 4).

The Catholic Christian community in America, as part of the large religious community and in association with all people of good will, faces a most challenging task in dealing with energy. Some matters are fairly clear: the primacy of serving human needs, the necessity of avoiding occasions of war, the duty of conserving energy wisely, the desirability of responsibly developing renewable enegy sources, to name a few. However, many of the central questions in the energy field are hard to define, much less to answer. The Catholic Christian community should be a continuous presence in the energy debate as long as issues so closely touching the welfare of humanity go unresolved.

It should be present through Catholic parishes, which can act to save energy in their own buildings, assist the poor, educate adults and children, and provide means for people to organize for advocacy.

It should be present through Catholic primary and high schools, which can emphasize the link between science and morality.

It should be present through Catholic colleges and universities, where theologians and ethicists can join with scientists, engineers and others to design practical ways to bring moral considerations to bear on energy policy and practice.[40]

It should be present through Catholic seminaries and novitiates, which can prepare priests and religious to approach matters of social justice with informed sensitivity.

It should be present through participation in interfaith groups and compatible secular coalitions, which can broaden support for laudable goals.

Finally, the Catholic community should be present through Catholic people of every calling who are willing to address energy issues with moral insight and commitment.

A sound viewpoint on energy rises above the perspective of the producer who cares nothing for the consumer or the consumer who ignores the producer's rights. It is a viewpoint that recognizes the transition to alternative sources of energy as a movement in history, a link between episodes in the development of civilization. In this movement lies creative potential for promoting human solidarity, for shaping what in Jesus' eyes would be a better world. Only through steadfast loyalty to a dream of justice can we bring that world to birth—as creatures and as fellow creatures.

Notes

1. Dr. V. Paul Kenny, professor of physics at the University of Notre Dame, served as technical consultant to the USCC subcommittee on energy. He comments, "Estimation of oil and gas reserves is more art than science, but it seems likely that we passed our domestic peak about 1970 and that world production will pass its peak between 1990 and 1995." A well-respected study concludes: "Even if imports of oil were maintained at the 1976 level of about 40 per cent, and oil and gas consumption grew at an annual rate of 2 per cent, conventional domestic oil and natural gas resources would not last much beyond the year 2000." Sam H. Schurr (project director), *Energy in America's Future: The Choices Before Us,* a study by the staff of Resources for the Future. Johns Hopkins University Press (Baltimore, 1979), p. 26.

2. The sources of energy used in the United States in 1979 were as follows: Oil, 47.5 per cent; natural gas, 25.4 per cent; coal, 19.6 per cent; hydroelectric, 4 per cent; nuclear, 3.5 per cent. Power Systems Sector, General Electric Co., *United States Energy Data Book* (Fairfield, Conn., General Electric Co., 1980), p. 7. The percentage of our oil that is imported has fallen from a high of 46.6 in 1977 (see note 6).

3. "The denial of (foreign) oil supplies—to us or to others—would threaten our security and provoke an economic crisis greater than that of the Great Depression fifty years ago, with a fundamental change in the way we live." President Jimmy Carter, State of the Union Address, Jan. 23, 1980.

4. Rev. John T. Pawlikowski, O.S.M., professor of social ethics at the Catholic Theological Union in Chicago, served as theological consultant to the USCC subcommittee on energy.

5. "National policies of conservation, fuel substitution and domestic supply enhancement which reduce oil imports have effects beyond the borders of the country which acts. They tend to lower energy prices, lessen stresses on the international financial system, and improve the prospects for political and economic stability. In doing so, they make both the country that reduces imports and all other oil importers better off." Schurr, pp. 418-19.

6. The United States imported 8.8 million barrels of oil a day in 1977 and 8.2 million barrels a day in 1979. *Energy Data Book,* p. 46. Preliminary estimates for 1980 put imports at less than 7 million barrels per day.

7. For electrical demand, see *Energy Data Book,* p. 15. The drop in gasoline sales, a recent phenomenon, has been widely reported. The current recession may well be responsible for part of this cutback, but the extent of its influence is unknown.

8. *The Washington Post,* Sept. 25, 1979, p. A10.

9. Committee on Nuclear and Alternative Energy Systems, National Academy of Sciences, *Energy in Transition, 1985-2010* (San Francisco, W. H. Freeman, 1980), p. 158.

10. "The United States has more mineable coal reserves than any other country, a supply that will last hundreds of years. Current annual excess production capacity in the industry stands at nearly 200 million tons." President's Commission on Coal, "Recommendations and Summary Findings" (Washington, D.C., Government Printing Office, 1980), p. 7. The U.S. Senate Committee on Energy and Natural Resources offers a more precise estimate: "Recoverable coal reserves amount to at least 150 billion tons, which is equal to at least two centuries of consumption at current levels." "Energy: An Uncertain Future" (Washington, D.C., Government Printing Office, 1978), p. 35.

11. Carroll L. Wilson (project director), *Coal: Bridge to the Future,* report of the world coal study (Cambridge, Mass., Ballinger Publishing Co., 1980), p. 144.

12. There is considerable uncertainty concerning the number of deaths that air pollution may be said to cause. One study comments: "Although we have given two estimates of deaths attributable to air pollution—9,000 and 14,000—we emphasize that reliable quantitative estimates of the overall health impact of air pollution do not exist." Hans H. Landsberg, et al., *Energy: The Next Twenty Years* (Cambridge, Mass., Ballinger Publishing Co., 1979), p. 365. Dr. Kenny adds: "Air-pollution epidemiology studies suggest that sulfate and particulate emissions from coal-fired plants may cause some 50,000 to 100,000 premature deaths yearly across the entire U.S. population."

13. This discussion of the carbon dioxide problem is drawn from a symposium before the Senate Committee on Governmental Affairs, July 30, 1979. The word "uncertainty" dominated the discussion. While the majority opinion is that increased levels of carbon dioxide will cause a warming of the atmosphere, for example, some scientists think it may produce a cooling. See also Wilson, pp. 147-50.

14. General Accounting Office, "Improvements Needed in Controlling Major Air Pollution Sources" (Washington, D.C., General Accounting Office, 1978).

15. General Accounting Office, "Questions on the Future of Nuclear Power: Implications and Trade-Offs" (Washington, D.C., General Accounting Office, 1979), pp. 1, 8.

16. *Energy Data Book,* p. 77.

17. Robert Stobaugh and Daniel Yergin, *Energy Future* (New York, Random House, 1979), p. 117.

18. Many estimates have been given as to the length of time nuclear wastes must be isolated from the environment. According to a panel discussion sponsored by the Forum of the National Academy of Sciences in Washington, D.C., Nov. 19, 1979, the most critical period is the first 1,000 years. A transcript of the discussion, titled "Nuclear Waste: What to Do With It?" is available from the National Academy of Sciences. See also Schurr, pp. 499-500.

19. Bishop Joseph Daley of Harrisburg issued a formal statement in the wake of the Three Mile Island accident calling for a moratorium on the licensing of new nuclear plants until the government can "guarantee" their safety.

20. The question of the connection between the U.S. nuclear power industry and nuclear arms proliferation is problematical. Dr. Kenny comments: "It is certainly technically feasible to apply sufficient overall security measures to ensure the integrity of our domestic reactor fuel cycle. . . . Reactor fuel supplied to nations overseas is the real focus of our proliferation problem. Recent attempts by the United States to dissuade the lesser-developed nations from further reliance on nuclear power have been rebuffed. Moreover, regardless of what nuclear stance this nation assumes, it is already clear that nuclear fuel and technology will be supplied to those who ask for it by other industrialized countries in both Western and Eastern Europe." For a more detailed discussion that draws similar conclusions but emphasizes the need for a non-proliferation policy, see Landsberg, pp. 442-46 and 454-65.

21. "Questions on the Future of Nuclear Power," p. 26. "The trends we have projected indicate that if actions are taken to limit or halt the growth of nuclear power, they must be accompanied by actions to severely limit electricity requirements or programs to expand coal supply or other non-nuclear fuels. Otherwise, serious shortfalls of electricity supply are likely to occur in the 1980s."

22. Granted that nuclear power represents a special case because it has been so highly politicized, such referenda might logically be held on all major energy projects where social costs and benefits must be weighed: for example, the construction of large dams, the opening of new coalfields, and the installation of windmill systems and large solar arrays.

23. This discussion of geothermal energy is based on General Accounting Office, "Geothermal Energy: Obstacles and Uncertainties Impede Its Widespread Use" (Washington, D.C., General Accounting Office, 1980).

24. For coal reserves, see footnote 10; for oil shale, see Schurr, p. 231; for biomass see Schurr, pp. 260-61.

25. There is still considerable uncertainty about the exact environmental impacts of synfuel production, but they would be substantial. For shale oil, see National Academy of Sciences, pp. 138-39. For coal liquids, see National Academy of Sciences, p. 181. For coal gas, see National Academy of Sciences, p. 143.

26. See Schurr. pp. 55-58.

27. The most obvious exception to this rule is the hydroelectric facility. When a dam bursts, people die and the local environment certainly suffers. Some solar systems—the solar power satellite is the most frequently cited example—may pose serious risks to humanity and nature.

28. As is well known, the Carter administration set a goal of obtaining 20 per cent of our energy from solar sources by the year 2000. The National Academy of Sciences study mentioned above, which has been widely attacked as being anti-solar, holds that this goal can only be reached if the government provides "vigorous incentives" to promote solar technologies (p. 346-49); in the absence of such incentives, the authors argue, solar will meet only 5 per cent of our energy needs in 2000. Stobaugh and Yergin, who are more optimistic on solar energy's prospects, say: "We believe that given reasonable incentives, solar could provide between a fifth and a quarter of the nation's energy requirements by the turn of the century" (p. 183). Denis Hayes, a leading solar advocate and head of the Solar Energy Research Institute, takes the whole world into account in his projection: "By the year 2000, such renewable energy sources could provide 40 per cent of the global energy budget; by 2025, humanity could obtain 75 per cent of its energy from solar resources." *Rays of Hope* (New York, W. W. Norton, 1977), p. 155.

29. See Schurr, p. 482: "Solar space and water heating may offer a near-term opportunity to shift from depletable to renewable energy sources. This technology may help to fill energy requirements and also supply a prototype for a series of long-term shifts as the energy sector changes over time. On institutional as well as technical grounds, therefore, the solar space and water heating enterprise has far-reaching implications that give it an important role among energy initiatives." This view of solar heating has wide support. Michael D. Yokell, formerly of the Solar Energy Research Institute, concludes in a recent article in *Public Interest Economics:* "Is the role for solar energy then limited to hot water and space heating in newly constructed buildings plus a few special applications? In the short run, the candid answer must be yes." Vol. 5, No. 1 (Spring 1980), pp. 1, 8.

30. See National Academy of Sciences, p. 40. "Unlike solar thermal conversion (photovoltaics) is a field in which fundamental research could yield dramatic returns, and recent technical progress has been very rapid."

31. In a speech at the Bio-Energy'80 World Congress in Atlanta April 24, 1980, Thomas E. Stelson, assistant secretary for conservation and solar energy at the U.S. Department of Energy, estimated that biomass could produce from 8 to 13 quads (using widely shared projections of demand, about 7 per cent to 10 per cent of total energy use) by the year 2000.

32. John F. O'Leary, former deputy secretary of energy, called supply interruptions "almost inevitable in the 1980s" in an editorial in the *Washington Post* (Jan. 22, 1980, p. A19). He also asked, "Will we see a repetition of the downslide of real prices in the years to come? The answer almost certainly is no, because the major factor contributing to falling prices—chronic and sustained surpluses—has disappeared. In fact, it is fair to predict that from this time forward, at least during the 1980s, we shall see constant upward pressure on price."

33. "Life-line rates" and "time-of-day rates" have been prominently mentioned in this connection. Time-of-day rates would encourage people to reduce their use of energy during certain hours in order to eliminate the need for costly "peak-load" facilities. Life-line rates would establish a basic charge for a certain minimum amount of power for necessary uses, and impose higher charges for energy consumed above that minimum. Life-line rates,

though good in concept, would have to be carefully structured to avoid discriminating against some of the very people they are intended to protect. For example, a childless middle-class couple where both husband and wife worked might use very little energy at home and thus qualify for the basic charge, while a poor woman with young children might require more power for heating, cooking, and so on, and fail to qualify.

34. Robert M. Wolcott, "Monolith in the Making," *Public Interest Economics,* Vol. 5, No. 1 (Spring 1980), pp. 2, 7.

35. For a skeptical though not hostile history of the oil industry, see Anthony Sampson, *The Seven Sisters* (New York, Viking Press, 1975).

36. Pope John XXIII quotes Pope Pius XI on this point and adds his own observations in *Mater et Magistra,* 35-40. See also Pope Paul VI, *Populorum Progressio,* 26.

37. The Community Services Administration has published a booklet telling people what to do when the heat fails as a result of a cutoff or for some other reason. Among the suggestions: wrap yourself in newspapers to avoid freezing. See Greg E. Welsh, "No More Heat? A Self-Help Booklet!" (Washington, D.C., Community Services Administration, 1979).

38. "However, where fuel transport costs are very high, or scale economies are weak or non-existent, decentralization may be more desirable. For example, if the direct rays of the sun are the fuel, the possible economic advantage of collecting and using that energy domestically for home heating, as opposed to collecting it for later distribution in a central-ized electrical network, becomes a calculation of great interest for energy planning." Schurr, pp. 324-25. "Indeed, because arrays of PV (i.e., photovoltaic) cells may show little or no scale economies, small- and medium-scale installations could well be a more intelligent use of this technology." Schurr, p. 331.

39. See Paul Keegan, "Employment Is the Name of the Game as Solar Advocates Press Their Case," *National Journal* (Dec. 15, 1979), pp. 2100-03.

40. In a speech to scholars and students in Cologne, West Germany, Nov. 15, 1980, Pope John Paul said: "Today it is the church that is the portal for reason and science that trust in capacity for truth, which legitimizes them as human capacities; for the freedom of science, through which it has dignity as a human, personal good; for progress in service to mankind, which needs it for the safety of its life and dignity."

The NCWC's Approach to Political and Social Reform

THE NATIONAL CATHOLIC WELFARE COUNCIL (NCWC) was a canonical body established in 1919 and renamed the National Catholic Welfare Conference in 1922. It exercised a role similar to that of the present National Conference of Catholic Bishops. Only bishops were members. The National Catholic Welfare Conference, Incorporated, was established in 1922 as a separate civil entity. Composed of bishops, priests, religious (i.e., members of a religious order, such as the Jesuits [the Society of Jesus] and the Sisters of Mercy), and laymen, it performed functions similar to those of the present United States Catholic Conference but on a smaller scale and in fewer areas.

The NCWC stressed the role of religion and education in leading individuals to virtue and in moving society toward Christian norms. The home, church, and school were emphasized as the prime teachers of religious and moral values. The bishops believed that no deep or lasting political or social reform could occur in the absence of sound religious and moral education.

The NCWC did not place the burden of educating Americans to virtue entirely upon home, school, and church. The bishops expected some aid from the state in the form of minimum standards of public morality, favorable attitudes toward religion, and a general moral tone.

The NCWC's concern to educate Catholics to virtue reflected great respect for the laity. Implicit in the bishops' view was the assumption that the laity, once converted, would infuse a Christian spirit into everything they did. Laypeople were expected to become better husbands, wives, and parents, and to perform more conscientiously the duties imposed by their work and citizenship.

The NCWC stressed the great political and social benefits that accrue to a nation if religion remains strong and education to virtue takes place in the family and in school. The bishops believed, with de Tocqueville, that religion properly practiced is the first of our political institutions. They saw their efforts to promote religion in all aspects of American life as political action of the most effective sort. This emphasis on moral and religious education, especially through the work of private individuals and groups but also, to some extent, by the state, reflected, albeit imperfectly, the approach to political reform characteristic of pre-modern political philosophy. Philosophers and theologians like Plato, Aristotle, Augustine, and Aquinas also spoke of education to virtue as the most important element in bringing about a just society.

Another characteristic of the NCWC was the promotion of reforms to ease the conflict between labor and capital. Cooperation between these groups was envisioned as a great step toward a kind of organic society—the kind of society advocated by the medieval, natural-law thinkers. The bishops did not hesitate to propose reforms that would bring about an organic society, because they saw no tension between the Christian natural-law teaching of the Middle Ages, which is the foundation of such a society, and the theory of natural rights upon which the American nation was founded. It follows from this that the National Catholic Welfare Conference would not recognize as fully American James Madison's statement, in *Federalist Ten*, that one principal objective of government is to protect the "different and unequal faculties of acquiring property"—in other words, to protect the right of individuals to pursue their self-interest.

The NCWC explicitly tried to look on all sides of important issues. For example, even though the bishops defended labor in season and out of season, they did not refrain from pointing out injustices committed by workers.

The NCWC tended to make few specific policy suggestions to civil authorities. "The Bishops' Reconstruction Program" of February 1919 (actually published before the official establishment of the NCWC in September of that year) was an exception. The NCWC did make general policy proposals, especially in the area of social order. For example, the bishops argued that labor should have a right to organize and be paid a living wage, and that the state ought to exercise some censorship over obscene materials. They spoke out on numerous occasions to denounce religious persecution in foreign lands. Toward the end of World War II, the bishops argued very forcefully, in several statements, that all nations were subject to the law of God. They supported the United Nations and expressed dismay that the Allies had allowed the Soviet Union to absorb Eastern Europe. They called upon the Allies to mount a massive relief effort to aid the war-torn countries of Europe. For all practical purposes, it can be said that throughout its nearly half decade of existence, the National Catholic Welfare Conference was not critical of American foreign policy.

Notes

CHAPTER ONE

1. Statements issued by the National Catholic Welfare Conference may be found in the following two volumes: Hugh J. Nolan, ed., *Pastoral Letters of the American Hierarchy, 1792-1970* (Huntington, Ind.: Our Sunday Visitor, 1971), and Raphael M. Huber, *Our Bishops Speak* (Milwaukee: Bruce Publishing Company, 1952).

2. It is important to note that my study does not attempt to assess the contribution that the bishops make to the political and social order through such agencies as the Campaign for Human Development and Catholic Relief Services. Furthermore, my study does not examine what is said and done by individual bishops in their dioceses.

3. Most of the bishops' statements can be found in J. Brian Benestad and Francis J. Butler, eds., *Quest for Justice: A Compendium of Statements of the United States Catholic Bishops on the Political and Social Order, 1966-1980* (Washington: USCC, 1981).

4. NCCB, "The Bicentennial Consultation: A Response," in *A Call to Action* (Washington: USCC, 1977), p. 137.

5. See especially Pope Leo XIII, *Rerum Novarum* (1891); Pope Pius XI, *Quadragesimo Anno* (1931); Pope John XXIII, *Mater et Magistra* (1961) and *Pacem in Terris* (1963); Pope Paul VI, *Populorum Progressio* (1967) and *Octogesima Adveniens* (1971); and Pope John Paul II, *Redemptor Hominis* (1979), *Dives in Misericordia* (1980), and *Laborem Exercens* (1981). Pope John Paul II has also spoken about the political and social order in speeches delivered in various places: Mexico, Poland, Ireland, the United States, Turkey, Africa, Brazil, France, Germany, Japan, the Philippines, and, of course, Rome, Italy. Nearly all these writings and speeches have been published in booklets or books by the Daughters of St. Paul, Boston, Massachusetts. See also the Second Vatican Council documents *Gaudium et Spes, Dignitatis Humanae Personae,* and *Lumen Gentium.* Some documents issued by the International Synod of Bishops also make a contribution to Catholic social thought; see Roman Synod of Bishops, *Justice in the World* (Washington: USCC, 1972), and *Synod of Bishops, 1974* (Washington: USCC, 1975).

6. Vatican II, *Gaudium et Spes,* #43, in Walter M. Abbott and Joseph Gallagher, eds., *The Documents of Vatican II* (New York: Guild Press, 1966). See

also Jean-Yves Calvez and Jacques Perrin, "The Limits of the Church's Intervention," in *The Church and Social Justice: The Social Teachings of the Popes from Leo XIII to Pius XII, 1878-1958* (Chicago: Regnery, 1961), pp. 54-74.

7. Jean Jacques Rousseau, *The Social Contract and Discourse on the Origin of Inequality* (New York: Washington Square Press, 1967), p. 46.

8. Pope John Paul II, *Brazil: Journey in the Light of the Eucharist* (Boston: Daughters of St. Paul, 1980), p. 40.

9. John Eagleson and Philip Scharper, eds., *Puebla and Beyond: Documentation and Commentary* (Maryknoll, N.Y.: Orbis Books, 1979), #534, citing Pope Paul VI's *On Evangelization in the Modern World*, #36.

10. See Leo Strauss and Joseph Cropsey, *History of Political Philosophy*, 2nd ed. (Chicago: Rand McNally, 1972), especially the essays on St. Thomas Aquinas and St. Augustine by Ernest L. Fortin; Pope Pius XI, *Quadragesimo Anno*, #127-49; Calvez and Perrin, *The Church and Social Justice*, pp. 13, 15, 126, 169, 172-73; Pope John XXIII, *Pacem in Terris*, #146-73, especially #165; Vatican II, *Gaudium et Spes*, #10, 15, 25, 26, 30, 31, 38, 43; and Pope Paul VI, *On Evangelization in the Modern World*, #20, 29, 36. These references are not intended to be comprehensive, of course, but they are representative of Catholic political and social thought. See chapter six for further indications of Pope John Paul II's views on the relation of virtue to the quality of the political order.

11. Vatican II, *Gaudium et Spes*, n. 192, p. 264. There is a mistranslation of this note in the Abbott and Gallagher edition of the council documents. They have: "If [the Church] civilizes, it is for the sake of evangelization." The translation should read: "If [the Church] civilizes, it is by evangelization." The French word *par* was mistranslated.

12. Ibid., #58, pp. 264-65

13. Ibid., #42, p. 242.

14. Pope John Paul II, *Brazil: Journey . . .*, p. 275.

15. Pope John Paul II, *John Paul II in Mexico* (London: Collins, 1979), p. 80.

16. Roger Heckel, ed., *The Social Teaching of John Paul II: Basis for Motivations and Ways of the Church's Intervention on Socio-Political Issues, Texts of John Paul, October 1978–February 1980* (Vatican City: Pontifical Commission *Iustitia et Pax*, 1981), F 19, p. 37.

17. Ibid., F 30, p. 41.

18. Eagleson and Scharper, *Puebla and Beyond*, #388, p. 177.

19. Pope John Paul II, *Brazil: Journey . . .*, pp. 159-60.

20. Jacques Maritain, *Integral Humanism*, trans. Joseph W. Evans (Notre Dame, Ind.: University of Notre Dame Press, 1973), p. 122.

21. Ibid., p. 121.

22. Pope Paul VI, *On Evangelization in the Modern World, Apostolic Exhortation, Evangelii Nuntiandi* (Washington: USCC, 1976), #26-27, pp. 20-21.

23. Pope John Paul II, *Brazil: Journey . . .*, p. 255.

24. Pope Paul VI, *Apostolic Letter on the Eightieth Anniversary of Rerum*

Novarum, Octogesima Adveniens (Washington: USCC, 1971), #50, p. 29. See also *Gaudium et Spes:*

Christians should recognize that various legitimate though conflicting views can be held concerning the regulation of temporal affairs [#75].

Often enough the Christian view of things will itself suggest some specific solution in certain circumstances. Yet it happens rather frequently, and legitimately so, that with equal sincerity some of the faithful will disagree with others on a given matter. Even against the intentions of their proponents, however, solutions proposed on one side or another may be easily confused by many people with the gospel message. Hence it is necessary for people to remember that no one is allowed in the aforementioned situations to appropriate the Church's authority for his opinion. They should always try to enlighten one another through honest discussion, preserving mutual charity and caring above all for the common good [#43].

25. Maritain, *Integral Humanism*, p. 304.

26. Karl Rahner, "The Function of the Church as Critic of Society," *Theological Investigations*, 12 (New York: Seabury Press, 1974), p. 243.

27. See Pope Leo XIII, *Rerum Novarum*, #16-31; Pope Pius XI, *Quadragesimo Anno*, #127-49; Calvez and Perrin, *The Church and Social Justice*, pp. 1-35, 55, 64, 89, 95; Jean-Yves Calvez, *The Social Thought of John XXIII*, trans. George J. M. McKenzie (Chicago: Regnery, 1964), pp. 85-93; Pope Paul VI, *Octogesima Adveniens*, #4, 42, 48; Pope Paul VI, *On Evangelization in the Modern World*, #3, 18, 20, 25-39, 68; Vatican II, *Gaudium et Spes*, #21, 40-45, 58, 76. For a discussion of Pope John Paul II's views on this subject, see chapter six.

28. Pope John Paul II, *Brazil: Journey . . .*, pp. 254-55.

29. Vatican II, *The Dogmatic Constitution on the Church, Lumen Gentium* (Washington: National Catholic Welfare Conference, 1964) #25, p. 47; #3, p. 35.

30. See especially Leo Strauss, "The Three Waves of Modernity," in *Political Philosophy: Six Essays by Leo Strauss*, ed. Hilail Gildin (New York: Bobbs-Merrill, 1975), pp. 81-98, and "What Is Political Philosophy?," in *What Is Political Philosophy? and Other Studies* (Glencoe, Ill.: The Free Press, 1959), pp. 9-55.

31. Ernest L. Fortin, review of Frederick D. Wilhelmsen, *Christianity and Political Philosophy*, in *Review of Politics*, 41, No. 4 (1979), 581.

CHAPTER TWO

1. See J. Brian Benestad and Francis J. Butler, eds., *Quest for Justice: A Compendium of Statements of the United States Catholic Bishops on the Political and Social Order, 1966-1980* (Washington: USCC, 1981), pp. 4-5, 23-47, 122-23. This volume is hereafter cited as *Compendium*.

2. Ibid., p. 57.

3. Ibid., p. 23.

4. Pope John Paul II, *Sources of Renewal: The Implementation of Vatican II* (San Francisco: Harper and Row, 1980), p. 61.

5. Pope Pius XII, Radio Message, Pentecost, June 1, 1941, A.A.S. XXXIII, 1941, p. 200; cited in Pope John XXIII, *Pacem in Terris,* #60.

6. Pope John Paul II, "Address to the Diplomatic Corps," *Origins,* 9, No. 35 (1980), 572.

7. Pope John Paul II, *John Paul II in Mexico* (London: Collins, 1979), p. 74.

8. See Pope John Paul II, *Pilgrim to Poland* (Boston: Daughters of St. Paul, 1979).

9. Pope John Paul II, *USA: The Messages of Justice, Peace, and Love* (Boston: Daughters of St. Paul, 1979), p. 50.

10. Ibid., p. 49.

11. Pope John Paul II, "Tensions of the Post-Conciliar Period; Address to the French Bishops," *Origins,* 10, No. 4 (1980), 52.

12. Pope John Paul II, *USA: The Messages of Justice, Peace, and Love,* pp. 54-55.

13. Pope Paul VI, *Apostolic Letter on the Eightieth Anniversary of Rerum Novarum, Octogesima Adveniens* (Washington: USCC, 1971), #30, p. 16.

14. Ibid., #31, p. 17.

15. Ibid., #26, p. 15.

16. Ibid., #35, p. 18.

17. USCC Administrative Board, "Political Responsibility: Choices for the 1980s," October 1979, citing *Gaudium et Spes,* #76, in *Compendium,* p. 6.

18. Ibid., citing Roman Synod of Bishops, *Justice in the World* (Washington: USCC, 1972), p. 43.

19. Ibid., citing *Pacem in Terris,* #160:

Neminem enim praetereat oportet, Ecclesiae ius itemque officium esse, non solum fidei morumque doctrinam tutari, sed etiam auctoritatem suam apud filios suos in regione rerum externarum interponere, cum diiudicare opus est quomodo doctrina eadem sit ad effectum adducenda.

A literal translation of this text is:

It must not be forgotten that the Church has both the right and the duty, not only to safeguard the doctrine of faith and morals, but also to intervene authoritatively in the temporal sphere when there is a question of judging how that same doctrine should be implemented.

This passage does not seem to apply to *partisan* policy statements. In those areas where reasonable Christians may disagree, the Church does not intervene authoritatively. See *Gaudium et Spes,* #43.

20. Ibid, pp. 6-7.

21. Ibid., p. 7.

22. NCCB, *Sharing the Light of Faith: National Catechetical Directory for Catholics of the United States* (Washington: USCC, 1979), p. 90, citing *Gaudium et Spes,* #39.

23. Ibid., citing Pope Paul VI's "Filmed Message to the Assembled Delegates of the Call to Action Conference."

24. Ibid., citing Roman Synod of Bishops, *Justice in the World,* p. 34.

25. *Compendium,* p. 102.

26. *Homily: The Red Mass* (Washington: USCC, 1975), n. pag.

27. *Compendium,* p. 15.

28. See *Compendium,* pp. 4-5. Instead of the key passage from *Justice in the World,* there is a quotation from Pope John Paul II's *Redemptor Hominis.*

29. J. Bryan Hehir, "The Ministry of Justice," *Network Quarterly,* 11, No. 3 (Summer 1974), 2. Commenting on Hehir's statement, Ernest Fortin made this thoughtful observation:

> Work on behalf of justice, we are being told, is a "constitutive dimension" of the Church's ministry, on a par with the celebration of the sacraments and the preaching of the word of God. One would have little reason to quarrel with this view if one were sure that the justice in question is that of the Sermon on the Mount and not the latest version of the modern egalitarian creed or what goes under the new name of "social justice." If social justice is so central an element of the gospel message, one wonders why no one ever bothered to talk about it prior to the middle of the nineteenth century, when the neologism was first put into circulation, probably by the Italian philosopher Taparelli d'Azeglio, who would have rendered us an even greater service had he taken the pains to spell out what he meant by it [*Center Journal,* 1, No. 3 (1982), 37-38].

30. International Theological Commission, "Declaration on Human Development and Christian Salvation," *Origins,* 7, No. 20 (1977), 308.

31. Saint Augustine, *The City of God,* trans. Marcus Dods (New York: Modern Library, 1950), p. 700.

32. International Theological Commission, "Declaration on Human Development," p. 312.

33. Pope Paul VI, "Closing Address," *Synod of Bishops, 1974* (Washington: USCC, 1975), p. 12.

34. Pope Paul VI, "Opening Address," *Synod of Bishops, 1974,* p. 5.

35. Pope Paul VI, *On Evangelization in the Modern World, Apostolic Exhortation, Evangelii Nuntiandi* (Washington: USCC, 1976), #32, p. 23.

36. Ibid., #22, p. 18.

37. NCCB, *Sharing the Light of Faith,* p. 90.

38. See "Address to the Latin American Bishops" in *John Paul II in Mexico,* pp. 66-83; see also two other addresses to Latin American bishops in *Brazil: Journey in the Light of the Eucharist* (Boston: Daughters of St. Paul, 1980), pp. 88-107, 332-54.

39. *Compendium,* p. 57.

40. Ibid., p. 59, citing *Gaudium et Spes,* #80.

41. Ibid., citing *Gaudium et Spes,* #81.

42. Ibid., p. 60, citing *Gaudium et Spes,* #82.

43. Ibid., p. 58, citing *Gaudium et Spes,* #79.

44. Ibid., p. 67, citing *Gaudium et Spes,* #78.

45. Ibid., p. 62, citing *Gaudium et Spes, #82.*

46. Ibid., p. 64.

47. Ibid., p. 60.

48. James S. Rausch, *Human Rights: Reflections on a Twin Anniversary* (Washington: USCC, 1973), n. pag.

49. J. Bryan Hehir, "A Challenge to Theology: American Wealth and Power in the Global Community," Catholic Theological Society of America: Proceedings of the Thirtieth Annual Convention, June 1975, p. 152.

50. Ibid.

51. Ibid., p. 154.

52. Ibid.

53. *Compendium,* p. 23.

54. Ibid., p. 43.

55. Ibid., p. 45.

56. Ibid., p. 44.

57. USCC, *Resolution of the United States Catholic Conference on the Twenty-fifth Anniversary of the Universal Declaration of Human Rights* (Washington: USCC, 1973), n. pag.

58. Pope John XXIII, *Pacem in Terris* (Washington: NCWC, 1963), #11 (modified translation).

59. Ibid., #9-27.

60. *Compendium,* p. 37.

61. Ibid., p. 41.

62. Ibid., p. 38.

63. Ibid., p. 41.

64. Pope John Paul II, *USA: The Messages of Justice, Peace, and Love,* p. 183.

CHAPTER THREE

1. "Human Life in Our Day, Chapter II: The Family of Nations," in J. Brian Benestad and Francis J. Butler, *Quest for Justice: A Compendium of Statements of the United States Catholic Bishops on the Political and Social Order, 1966-1980* (Washington: USCC, 1981), p. 57. This volume is hereafter cited as *Compendium.*

2. James Finn, "War and the Individual Conscience," in James S. Rausch, ed., *The Family of Nations* (Huntington, Ind.: Our Sunday Visitor, 1970), p. 82.

3. Ibid., p. 81.

4. Gordon Zahn, "The Bishops and Selective Conscientious Objection," in Rausch, *The Family of Nations,* p. 87.

5. *Compendium,* p. 76.

6. Ibid., p. 74.

7. Ibid., p. 76, citing *Gaudium et Spes,* #78.

8. Ibid., citing *Gaudium et Spes,* #79.

9. Vatican II, *Gaudium et Spes,* #256, in Walter M. Abbott and Joseph Gallagher, eds., *The Documents of Vatican II* (New York: Guild Press, 1966), pp. 292-93.

10. H. Vorgrimler, ed., *Commentary on the Documents of Vatican II* (New York: Herder and Herder, 1969), V, 353.

11. James R. Jennings, ed., *Just War and Pacifism: A Catholic Dialogue* (Washington: USCC, 1973).

12. *Compendium,* p. 75.

13. Ibid.

14. Jennings, *Just War and Pacifism,* p. 25.

15. Ibid., p. 36.

16. Ibid.

17. Ibid., p. 51.

18. Ibid., p. 52.

19. Ibid., p. 51.

20. Peter L. Gerety, *U.S. Foreign Policy: A Critique from Catholic Tradition* (Washington: USCC, 1976), p. 3.

21. *Compendium,* p. 44.

22. John Cardinal Krol, "Testimony Delivered Before the Senate Foreign Relations Committee," *Origins,* 9, No. 13 (1979), 197.

23. J. Bryan Hehir, "Moral Doctrine on Modern War: National Defense and the Nuclear Age," testimony before the House Armed Services Committee, March 1980, *Origins,* 9, No. 42 (1980), 679.

24. J. Bryan Hehir, "The New Nuclear Debate: Political and Ethical Considerations," in *The New Nuclear Debate* (New York: Council on Religion and International Affairs, 1976).

25. Ibid., p. 42.

26. Ibid., p. 43, citing Paul Ramsey, *The Just War: Force and Political Responsibility* (New York: Scribner, 1968), p. 237.

27. Ibid., p. 50.

28. Ibid., pp. 52-53.

29. J. Bryan Hehir, "The Arms Race: From Prophecy to Policy," testimony before the House Armed Services Committee, April 1978, in *The Arms Race: From Prophecy to Policy* (Washington: USCC, 1978), p. 12.

30. John Cardinal Krol, "Testimony Delivered Before the Senate Foreign Relations Committee," p. 197.

31. J. Bryan Hehir, "Testimony Presented to the House Committee on Armed Services on the Annual Report of the Secretary of Defense (FY 81)," *Origins,* 9, No. 42 (1980), 678-80.

32. U.S. Bishops, "Pastoral Letter on Marxist Communism," *Origins,* 10, No. 28 (1980), 433.

33. James S. Rausch, "Open Letter to the Honorable Henry A. Kissinger," 7 April 1976 (Washington: USCC, 1976).

34. This observation is based upon several conversations I have had with Father Hehir over the past eight years.

35. James S. Rausch, *Proposed Reforms of U.S. Overseas Investment and Trade Policies for the 1970s* (Washington: USCC, 1973), p. 2.

36. Ibid., p. 17.

37. Ibid., p. 11.

38. Ibid., p. 12.

39. Ibid., p. 15.

40. *Compendium*, p. 108.

41. Ibid., p. 109.

42. Ibid., p. 109, citing *Octogesima Adveniens, #*44.

43. Ibid., pp. 111-12.

44. Ibid., p. 112.

CHAPTER FOUR

1. *Origins,* 10, No. 5 (1980), 67.

2. J. Brian Benestad and Francis J. Butler, eds., *Quest for Justice: A Compendium of Statements by the American Catholic Bishops on the Political and Social Order, 1966-1980* (Washington: USCC, 1981), p. 23. This volume is hereafter cited as *Compendium.*

3. NCCB/USCC, *The Plan of Pastoral Action for Family Ministry: A Vision and Strategy* (Washington: USCC, 1978).

4. *Compendium*, p. 263.

5. Eugene A. Marino, "The Full Employment and Balanced Growth Act of 1976," testimony before the U.S. House of Representatives, Subcommittee on Equal Opportunity, March 15, 1976, in *Full Employment and Economic Justice* (Washington: USCC, 1977), p. 29.

6. *Compendium*, p. 270.

7. Ibid., p. 298.

8. Ibid., p. 313.

9. Ibid., pp. 313-14.

10. USCC, Catholic Hospital Association, and National Conference of Catholic Charities, *Statement on National Health Insurance before the Committee on Ways and Means* (Washington: USCC, 1974), pp. 2-3.

11. Ibid., p. 2.

12. Ibid., pp. 4-5.

13. *Compendium*, p. 394.

14. Ibid., p. 397.

15. Ibid., p. 399.

16. Ibid., p. 411.

17. Ibid., p. 322.

18. Ibid., p. 323.

19. Ibid., p. 324.

20. Ibid., p. 325.

21. Ibid., p. 327.

22. Ibid., p. 328.

23. Ibid.

24. Ibid., p. 329.

25. Ibid., p. 324.

26. Ibid., p. 359.

27. Ibid.

28. Ibid.

29. Ibid., p. 360.

30. Ibid., p. 373.

31. Ibid., p. 383.

32. Ibid., p. 319.

33. Ibid., p. 333, p. 340.

34. Ibid., p. 346.

35. Ibid., p. 221.

36. Ibid., p. 225.

37. Ibid., p. 226.

38. Ibid., p. 8.

39. U.S. Bishops, "Statement on Capital Punishment," *Origins,* 10, No. 24 (1980), 373-77.

40. *Compendium,* p. 208.

41. Ibid., p. 214.

42. Ibid., p. 226.

43. Ibid., p. 231.

44. NCCB/USCC, *Documentation on the Right to Life and Abortion* (Washington: USCC, 1974).

45. USCC, "Testimony on Constitutional Amendments Protecting Unborn Human Life before the Subcommittee on Constitutional Amendments of the Senate Committee on the Judiciary," in NCCB/USCC, *Documentation,* p. 2.

46. NCCB/USCC, *Documentation,* p. 56; also in *Compendium,* p. 154.

47. USCC, "Testimony before [Senate] Subcommittee on Constitutional Amendments," in NCCB/USCC, *Documentation,* pp. 17 and 22.

48. NCCB/USCC, *Documentation on Abortion and the Right to Life II* (Washington: USCC, 1976), pp. 45-57; also in *Compendium,* pp. 159-69.

49. NCCB/USCC, *Documentation II,* p. 50; *Compendium,* pp. 162-63.

50. NCCB/USCC, *Documentation II,* p. 50; *Compendium,* p. 164.

51. NCCB/USCC, *Documentation II,* p. 52; *Compendium,* pp. 164-65.

52. USCC, "Testimony on Constitutional Amendments Protecting Unborn

Human Life before the Subcommittee on Civil and Constitutional Rights of the House Subcommittee on the Judiciary," in NCCB/USCC, *Documentation II,* pp. 1-36.

53. *Compendium,* p. 292. Other statements can be found in the records of congressional hearings. For example: "Tax Credits for Nonpublic Education, Hearings before the Committee on Ways and Means, House of Representatives, 92nd Congress, 2nd Session, on HR16141 and Other Pending Proposals," Part III of three parts, September 7, 1972, pp. 579-611.

54. USCC, *Teach Them: Statement on Catholic Schools* (Washington: USCC, 1976), p. 10.

55. *Compendium,* p. 19, p. 9. The other four policy positions are:

(1) Sufficient public and private funding to make an adequate education available for all citizens and residents of the United States of America and to provide assistance for education in our nation's program of foreign aid. (2) Governmental and voluntary action to reduce inequalities of educational opportunity by improving the opportunities available to economically disadvantaged persons. (3) Orderly compliance with legal requirements for racially integrated schools. (4) Voluntary efforts to increase racial ethnic integration in public and non-public schools.

56. NCCB, *To Teach as Jesus Did: A Pastoral Message on Catholic Education* (Washington: USCC, 1973), #111, p. 31; see also USCC, *Teach Them,* p. 4.

57. USCC, Administrative Board, "Statement on Prayer in Public Schools," *Origins,* 3, No. 15 (1973), 231.

58. NCCB/USCC, *The Plan of Pastoral Action for Family Ministry,* p. 6, quoting *Gaudium et Spes,* #47.

59. NCCB, *Sharing the Light of Faith: National Catechetical Directory for Catholics in the United States* (Washington: USCC, 1979), p. 13.

60. *Compendium,* p. 416.

61. Ibid., p. 421.

62. Ibid., p. 428.

63. Ibid., p. 173.

64. Ibid., p. 170.

CHAPTER FIVE

1. This series, *The Social Teaching of John Paul II* (Vatican City: Pontifical Commission *Iustitia et Pax*), includes the following: (1) *General Aspects of the Social Catechesis of John Paul II,* ed. R. Heckel; (2) *The Human Person and Social Structures,* ed. R. Heckel; (3) *Religious Freedom,* ed. R. Heckel, with a supplement, *Religious Freedom and the Helsinki Final Act;* (4) *The Theme of Liberation,* ed. R. Heckel; (5) *Human Labor,* ed. R. Rossi; (6) *The Person, the Nation, and the State,* ed. W. Murphy; (7) *Human Rights,* ed. G. Filibeck; (8) *Basis for Motivations and Ways of the Church's Interventions on Socio-Political Issues,* ed. R. Heckel.

2. Hugh J. Nolan, ed., *Pastoral Letters of the American Hierarchy, 1792-1970* (Huntington, Ind.: Our Sunday Visitor, 1971), pp. 679-705; J. Brian Benestad and Francis J. Butler, eds., *Quest for Justice: A Compendium of Statements of the United States Catholic Bishops on the Political and Social Order, 1966-1980* (Washington: USCC, 1981), pp. 23-47. The latter volume is hereafter cited as *Compendium*.

3. *Origins*, 10, No. 24 (1980), 369.

4. See Leo Strauss, *Natural Right and History* (Chicago: University of Chicago Press, 1953), pp. 1-81. See also note 58 of chapter six of this book (p. 198) for a brief discussion of historicism.

5. See John Locke, *Second Treatise of Government*, chapter five, "Of Property," and Pope John Paul II, *Laborem Exercens*, #14.

6. Pope John Paul II, *On Human Work, Laborem Exercens* (Boston: Daughters of St. Paul, 1981), pp. 34-35.

7. Pope Pius XI, *Quadragesimo Anno*, #79, as cited in Jean-Yves Calvez and Jacques Perrin, *The Church and Social Justice: The Social Teachings of the Popes from Leo XIII to Pius XII* (Chicago: Regnery, 1961), pp. 331-32.

8. Ibid., p. 332. For a fuller treatment, see also pp. 328-37. It is important to note that the principle of subsidiarity allows, indeed requires, as much government intervention as necessary. Therefore it is incorrect to say that subsidiarity needs a counterprinciple, viz., "socialization." The important concept of "socialization," as elaborated by Pope John XXIII in *Mater et Magistra*, is misunderstood if seen as a counterprinciple to subsidiarity.

9. Oswald von Nell Breuning, "Social Movements," in Karl Rahner et al., eds., *Sacramentum Mundi*, 6 (New York: Herder and Herder, 1970), 110.

10. See *Compendium*, pp. 176-206.

11. Pope John Paul II, *Brazil: Journey in the Light of the Eucharist* (Boston: Daughters of St. Paul, 1980), p. 352.

12. Ibid., p. 350.

13. *The Social Teaching of John Paul II: Basis for Motivations and Ways of the Church's Interventions on Socio-Political Issues*, ed. R. Heckel (Vatican City: Pontifical Commission *Iustitia et Pax*, 1981), F 14a, p. 34.

14. See Aristotle, *Nichomachean Ethics*, trans. Martin Ostwald (Indianapolis: Bobbs-Merrill, 1962); Aristotle, *The Politics of Aristotle*, ed. and trans. Ernest Barker (New York: Oxford University Press, 1962); Plato, *The Republic of Plato*, trans. Allan Bloom (New York: Basic Books, 1968); Saint Thomas Aquinas, *The Political Ideas of Saint Thomas Aquinas*, ed. Dino Bigongiari (New York: Hafner, 1953); Saint Augustine, *City of God*, trans. Marcus Dods (New York: Modern Library, 1950); Leo Strauss and Joseph Cropsey, *History of Political Philosophy*, 2nd ed. (Chicago: Rand McNally, 1972), especially the articles on Saint Thomas Aquinas and Saint Augustine by Ernest L. Fortin; Leo Strauss, *Natural Right and History* (Chicago: University of Chicago Press, 1953); Leo Strauss, *What Is Political Philosophy? and Other Studies*, (Glencoe, Ill.: The Free Press, 1959);

Leo Strauss, *Political Philosophy: Six Essays by Leo Strauss,* ed. Hilail Gildin (New York: Bobbs-Merrill, 1975).

15. Joseph Bernardin, "Opening Address to Fall 1977 U.S. Catholic Bishops' Meeting," *Origins* 7, No. 24 (1977), 372.

16. Thomas Fleming, "Divided Shepherds of a Restive Flock," *New York Times Magazine,* 16 January 1977, p. 9.

17. "The Bishops' Program for Social Reconstruction" (1919) in Nolan, *Pastoral Letters,* p. 211.

18. USCC, Administrative Board, "Registration and the Draft," *Origins* 9, No. 38 (1980), 607.

19. Pope John Paul II, "World Day of Peace Message," *Origins* 10, No. 30 (1981), 468.

20. On Hehir's view of leverage, see "Human Rights and U.S. National Interest," a paper he prepared for the Marquette University Symposium on Faith and Politics, February 27, 1982.

21. *Populorum Progressio, #42.*

22. Ibid., #29.

23. Ibid., #41, #20.

24. *Compendium,* p. 93.

25. Thomas Aquinas, *Aquinas: Selected Political Writings,* ed. A. P. D'Entreves (Oxford: Basil Blackwell, 1948), p. 75. As columnist George Will put it:

> Citizens are social artifacts, works of political art. They carry the culture that is sustained by wise laws, and traditions of civility. At the end of the day, we are to judge a society by the character of the people it produces. That is why statecraft is, inevitably, soulcraft [*The Pursuit of Happiness and Other Sobering Thoughts* (New York: Harper and Row, 1978), p. xvii].

26. J. Bryan Hehir, "Religious Organizations and International Affairs," *Network Quarterly* 4, No. 3 (1976).

27. Garry Wills, *Bare Ruined Choirs: Doubt, Prophecy, and Radical Religion* (Garden City: Doubleday, 1972), p. 83.

28. Ibid., p. 147.

29. Ibid., pp. 149-50.

30. Ibid., p. 151.

31. Alexis de Tocqueville, *Democracy in America II* (New York: Vintage, 1945), p. 156.

32. Pope John Paul II, *Brazil: Journey . . .,* p. 96.

33. Ibid., p. 97.

34. Peter Berger has made some interesting observations about the way religion is being related to the political order:

> The religio-political extravaganza on the right has reminded fair-minded observers of the comparable extravaganza on the left—a phenomenon which, far from having been laid to rest with the late 1960s, is still going full blast and has been institutionalized in important agencies of mainline religion in this country. . . . the specificity with which the political implications of Christian faith are spelled out on the right can be matched, *pronunciamento* by *pronunciamento,* on the left [Peter L. Berger, "The Class Struggle in American Religions," *The Christian Century,* 98, No. 6 (1981), 194].

35. USCC, Committee on Social Development and World Peace, "The Family Farm," *Compendium,* p. 411.

36. Ibid.

37. "Declaration of Concern," *Origins,* 7, No. 28 (1977), 441.

38. Ibid., pp. 441-42.

39. Ibid., p. 441.

40. Pope John Paul II, *Brazil: Journey . . .,* p. 349.

41. John Eagleson and Philip Scharper, eds., *Puebla and Beyond: Documentation and Commentary* (Maryknoll, N.Y.: Orbis Books, 1979), p. 102.

42. Pope John Paul II, *Brazil: Journey . . .,* p. 351.

43. Pope John Paul II, *Letters to All the Bishops of the Church and All the Priests of the Church on the Occasion of Holy Thursday, 1979* (Boston: Daughters of St. Paul, 1979), p. 29.

44. Pope John Paul II, *Brazil: Journey . . .,* p. 124.

45. Pope John Paul II, *Sources of Renewal: The Implementation of Vatican II* (San Francisco: Harper and Row, 1980), p. 53.

46. Pope John Paul II, "Dedication to Christ and His Word," in *Ireland: In the Footsteps of St. Patrick* (Boston: Daughters of St. Paul, 1979), p. 122.

47. Pope John Paul II, "No One Can Exclude Christ From the History of Mankind," in *Pilgrim to Poland* (Boston: Daughters of St. Paul, 1979), p. 65.

48. Pope John Paul II, "Gratitude for the Gift of the Spirit," in *Pilgrim to Poland,* p. 37.

CHAPTER SIX

1. Pope Pius XI, "On Reconstructing the Social Order," in *The Church and the Reconstruction of the Modern World,* ed. T. McLaughlin (Garden City, N.Y.: Doubleday, 1957), #129, p. 264.

2. Pope Paul VI, *On Evangelization in the Modern World* (Washington: USCC, 1976), #22, p. 23.

3. Pope John Paul II, *Sign of Contradiction* (New York: Seabury Press, 1979), p. 23.

4. Pope John Paul II, *Redemptor Hominis* (Washington: USCC, 1979), p. 28.

5. Wilson Carey McWilliams, "American Pluralism: The Old Order Passeth," in *The Americans 1976: Critical Choices for Americans,* II, eds. Irving Kristol and Paul Weaver (Toronto: Lexington Books, 1976), p. 318.

6. Wilson Carey McWilliams, "Equality as the Moral Foundation for Community," in *The Moral Foundations of the American Republic,* ed. Robert H. Horowitz (Charlottesville, Va.: University Press of Virginia, 1977), p. 212.

7. Pope John Paul II, "Freedom of Assistance in the Contemporary State," in *Talks of John Paul II* (Boston: Daughters of St. Paul, 1979), p. 321.

8. Pope John Paul II, "A Message of Hope to the Asian People," *Origins,* 10, No. 39 (1981), 614.

9. Pope John Paul II, "No One Can Exclude Christ from the History of Mankind," in *Pilgrim to Poland* (Boston: Daughters of St. Paul, 1979), pp. 71-72.

10. Saint Augustine, *The City of God*, trans. Marcus Dods (New York: Modern Library, 1950), p. 700; Immanuel Kant, *Zum Ewigen Frieden Ein Philosophischer Entwurf* (Stuttgart: Reclam, 1972), p. 47. The translation is that of Leo Strauss in *Political Philosophy: Six Essays by Leo Strauss* (New York: Bobbs-Merrill, 1975), p. 87.

11. Pope John Paul II, "Address to the United Nations," in *USA: The Messages of Justice, Peace, and Love* (Boston: Daughters of St. Paul, 1979), p. 49.

12. Pope John Paul II, "The World as an Environment for Humanity," UNESCO speech, *Origins*, 10, No. 4 (1980), 64.

13. Ibid., p. 60.

14. Ibid., p. 62.

15. Ibid., p. 64.

16. Karol Wojtyla, "Il Problema del Constituirsi della Cultura Attraverso la 'Praxis' humana," *Revista di Filosophia Neoscolastica*, 3 (1977), 519.

17. Ibid.

18. Pope John Paul II, "A City Must Have a Soul," in *USA: The Messages of Justice, Peace, and Love*, p. 100.

19. Pope John Paul II, "No One Can Exclude Christ . . .," pp. 67-68.

20. Pope John Paul II, "Unity of Polish Bishops: A Recognized Source of Spiritual Strength," in *Pilgrim to Poland*, p. 151.

21. Pope John Paul II, "Plea for Spiritual Unity of Christian Europe," in *Pilgrim to Poland*, p. 90.

22. John Whale, ed., et al., *The Man Who Leads the Church: An Assessment of Pope John Paul II* (San Francisco: Harper and Row, 1980), pp. 257-58.

23. See *Insegnamenti di Paolo VI*, XIII (1975), p. 1568 (Close of the Holy Year, December 25, 1975).

24. Pope John Paul II, *Dives in Misericordia, On the Mercy of God* (Boston: Daughters of St. Paul, 1980), p. 43.

25. Ibid., p. 45.

26. Ibid., p. 41.

27. Ibid., pp. 43-44.

28. Ibid., p. 43.

29. Ibid., p. 45.

30. Leo Strauss, *Political Philosophy: Six Essays by Leo Strauss*, ed. Hilail Gildin (New York: Bobbs-Merrill, 1975), p. 85.

31. Ibid., p. 87.

32. Leo Strauss, "The Crisis of Our Time," in *The Predicament of Modern Politics*, ed. Harold J. Spaeth (Detroit: University of Detroit Press, 1964), p. 54.

33. Ibid.

34. Leo Strauss, *What Is Political Philosophy? and Other Studies* (Glencoe, Ill.: The Free Press, 1959), p. 281.

35. Pope John Paul II, *John Paul II in Mexico* (London: Collins, 1979), pp. 73-74.

36. Pope John Paul II, "Tensions of the Post-Conciliar Period: Address to the French Bishops," *Origins* 10, No. 4 (1980), 52.

37. Karl Barth, "Evangelical Theology in the Nineteenth Century," in *Humanity of God* (Richmond: John Knox Press, 1960), p. 21.

38. Pope John Paul II, *Sign of Contradiction,* p. 199.

39. Pope John Paul II, *Redemptor Hominis,* p. 76.

40. Pope John Paul II, *Letters to All the Bishops of the Church and All the Priests of the Church on the Occasion of Holy Thursday, 1979* (Boston: Daughters of St. Paul, 1979), p. 6.

41. Ibid., pp. 29-30.

42. Pope John Paul II, "Address to the Puebla Conference," in *John Paul II in Mexico,* pp. 67-83.

43. Ibid., p. 82.

44. Ibid., p. 79.

45. Pope John Paul II, *Brazil: Journey in the Light of the Eucharist* (Boston: Daughters of St. Paul, 1980), pp. 346-47.

46. Gaston Fessard, *Eglise de France, prends garde de perdre la foi* (Paris: Julliard, 1979). See also Gaston Fessard, *Chrétiens, marxistes, et théologie de la libération: Itinéraire du Père J. Girardi* (Paris: Lethielleux, 1978). See the review of these books by Ernest Fortin in *Review of Metaphysics,* 35, No. 1 (1981), 128. On Fessard's view of the French bishops Fortin writes:

> The story that these two books tell is not a happy one. Fessard is persuaded that in Marxism the Church faces a deadly and insidious rival, given to the use of "seduction" as a means of securing the "compromises" that will eventually "corrupt" and "destroy" its enemies. His basic thesis is that Marxism forms a unitary system whose premises and the practice they inspire are fundamentally at odds with the Christian faith. Much as some churchmen would like to separate them, historical materialism is indissolubly wedded to the philosophic materialism in which it finds its roots. By acquiescing in a typically Marxist critique of capitalist society while rejecting Marx's atheism, the bishops, their theologians, and their spokesmen unwittingly commit themselves to a view of human life that, as Christians, they are bound to repudiate.
>
> Fessard does not doubt that their recent statements stem from the impulses of a generous heart. What troubles him is that the authors and promulgators of these statements are blind to their larger implications and hence guilty of inconsistency. Where Paul VI had spoken of the "dynamism of the Faith," the bishops speak of the "dynamism of the labor movement." They now subscribe as a matter of course to the Marxist notions of "class conflict" (often extended so as to include the Church itself) and of the "collective memory of the working class." Even the idea of a valid "socialist option with Marxist reference" barely gives them pause to reflect. True, they still prefer the word "socialisms" in the plural to "socialism" in the singular, as if to signify their desire to stand above party politics; but since one and only one brand of socialism is intended, the precaution is illusory and ineffectual. The few among them who try to buck the trend meet with little success. They are mercilessly set upon, sometimes by their

own colleagues, and pursued with an inquisitorial animus that has no parallel in history. Therein lies the tragedy. Unable to articulate or agree upon a coherent position of its own, the hierarchy has no other course but to "react" passively to pressures from without. This, more than anything else, is what is responsible for the chaotic state of the Church in France.

47. Pope John Paul II, Pope John Paul I, Pope Paul VI, *To the Church in America* (Boston: Daughters of St. Paul, 1981), p. 55.

48. Margaret O'Brien Steinfels, "Postscript: What Is to Be Done?," in *Challenge to the Laity,* ed. Russel Barta (Huntington, Ind.: Our Sunday Visitor, 1980), pp. 132-33.

49. *Origins,* 10, No. 24 (1980), 378-84.

50. Ibid., p. 381.

51. John Coleman, S.J., "What Is an Encyclical? Development of Church Social Teaching," *Origins,* 11, No. 3 (1981), 35-36. For a reflection on this article see J. Bryan Hehir, "Challenge of a Tradition," *Commonweal* 108, No. 17 (1981), 522. See also John Locke, "Of Property," chapter 5 in *The Second Treatise of Government.*

52. See Thomas Hobbes, *Leviathan,* especially chapter 11; John Locke, *Second Treatise of Government;* and Leo Strauss, *Natural Right and History* (Chicago: University of Chicago Press, 1953), pp. 165-251.

53. Vatican II, *Gaudium et Spes,* #41.

54. *Octogesima Adveniens,* #26, #35.

55. *The Social Teaching of John Paul II: Human Rights,* ed. G. Filibeck (Vatican City: Pontifical Commission *Iustitia et Pax*), A 1p, p. 11.

56. Ibid., B 50a, p. 50.

57. Peter L. Berger, "The Class Struggle in American Religion," *The Christian Century,* 98, No. 6 (1981), 194.

58. Another important contribution of political philosophy is to provide insight into the nature of historicism. Leo Strauss said this about historicism:

Whereas, according to the ancients, philosophizing means to leave the cave, according to our contemporaries all philosophizing essentially belongs to a "historical world," "culture," "civilization," "weltanschauung," that is, to what Plato had called the cave. We shall call this view historicism. . . . We are forced to suspect that historicism is the guise in which dogmatism likes to appear in our age. It seems to us that what is called "experience of history" is a bird's eye view of the history of thought, as that history came to be seen under the combined influence of belief in necessary progress (or in the impossibility of returning to the thought of the past) and of the belief in the supreme value of diversity or uniqueness (or of the equal right of all epochs or civilizations) [*Natural Right and History* (Chicago: University of Chicago Press, 1953), pp. 12, 22].

Many thinkers both critically and uncritically assume the truth of the historicist claim. An example of reliance on historicist premises can be found in a 1981 book by the Reverend Francis Murphy, C.S.S.R., entitled *The Papacy Today.* Murphy's fundamental criterion for judging the papacy is success or failure in accommodating the Church's spiritual message to the consciousness of contemporary man. He is very upset with the papal prohibition of artificial contraception; it does not reflect "the moral awareness of [the Church's] responsible theologians and well-informed laity." Murphy is also critical of the *Declaration on Certain Questions Concerning Sexual Ethics (Persona Humana)* issued by the Vatican Congregation for the Doctrine of the Faith in December 1975. This document reaffirmed traditional Catholic teaching on abortion, birth control, extramarital sex, masturbation, and homosexuality. Murphy says this is an attempt "to force the Church's moralists to comply with the document's absolutes—an impossible task, due to fundamental divergencies of human experience and opinions on these matters; as well as to the cultural traditions of peoples and nations" *(The Papacy Today* [New York: Macmillan, 1981], p. 215). Murphy is advocating a version of the historicist contention that truth is the perspective of an age discernible by being attentive to the culture, the prevailing mores, or the opinions of responsible theologians and well-informed laity.

A thorough study of the influence of historicism on Catholic theology has yet to be done.

59. *Origins,* 11, No. 24 (1981), 379.

60. Richard Current, ed., *The Political Thought of Abraham Lincoln* (Indianapolis: Bobbs-Merrill, 1967), p. 138.

61. George Will and Michael Novak, *Solzhenitsyn and American Democracy* (Washington: Ethics and Public Policy Center, 1981), p. 6. Pope John Paul II made the same point as Will in an address to the United Nations:

A critical analysis of our modern civilization shows that in the last hundred years it has contributed as never before to the development of material goods, but that it has also given rise, both in theory and practice, to a series of attitudes in which *sensitivity to the spiritual dimension of human existence is diminished* to a greater or less extent, as a result of certain premises which reduce the meaning of life to the many different material and economic factors—I mean to the demands of production, the market, consumption, the accumulation of riches, or of the growing bureaucracy with which an attempt is made to regulate these very processes. Is this not the result of having subordinated man to one single conception and sphere of values? [*USA: The Messages of Justice, Peace, and Love,* p. 51].

Index of Names and Documents

NAMES

ABC (American Broadcasting Company), 88
Acting Person, The (Karol Wojtyla/John Paul II), 122
Afghanistan, 53
Africa, 40, 53-54
Albania, 40, 54
American Civil Liberties Union, 111-12
American Indians (Native Americans), 35, 63, 65, 73-74, 88-89
American Society of Christian Ethics, 49
Americans for Democratic Action, 111
Angola, 41
Aquinas, Thomas, xii, 6, 47, 108, 122, 137
Aristotle, 100, 122, 137
Armed Services Committee, U.S. House, 49, 52
Atlantic Ocean, 126
Augustine, Saint, xii, 6, 23, 100, 122-23, 137
Auschwitz, 127

B-52 bombers, 52
Bacon, Francis, 139
Bare Ruined Choirs (Garry Wills), 108
Barth, Karl, 132
Berger, Peter, 138
Bernardin, Joseph, 74-75, 100
Berrigan, Daniel, 19
Berrigan, Philip, 19
Bishops' Committee on Farm Labor (NCCB), 71
Bolivia, 40
Boston, 84
Brazil, 5, 7, 40, 115
Byrd Amendment (Military Procurement Act, 1971), 40

California, 70-72
California Agricultural Labor Relations Act, 71
Cambodia (Kampuchea), 39, 54
Canada, 57
Capitol Hill, 19
Carberry, John Cardinal, 101
Catholic Action, 7
Catholic Hospital Association, 67
Catholic Mind, 110
"Challenge to Theology: American Wealth and Power in the Global Community, A" (J. Bryan Hehir, 1975), 30
Chicago, 114
Chile, 40, 58
China, People's Republic of, 54
Civil Rights Act of 1964, 109
Coleman, John, S.J., 137
College of Cardinals, 138
Committee on the Judiciary, U.S. House, 82
Communication, USCC Department of, 88
Congress, U.S., 55, 57, 62, 64, 66
Constantine, 46
Constitution, U.S., 20, 79-80, 83-84
Coste, René, 44, 104
Crete, 5
Cuba, 54
Czechoslovakia, 40, 54

"Declaration of Concern" (Chicago Catholics, 1977), 114-15
Declaration of Human Rights, U.N., 27, 29, 79, 83, 138
Declaration of Independence, 79-80, 83
"Declaration on Human Development and Christian Salvation" (Interna-

Note: This index was prepared by Richard E. Sincere.

DOCUMENTS OF THE AMERICAN CATHOLIC BISHOPS

PAPAL AND CONCILIAR DOCUMENTS

Ethics and Public Policy Reprints

Reprints are $1 each. Postpaid if payment accompanies order.
Orders of $20 or more, 10 per cent discount.